CONFESSIONAL CINEMA

Religion, Film, and Modernity in Spain's Development Years, 1960–1975

Confessional Cinema

Religion, Film, and Modernity in Spain's Development Years, 1960–1975

JORGE PÉREZ

UNIVERSITY OF TORONTO PRESS
Toronto Buffalo London

Toronto Buffalo London
www.utppublishing.com

ISBN 978-1-4875-0108-2

Toronto Iberic

Library and Archives Canada Cataloguing in Publication

Pérez, Jorge, 1976–, author
Confessional cinema : religion, film, and modernity in Spain's development years, 1960–1975 / Jorge Pérez.

(Toronto Iberic; 24)
Includes bibliographical references and index.
ISBN 978-1-4875-0108-2 (hardcover)

1. Religion in motion pictures. 2. Motion pictures – Spain – History. 3. Motion pictures – Religious aspects – Catholic Church. 4. Catholic Church – In motion pictures. 5. Spain – Religion – 20th century. 6. Spain – Intellectual life – 20th century. 7. Spain – History – 1939–1975. I. Title. II. Series: Toronto Iberic; 24

PN1995.9.R4P47 2017 791.43'682746 C2017-900133-7

University of Toronto Press acknowledges the financial assistance to its publishing program of the Canada Council for the Arts and the Ontario Arts Council, an agency of the Government of Ontario.

Canada Council for the Arts Conseil des Arts du Canada

Funded by the Government of Canada Financé par le gouvernement du Canada

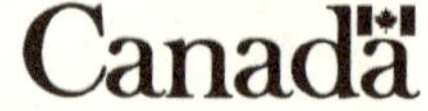

Contents

Figures

Acknowledgments

This book would not have been possible without the support of a number of people and institutions. I am very grateful to the University of Kansas for providing me with numerous ways of support of this project from its inception. A sabbatical semester in spring 2011 allowed me to spend three months in Madrid doing archival research. The College of Liberal Arts and Sciences granted me three consecutive General Research Funds (for the summers of 2010, 2011, and 2012) that were crucial to jump-start the project, and several College Travel Grants allowed me to present my work in professional conferences and symposia. The Hall Center for the Humanities gave me a Travel Grant to support my trip to Spain during my sabbatical semester and, furthermore, awarded me with a Research Fellowship in spring 2014 that enabled me to write the bulk of the manuscript. I want to thank its director, Victor Bayley, for allowing me to stay in residence through the summer, and all the other members of the staff of the Hall Center for their kindness and hospitality. My fellow residents, Bruce Hayes and Laura Mielke, deserve a special mention for their collegiality and encouragement. Credit to Bruce for his idea of weekly "accountabili-teas" to report on our writing progress and to help put things in perspective. I still remember often and fondly those seven months of writing in bliss.

Some sections of chapters 2 and 3 originally appeared as an article entitled "'¡Hay que motorizarse!': Mobility, Modernity, and National Identity in Pedro Lazaga's *Sor Citroen*," in the *Arizona Journal of Hispanic Cultural Studies* vol. 11 (2007), and a brief section of chapter 4 will appear in the volume *Spanish Erotic Cinema* (forthcoming from Edinburgh University Press, 2017). I wish to express my gratitude to the publishers for their permission to use this material here. I also want to thank

Victoria Bernal from EGEDA for helping me with the always arduous task of securing permissions for images. I presented material from the manuscript at invited talks at UCLA, University of Miami, Real Colegio Complutense at Harvard University, University of Texas at Austin, and Southern Missouri State University. The suggestions and questions I got in those venues helped sharpen my ideas.

I want to thank my editor at the University of Toronto Press, Siobhan McMenemy, for her guidance throughout the process and for her incisive suggestions to improve the manuscript. I also want to thank the editor of the Toronto Iberic series, Bob Davidson, for believing in this project and for his support for publication. The three anonymous readers of the press could not have been more helpful with their detailed suggestions and critiques of the first draft of the manuscript. It is a luxury to have expert scholars reading my work with that level of attention to detail.

I am indebted to the kindness and professionalism of the staff of the Filmoteca Española and the Biblioteca Nacional in Madrid for granting me access to their film archives and materials. Special recognition goes to Trinidad del Río, who has been super helpful and kind over the years. Miguel Soria was also helpful in finding some suitable images to include in the book and in preparing digital versions of them according to publishing standards. Special appreciation to Keah Cunningham and Jonathan Perkins from EGARC at the University of Kansas for their help preparing film stills in high resolution.

Many colleagues at the University of Kansas have been supportive of this project. Jonathan Mayhew helped me polish chapter 1 with his superb editing skills. Santa Arias and Verónica Garibotto have offered unparalleled support and friendship over the years. Perfectionist Santa is a model of professionalism who has inspired me to strive to write the best possible book. I owe Verónica for taking the lead in finalizing the details of a co-edited book project so that I could focus on completing the revisions of this book. I wrote most of this book while serving as associate chair. I will always be grateful to the department chair during that time, Stuart Day, for alleviating my administrative tasks so that I could complete my book before it was my time to step up as department chair. While he never said so, I know this meant he had to take on more duties that pushed him away from his own scholarship.

Many colleagues and friends from other institutions have also helped me during the writing of this book. Silvia Bermúdez, Justin Crumbaugh, Santiago Fouz-Hernández, Roberta Johnson, Jordi Marí,

Susan Martin-Márquez, Tatjana Pavlović, and Barbara Zecchi have all been incredibly supportive, sharing bibliographical references, writing me letters of support for grants, or simply with the example of their own scholarly work. Silvia Bermúdez was always there to listen to every crisis I had during the completion of this book. Justin Crumbaugh has a special place in this book as my "field work buddy." We crossed paths in Madrid several summers and, especially, during our sabbatical leaves, when we were both carrying out the initial archival work for our book projects. While our projects were different in topic and methodology, some overlaps led to mutual sharing of knowledge and references. Most importantly, it was awesome to have a friend to enjoy the Madrid nightlife after the long daily sessions at the library.

A number of friends and family members have also been instrumental over the years. My Lawrence friends, Steve Maceli and John Connolly, the most fabulous couple, helped me keep my mental sanity by pushing me away from the computer into all kinds of fun social events, including periodic trips to go dancing with Steve in KC. My brother and my mother were the best research assistants I could ever have. They collected for me films, books, and other useful materials that I could not get myself because of the geographical distance. My mom also listened to all my frustrations in our daily skype chats during my lunch break. My partner, Matthew Henderson, deserves special thanks for his patience, loving support, and for editing several parts of the manuscript to correct my tendency to write long sentences in English. He came into my life when I was starting the writing process, and had to experience first-hand all the ups and downs of writing and publishing an academic book. I know it is not easy to live with an academic, as he had to spend many nights and weekends playing video games and watching television shows on his own so that I could get back to the manuscript. *Pelirrojo*, I promise I will make it worth it from now on.

A Note on Translations

English quotations from José María Escrivá de Balaguer's *Camino* are from *The Way* (Scepter, 1979). All other translations are my own.

CONFESSIONAL CINEMA

Religion, Film, and Modernity in Spain's Development Years, 1960–1975

Introduction

Film, Religion, and the *Desarrollismo* Period

The purpose of this book is to analyse how cinema engaged the enduring yet shifting role of religion in the modernization process Spain underwent in the last fifteen years of Francisco Franco's dictatorship. Film is a cogent case study to examine the significance of religion not from a theological point of view, but rather as a sociopolitical force and cultural determinant in the Spanish public sphere of this period, known as *desarrollismo* (development years) (1960–75). The overarching motivation of my project is to interrogate the assumption that, after 1957, when the so-called technocrats came on board and the Franco regime recast itself in a secularized and modernizing fashion, religion vanished from the cultural field. A striking trend of Spanish cinema during the development years that remains largely unexplored is the vitality and popularity of religious films in an epoch that has been interpreted as a secular age and one that many historians refer to as "the secularization decade" of Western Europe (McLeod 140). However, they have been virtually erased from the history of Spanish cinema.

Two reasons lie behind this omission. The first one has to do with the rigid schemes employed to conceptualize this particular era of Spanish cinema. As Santos Zunzunegui has noted, along with other re-examinations of the 1960s (Faulkner, *A Cinema*; Triana-Toribio), film production during this period has been typically mapped with a twofold structure that divides acceptable and unacceptable critical routes to follow. In the foreground, the *Nuevo Cine Español* (with its supposed Catalan counterpart, the *Escuela de Barcelona*) looms large, while genre films appear all clustered and cornered in a background "sin más interés que el puramente estadístico" (with no more than purely statistical interest) (29). In this prevailing assessment of the history of Spanish cinema, religious films barely appear as part of that infamous background that Domenèc Font called "clerigallas residuales" (residual clerical films), despicable remnants of the religious films produced in the 1940s and 1950s that carried the ideological torch of the regime (*Del azul* 328–30). Hence they do not seem to merit critical attention.

The second reason, which I plan to evaluate more in depth in this book, relates to the broader tendency to theorize the development years through the prism of a secularist position that obliterates religion from the cultural archive of the period. Most scholarly accounts on the development years and on the transition to democracy in Spain presume that religion was an obstacle to modernization in the 1960s and 1970s. In fact, as Noël Valis has argued, we could extend this statement in chronological terms to the wider period of modern Spain (8). These views presuppose that the Catholic Church and religious beliefs vanished from the Francoist milieu overnight. For example, Tatjana Pavlović asserts that, with the technocratic mutation, "Franco's regime ceased to be providential and became technocratic. Spaniards would no longer be preparing for the heavenly paradise, but enjoying an earthly one" (*The Mobile* 1). For Nathan Richardson, an important aspect of the development period was the "ever-accelerating pace of creative destruction reshaping Spanish space and place," which was for him a secular affair with "little spiritual impulse" (*Constructing* 147). I intend to question the tendency of some of these scholars to become fascinated with the siren song of the "speed" of changes and, thereby, to outline an ironically static – in the sense of monolithic – view of the period that writes off religion as irrelevant and no longer operative.

A Paramount Case Study

Cinema is a suitable vehicle to explore the modernity-religion interface and to probe assumptions about the wane of religion in modern Spanish culture for a number of reasons. It emerged at the end of the nineteenth century as an emblem of modernity that integrates its defining features: "technology mediated by visual and cognitive stimulation; the re-presentation of reality enabled by technology; and an urban, commercial, mass-produced technique defined as the seizure of continuous movement" (Charney and Schwartz 10). Despite being born in a technological civilization and having a profane origin, the quintessentially modern film industry was hardly the work of the devil destined to ruin religious visions of the world. Nor was it a channel to destroy the aura of ritual and worship formerly surrounding art, as Walter Benjamin deemed the effects of the mechanical reproduction integral to film. For the first time in history, Benjamin famously contended, "mechanical reproduction emancipates the work of art from its parasitical dependence on ritual" (224), thus serving up the possibility of radical collective ways of production and reception. For Benjamin, "the liquidation of the traditional value of the cultural heritage" (221) brought by mechanically reproduced art works such as film made them agents of secularization and, furthermore, potentially revolutionary artistic forms.

The mechanical reproduction of film did not dislodge cinema from the aura of religious ritual. In fact, although cinema was a product of capitalist civilization, it was also a spectacle whose liturgy ensued from the Sunday visits to the churches. As Edgar Morin argued in *The Stars*, "The movies, machines for doubling life, summon the heroic and amorous myths to incarnation on the screen, start again the old imaginary processes of identification and projection from which gods are born. The religion of the stars crystallizes the projection-identification inherent in all participation in the film" (82). The weekly worship of saints was replaced by the worship of film stars, whose glamorous lives were as invented or embellished as the lives of saints to fill the void left by the secularization of society. Provocatively, Morin further claimed that "no one who frequents the dark auditoriums is really an atheist" (57). Thus, a more accurate assessment of the relationship between religion and cinema would be, as Melanie Wright states, that "[r]eligion has not been displaced by a new medium: it has colonized it, and has found itself challenged and altered in the course of the encounter" (2). Many scholars who investigate the intersections between film and religion have argued that cinema could be seen as a feasible and productive location of spiritual relevance in the modern world (Deacy, *Faith* vi; Lindvall 217; Lyden 12). André Bazin had previously stated that the link between film and religion was as old as film itself, since "[t]he cinema has always been interested in God" (61). For scholars with a theological approach to film criticism, the film industry operates as a secular production machine that has assumed some of the roles that one would ascribe to traditional religious institutions. Secular media such as film "can and do raise vital questions about the spiritual landscape and normative values of society" (Deacy, *Faith* vi) and are capable of filling the void left by the waning of traditional religion (Deacy, *Screen Christologies* 9).

Film, despite being a non-spiritually rooted modern art, arose closely linked to religion, as pioneering industries such as those in France and the United States were already producing their first Bible-inspired films by 1897; that is, only two years after the invention of the *cinématographe*. The inventors of film, the Lumière brothers, made *The Passion* in 1897 and Georges Méliès made *Walking on Water* in 1899. In the United States, the Thomas Edison Company "released *The Passion Play of Oberammergau* in 1898" (Nolan 9). The case of Spain is somewhat comparable. During the Franco regime, the historiography of Spanish cinema claimed that the first Spanish motion picture was Eduardo Gimeno's *Salida de la misa de doce del Pilar* (1899), a cinematic testimony of churchgoers coming out of midday Mass. Although Jon Letamendi and Jean-Claude Seguin have demonstrated that the first Spanish motion picture was actually *Riña en un café* (Fructuós Gelabert, 1897) and have documented the ideological manipulation behind what we could term the "foundational fallacy" of Spanish cinema, it is still telling that some of the early displays of filmmaking in Spain emerged so closely related to religious devotion and to the Church.[1]

Film is also pertinent as a case study because it was regarded as the utmost significant channel of social communication by the Catholic Church. Counting until the epoch of the Vatican II Council, more than 130 papal documents discussing the role of film in society had been disseminated. In general terms, we can identify three stages in the position of the Roman Catholic Church in relation to film. The initial indifference led to a phase of rejection and distrust of films' malicious effects on society's morals.[2] From the 1950s on, the official discourse of the Church, while not abandoning suspicion, began leaning towards an interest in the value of films for educational and missionary purposes. This change of attitude could be best seen in the switch from a defensive scheme, one in which cinema was understood as a potential enemy, to one in which films were embraced as instruments for the apostolate (Orellana, *Como en un espejo* 188). While there is abundant scholarship in relation to the role of the Church in the censorship of Spanish films (González Ballesteros; Gubern, *La censura*; Heredero 49–69; Martínez Bretón; Sanz Ferreruela, *Catolicismo y cine*), far less attention has been paid to its involvement in the production of films. It is undeniable that the Church has been a crucial pressure group to clean up movies in Spain and elsewhere.[3] The Church's crusade against the film industry forced producers and directors to eliminate certain scenes, to reshoot parts of films, or to add another beginning or ending to accommodate the products to the rigid moral standards of the clerical censors. Until well into the 1960s, the Church had a great deal of say in what Spanish audiences could or could not see. But there is more to the story of the Church's involvement in the film industry. The Church also generated mechanisms to become an active agent of filmmaking. Motion pictures of and by the Church told influential stories that had popular appeal, and reimagined the shape of Spanish Catholicism and sometimes also the notion of Spanish national identity.

After the mid-1940s, the Church gained more political capital to the detriment of the Falangist factions of the regime, and its influence in the film industry increased. In the late 1940s, the journal *SIPE* announced a cycle of missionary films that was institutionally sponsored through the "Concurso de Guiones Cinematográficos sobre las Misiones Españolas" organized by the Consejo Superior de Misiones ("Concurso" 48). Films such as *Viento de siglos* (Enrique Gómez, 1945), *Misión blanca* (Juan de Orduña, 1946), *La manigua sin Dios* (Arturo Ruiz Castillo, 1949), and *La mies es mucha* (José Luis Sáenz de Heredia, 1949) benefited from the institutional urge to appropriate film as a propagandist medium. These films served to legitimize the imperialistic undertones of the project of national identity that the regime promoted.[4] The signing of the Concordate with the Vatican (1953), which sanctified the confessional nature of the Spanish state, contributed to this re-Catholization of culture. The results of this arrangement are well known: the compulsory religious education in all pedagogical institutions; the tax exemptions for the Church along with generous financial support from the government; and the green light conferred on the Church to exercise control over the censorship of all publications, media, and the arts. This political climate, along with the Vatican's call to take on an active role in the film industry at the service of the apostolate, fostered the bourgeoning of production companies in the orbit of the Church to make religious films. These films constructed images of Catholicism closely tied to the political project of the Franco regime. In this way, they operated as a well-oiled propagandist machine that we could refer to as "celluloid National-Catholicism," in the sense of providing the cinematic version of the political co-optation of religion by the regime.

The most notable example was the production company Aspa Films. After the success of the initial instalment, *Balarrasa* (José Antonio Nieves Conde, 1951), scriptwriter Vicente Escrivá teamed with director Rafael Gil to make a series of profitable and institutionally acclaimed religious films commissioned by Aspa.[5] Interestingly enough, these films were less concerned with presenting an orthodox account of theological notions than with addressing wider sociopolitical issues. *La señora de Fátima, Murió hace quince años,* and *El canto del gallo* tackle the crusade against communism, while *La guerra de Dios* proposes a Catholic notion of economic justice as the recipe to solve class issues in the Asturias mines.[6] Aspa Films represents the tip of the iceberg of a larger infiltration of the Church in the Spanish cinema industry in the 1950s. The scope of that infiltration reached all facets of the industry, including distribution and exhibition, cine-clubs (such as the cine-club Monterols in Barcelona, organized in an Opus Dei college dormitory), an editorial press that released many titles on the topic of film and religion (Rialp), and even the organization of film festivals. The barely known Semana de Cine Católico in Zaragoza was the launching platform for the more prominent Semana del Cine Religioso de Valladolid, which began in 1956 and influenced official policy regarding film censorship.[7]

The Church's involvement in the film industry diminished from the 1960s on, which has led film historians to create a straightforward cause-effect relationship between the political and economic policies of the technocrats and the declining weight of religion in the film industry. For example, Carlos Heredero argues that "en 1962 el ciclo de cine religioso se encuentra ya prácticamente agotado" (the cycle of religious cinema is pretty much over in 1962) (59). A careful look reveals that the religious cycle was far from exhausted by 1962. Other influential critics have acknowledged the continued production of religious films throughout the *desarrollismo,* but they have regarded them as continuations of formulaic templates from the 1940s and 1950s (Torreiro, "¿Una dictadura?" 333). For Diego Galán, religious films simply followed the pattern of the historical cinema of the 1940s and early 1950s. Thus, Galán denies religious cinema any specificity and renders it as a transitional genre between the historical film and the folkloric film ("El cine" 97). In these reductionist views, religious cinema appears as some sort of fixed, trans-historical entity independent of its context of production.

The significant number of religious films produced in this period indicates that large audiences still craved these films. Suffice it to say here that some of its subgenres, such as the "hagiographic film" that I will address in chapter 1, thrived in the 1960s. The missionary subgenre, though no longer the big gun of pro-regime film propaganda that it was in the late 1940s and early 1950s, continued to be produced in films such as *Cristo negro* (Ramón Torrado, 1963), *Piedra de toque* (Julio Buchs, 1963), and *Encrucijada para una monja* (Julio Buchs, 1967). Also, examples can be found of biblical and "Jesus films" such as *Milagro a los cobardes* (Manuel Mur Oti, 1962), *Los jueces de la Biblia* (Francisco Pérez Dolz, 1966), *El Cristo del océano* (Ramón Fernández, 1971), and *Proceso a Jesús* (José Luis Sáenz de Heredia, 1973). Clerical comedies and melodramas also lingered on Spanish screens in the 1960s and 1970s. *Canción de cuna* (José María Elorrieta, 1961), *El padre Manolo* (Ramón Torrado, 1966), *Sor Citröen* (Pedro Lazaga, 1967), *Sor Ye-Yé* (Ramón Fernández, 1967), and *¡Se armó el belén!* (José Luis Sáenz de Heredia, 1969) were some of the most popular ones. In the dissident camp, Luis Buñuel made a number of key films in which religion featured prominently: *Nazarín* (1958), *Viridiana* (1961), *El ángel exterminador* (1962), *Simón del desierto* (1965), *La Voie Lactée* (1968), and *Tristana* (1970). Continuing his famous anti-clerical and sacrilegious attitude, all of them were harsh critiques of organized religion and, above all, of the Catholic Church. Oppositional filmmakers of the *Nuevo Cine Español* took on Buñuel's anti-clerical legacy and embraced the trend of late-Franco cinema to approach the public dimension of religion. Notably, Basilio Martín Patino's *Canciones para después de una guerra* (1971) and *Caudillo* (1974) and Carlos Saura's *La prima Angélica* (1974) and *Cría cuervos* (1975) comprised a critical commentary on the confessional status of the Spanish state.

Religious cinema, or films concerned with religion, survived the secularization process, for they remained popular and profitable during the 1960s and beyond. Film historians, though, have not cared much about the symbiosis between religion and film in late Francoism. It is significant that the few comprehensive studies on the relationship between film and the Catholic Church under Franco limit their scope to the first half of Francoist dictatorship. Juan Antonio Martínez Bretón's *Influencia de la Iglesia católica en la cinematografía española (1951–1962)* (1987) and, more recently, Fernando Sanz Ferreruela's *Catolicismo y cine en España (1936–1945)* (2013) seem to confirm Heredero's contention that by 1962 the interdependence between religion and film was over. The only exceptions are the scholarship on Luis Buñuel and Elizabeth Scarlett's recently published *Religion and Spanish Film* (2015). By analysing in depth the persistence of religious themes in contemporary Spanish cinema, Scarlett's book is a pioneering effort that confirms that modernity did not obliterate religion from Spanish cultural production. But even Scarlett pays little attention to the development years except for a brief section about the engagement with religion of oppositional directors such as Carlos Saura and Víctor Erice (102–10). I want to correct this oversight of the historiography of Spanish cinema, which is in part linked, as I will explain later in this introduction, to the secularist framework employed to examine cultural production during the modernization process. But before I embark on this critical pathway, a few definitions and clarifications are in order. I need to define my object of study in more specific terms, since the category "religious film" is not self-explanatory.

Religious Film, Religion in Film, or Religion and Film?

The notion of "religious film" has been and still is a highly disputed concept. In the 1950s, French theorists Amédée Ayfre and Henri Agel initiated a critical conversation about the issue of spirituality in film that stirred a big debate in European film circles. A salient component of that debate entailed outlining a precise definition of what a religious film is and what it should include. And it is very telling in this regard that Ayfre started his book *Dios en el cine* with the following statement: "Cuando se aborda el problema del cine religioso, inmediatamente se advierte cuán difícil es circunscribir dicho problema" (When dealing with the problem of religious cinema, one immediately notices how hard it is to demarcate that problem) (15). So, religious cinema is a "problem," so big that it becomes almost a riddle to solve. In Spain the debate about this "problem" was nothing short of heated. Not only Church-based publications such as *Revista Internacional del Cine, SIPE,* and *Ecclesia* but also film journals and magazines such as *Film Ideal, Otro Cine,* and *Cinema Universitario* and cultural magazines such as *Ateneo* and *Triunfo* (all from varied ideological positions) devoted substantial space to this issue, including articles in response to opinions expressed in the other venues. Influential intellectuals of the calibre of José Luis Aranguren, José María García Escudero, and Carlos Fernández Cuenca were some of the main discussants in this debate. All of them defended the existence of a "cine religioso," which García Escudero claimed should deal with "la relación entre lo humano y la transcendencia" (the relationship between the human sphere and the transcendental sphere) (*Una política* 151). In no less than five books and many journal articles that García Escudero published about the issue of religious films, one would not find a much more elaborate definition than the one mentioned above.[8]

Other voices were no more explicit. Most of the discussions – including the pioneering contributions by Agel and Ayfre – pivoted around what religious films were not and illustrated these negative definitions with examples from Hollywood and Spanish cinema as well as from other latitudes. In his famous "Historia en cien palabras del cine español," García Escudero regarded all Spanish religious films made until the mid-1950s as "un cine religioso sin autenticidad" (a religious cinema without authenticity) (*Cine español* 21), which deploys clichés such as "el envaramiento de los personajes, la lentitud de movimientos, la solemnidad de las voces, el fuerte subrayado musical" (the stiffness of the characters, the slowness of the movements, the solemnity of the characters' voices, the heavily emphatic musical score) to give the impression of a supernatural presence (*Una política* 195, 196). Spanish films that passed as religious were for García Escudero sugar-coated cinema, "servido con dos y tres terrones" (served with two and three lumps of sugar), and offered an exemplary tale with a moral message (*Cine español* 31). Similar to García Escudero, José María Pérez Lozano considered Spanish religious cinema a "cine anodino, beato, ñoño" (anodyne, pious, insipid cinema) (90). The Aspa cycle of religious films was the main target of these critics' darts. The editorial in the third issue of *Cinema Universitario* lambasted "ese deleznable cine religioso del 'curascope' de Aspa Films" (that atrocious religious cinema of the "curascope" of Aspa Films) ("Sacerdocio y Curascope" 3). In *Film Ideal*, Juan Ripoll pointed out in a panoramic article that "el mercado se saturó de actores vestidos de sacerdotes y monjas en películas entre ingenuas, falsas o relamidas" (the market got saturated with actors dressed as clergy in naive, fake, or disingenous films) (7).

In the 1990s, Carlos Heredero maintained the same differentiation between "cine religioso," corresponding to European auteurs such as Carl Theodor Dreyer, Ingmar Bergman, and Pier Paolo Pasolini, and "cine protagonizado por los ministros de la Iglesia" (films starring Church ministers), which was what, according to him, the totality of Spanish production did (192). A common ground of all these accounts is that true religious cinema was largely absent in the Spanish film industry (and elsewhere). Instead of opening up to a transcendental sphere through the exploration of the human condition – García Escudero's definition of religious film – these films merely included clerical characters in mawkish productions for simplistic spiritual indoctrination. But what no one explained in clear terms was how films should reach that transcendental sphere. The masters Agel and Ayfre were no less abstract in this regard. For Henri Agel, the sacred in film appeared in the paradigmatic example of Carl Dreyer's *The Passion of Joan of Arc* (1928) as "la transformación de lo real hasta la ascesis" (the transformation from reality to divinity) (*El cine* 26), and for Ayfre in the depiction of "acontecimientos humanos concretos en los cuales está copresente el misterio entero del universo" (concrete human events in which the mystery of the entire universe is present) (quoted in Agel, *El cine* 26). Despite the examples, it still unclear to me how the films described reached that ascetic domain or transcended the real. Even García Escudero, a confessed follower of both Agel and Ayfre, was aware of the slippery terrain one gets into when searching for a "true" religious cinema, as he wondered "¿hasta qué punto es realizable?" (To what extent is it feasible?) (*Palabras* 35).

Several decades of critical writing have not solved the "problem" of defining in concrete terms what "true" religious cinema is. Current debates are far from unanimous. For some critics, religious cinema is a genre recognized in thematic terms (Rodríguez Rosell 30–3); for others it is not a genre, since it does not have a specific content or aesthetics, but rather it is any film that deals with the relationship between human beings and God (Claveras 16). Ultimately, what religious cinema is or is not depends on the approach each particular scholar takes, whether it is a scrutiny with a theological lens or based solely on cinematographic properties. The vast majority of film critics who have commented negatively on religious films have tried in vain to find a common ground in a cluster of films that are supposed to constitute a film genre. In my view, they have failed to do so because they have mixed assessment criteria. They have tried to identify and explain a genre by using aesthetic measures of auteurist cinema and, above all, a Kantian notion of art as a "sublime" activity that rests on transcending the vulgarity of ordinary life. In this sense, what is at stake in the adverse assessments of commercial religious cinema by Agel, Ayfre, García Escudero, and Heredero is pure aesthetic taste. Along these lines, Paul Schrader's "transcendental style" is the most systematic attempt to theorize a cinematic style that seeks to "express the Holy itself" (7). Giving examples of the work of the auteurs Yasujiru Ozu, Robert Bresson, and Carl Dreyer, Schrader argues that this transcendental style departs from Hollywood's pyrotechnics, which he calls a poetics of "abundant means" (154), and instead produces a style of "sparse means" (154), which is characterized by minimalist technical resources. By toning down the role of the camera work, editing, and plot twists, the transcendental style of these auteurs focuses on finding a way out of the hollow details of everyday life and into the sacred domain. Or so Schrader thought.

When critics like Schrader celebrate the scarce examples of true religious cinema in the brilliance of auteurs such as Dreyer and Ozu in opposition to the ostentatious popular religious films, they are drawing a line of cultural distinction that has little to do with spiritual issues. They are proposing a theory of "pure taste" with implications of religious transcendence that rests on the denial of what is considered "impure," understood as simplistic technical conventions that overstate the insertion of the supernatural in everyday life. If what we are dealing with here are aesthetic tastes, it is important to bear in mind that those are, as Pierre Bourdieu stated in *Distinction*, "the practical affirmation of an inevitable difference. It is no accident that, when they have to be justified, they are asserted purely negatively, by the refusal of other tastes" (56). To legitimize a certain aesthetic taste concerning religious films inextricably entails rejecting "facile effects" (486), what Schrader called the poetics of "abundant means" of Hollywood religious productions and García Escudero deemed sugar-coated cinema in the context of Spanish religious films. Thus, the "problem" of defining religious cinema is a matter of taste and cultural distinction, which in its essence is tied to disgust with the vulgarity of the ordinary. The quest for a definition of religious film has therefore involved aversion to commercial films that included religious messages easily digested for mainstream audiences.

By applying these codes of aesthetic distinction to the notion of "religious films," these critics privilege form over function, and the style of representation over the particular object represented. This presupposes the existence of an audience that can apply what Bourdieu calls an "aesthetic disposition," which he defines as "the aptitude for perceiving and deciphering specifically stylistic characteristics" (50). *Confessional Cinema* shows that the interface between religion and film cannot be fathomed only in aesthetic terms. Consideration of the visual styles of the films under scrutiny will be crucial to gauge how they engaged the topic of religion and appealed to audiences. For instance, I will show the significance of the uses of lighting techniques to endorse or challenge the sacred envisioning of national identity during the Franco regime in the hagiographic films that I analyse in chapter 1. Another prominent example is the recurrent deployment of crosscutting as the preferred editing pattern to showcase the synergy between technological modernization and post–Vatican II Catholicism in the comedies of development that I examine in chapters 2 and 3. However, attention to how these filmic texts interacted with other related social discourses in their historical matrix is equally important. As the title of the book suggests, we should perhaps think of these films as "confessional" rather than "religious," in the sense that they arose tied to or as a critical commentary on the confessional status of the Spanish state under Franco.

This is why it is perhaps more fruitful to think of the relationship between religion and film not as a specific style or a genre but in broad terms, and then narrow down a specific corpus of films that are relevant to one's focused research questions. Hence, given that my focus in this book is the impact of religion on the Spanish public sphere, I examine films with narratives that address issues pertaining to religious communities (convents, monasteries, religious missions, and so on) and/or feature religious characters (clergy, saints, and biblical characters). I deal with the links of these religious communities and characters to the broader context of late Franco Spain. The critical literature on these films has thus far insisted that they are not truly religious films, since they do not deal with *religion in film* but only with external aspects of religion or with religion as a pretext to address something else. My inquiry will be driven by the consideration of that "something else."

I am aware that the films under scrutiny offer scope for other kinds of readings. Besides a formalist method that assesses their aesthetic value, these films could be subjected to a theological approach that would involve examining how they encapsulate or communicate religious meanings and theological notions such as good and evil, salvation, grace, redemption, and so on. A theological reading of a film means looking for how that film engages, explains, or questions a particular religious idea, tradition, or text (Bird; Deacy, *Faith in Film*, *Screen Christologies*; Marsh and Ortiz; May).[9] As I said at the beginning of this introduction, I am not concerned with theological interpretations of film, among other reasons because I am not well equipped to make theological claims. I am aware that my non-doctrinal approach may be off-putting to those readers who approach religious films from a doctrinal perspective. I am not concerned with the degree of fidelity to religious texts or theological doctrines. Instead, my concern is with the links of film texts – their narratives and visual styles – to their contexts of production, distribution, and reception within the broader historical matrix of the modernization process in the last phase of the Franco regime and the crucial role that religion played in that period. The goal of the next section is precisely to argue that theories of the modernization of Spain that neglect the significance of religion in that process are inadequate or, at least, incomplete.

The "Secularization Thesis" of Spanish Modernity

The case study of Spanish cinema during the development years compels us to reframe the debate over secularization and to rethink the all-too-familiar conception of religion as opposed to modernity in the 1960s. In so doing, my work is informed by the turn across the humanities and social sciences to employ what has been termed "post-secular theory" to approach the study of religion. Post-secular theory interrogates the mainline narrative of secularization by questioning the categorical divide between the secular and the religious, reason and faith (Kaufmann, Rivett). Within Peninsular studies, William Viestenz has contributed to debates on post-secularism by analysing through the case study of post-war literature how Franco "conceptualized his right to sovereignty around a political theology" so that sacred concepts transferred to the secular terrain to underpin his project of national identity (3).[10] Although the post-Franco period was not the focus of his study, Viestenz also argues that modern liberal democracies such as contemporary Spain "tend to revert to a hierarchical, top-down form of governance that resembles a divine mandate" (4), thus pointing out how liberalism has not succeeded in fully separating itself from religious roots. Political thought still resorts to theological concepts in Spain and elsewhere. This is why a recalibration of the role of the sacred in contemporary societies is in order.

Granted, the term "post-secular" has been contested for being potentially confusing, since it is not clear when the secular age ceased to be current and became "post" (Calhoun, "Secularism" 78). Proponents of post-secular thinking point out different turning points between the "secular" and the "post-secular," thereby making one wonder whether or not those dates are somewhat arbitrary choices. For some post-secular scholars, the events of 9/11 and the subsequent political resurgence of the religious Right would mark that epistemic shift (Rivett); for philosopher Jürgen Habermas, it begins in the "epochmaking change of 1989–1990" (1).[11] Instead of envisioning a post-secular society that emerges at some indeterminate point, perhaps it is more effective to rethink the secular society in which we live as one in which the strict boundaries between the sacred and the secular spheres have dissolved. As William Viestenz suggests, instead of a "return of the sacred" after an era of secularity, it might be better to think of post-secularism as a renewed epistemological position which recognizes that secularity never did away with the sacred (8). Quibbles about nomenclature aside, the main lesson we can extrapolate from post-secular thinkers is that we need to go beyond a limited secularist notion of society, since the sacred still underpins political imagination. This would help us offer a more nuanced account of cultural production of *desarrollismo* and elude what Charles Taylor calls "the myth of the Enlightenment": the customary opinion that perceives the Enlightenment "as a passage from darkness to light" ("Why We Need" 52). This prevailing view of the Enlightenment explains modernity through a "subtraction story," that is, modernity is what is left once human beings emancipate themselves from the "illusions" or "limitations of knowledge" of religious beliefs (*A Secular* 22). Correspondingly, the modern subject is defined subtractively, as a mere residue of his/her previously oppressed status. Although Taylor is challenging the broader Western fixation with the distinction between secular reason and religious reason, regarded as "epistemically fragile" and consequently useless in the public sphere (49), his point is no less valid for scholarly debates about modernity in Spain.[12]

Peninsularists have taken at face value the "secularization thesis" of Western modernity. This thesis draws on the ideas of some of the great social theorists, with Karl Marx, Sigmund Freud, Max Weber, and Émile Durkheim among them, who predicted that the modernization of society would bring a decline in religious beliefs and the social significance of religion. The trend to value rationalization and scientific understandings of the world would simultaneously bring a devaluation of spiritual values, a process that Max Weber famously referred to as the "disenchantment of the world" (*From Max Weber* 155). In this dominant narrative of modernity, secularization appears as a required constituent. However, as Max Weber affirmed, modern Western rationalism was an ideal type against which specific cases in each national context should be compared to delineate their unique pathways to modernity (*The Methodology* 43). Post-Weberian secularist accounts of modernity have tended to neglect this caveat. They have promised secularization as a universal and unitary process when in reality it is a multidimensional and historically contingent set of processes that materializes in myriad ways in each specific context.

José Casanova contends that the normative narrative of secular modernity encompasses three different propositions or sub-theses that are not inextricably linked: 1) Secularization as the differentiation of public spheres that entails the separation between state and Church; 2) secularization as the decrease in church attendance and religious vocations;

and 3) secularization as the privatization of religion to the extent that it becomes practically imperceptible (*Public* 7). Casanova further argues that the first sub-thesis, the one that differentiates between a secular sphere of activity – the state, the market, and modern science – and a religious sphere, is the crucial component of the theory of secularization linked to modernization. But the other two sub-theses, usually taken as the inseparable by-product of the differentiation of spheres in the modern world, are not defendable and constitute "the main fallacy" of the dominant theory of secularization (19–20).[13] Scholars like José Casanova who have questioned the tenability of the secularization thesis in its dominant configuration (Asad, Katznelson and Stedman Jones, Mendieta and VanAntwerpen, Turner, Taylor) do not mean to suggest that we should get rid of the theory of secularization altogether. Instead, they maintain that we should reformulate it in a way that is elastic enough to account for the diverse contexts of modern societies. For example, it is a slippery move to apply the mainline secularization theory to the context of Spain, since some of the processes of secularization began when Spain was still a confessional state. The differentiation of secular and religious spheres was not legally sanctioned until the 1978 Constitution. This means that even Casanova's first sub-thesis is a pattern in ideal-typical circumstances that is not universally valid. Secularization in Spain in the sense of a decline in religious vocations began in the 1960s, though the decline in religious beliefs and practices is much harder to prove, since sociological surveys were infrequent and often controlled from above (Longhurst 21). As we can see, secularization – or some components of it – was a reality of the development years, but as a particular historical trend in Spain that was negotiated differently than in other Western societies and not as the inevitable outcome of modernization.

Accounts that take for granted the secularization thesis can be tied to an ideological discourse or world view that we should more properly call "secularism." The concept of "secularism" originated in the mid-nineteenth century in relation to the political doctrine of liberalism (Asad 23–34, Turner 128), and until recently it was thought to go in tandem with modern progress (Calhoun, Juergensmeyer, and VanAntwerpen 9). Janet R. Jakobsen and Ann Pellegrini argue that secularism is a discourse in the Foucauldian sense that is part of a larger political project. The main goal of this project is to legitimize modernity as a dominant political goal (7), which Judith Butler aptly calls "hegemonic secularism" (105). Secularism is central to the main narrative of the Enlightenment and its critique of religion as a backward influence, and it is thus offered as universal in opposition to the particularities of religion. But this discourse cannot be taken as universal because, as Max Weber argued in *The Protestant Ethic and the Spirit of Capitalism*, it is tied to a particular development in history that, furthermore, has religious roots: a specific, Euro-American secularism that is market-based and that has its origin in the economic ethic of Calvinism. Cultural interpretations of Spain's modernity since the 1960s have endorsed, however unconsciously, this secularist universal narrative – although of Euro-American Protestant origin – without problematizing whether or not it suits the specific context of a Catholic confessional state like Spain until 1978.

Conceptualizations of cultural modernity in Spain since the 1960s have been so inextricably secularist because of the loaded meaning that religion has had for scholars of Spanish cultural studies in relation to Francoism. Religion was a master-code of the early Franco regime and was equated with the role of the Catholic Church in legitimizing Francoism after the Civil War.[14] For oppositional forces to the regime – and for academics who have mostly aligned with those oppositional forces – modernity became a political goal associated by default with European secularized nation-states, which were considered emblems of democracy and social progress, and disassociated from the regime and, consequently, from the sacred. In this way, secular modernity became an ideal and, simultaneously, a curse, in a similar sense to what Carlos Alonso describes as the burden of modernity in the Latin American context (3). It is a curse because the desire to overcome any particular expression that may seem too local or insular and that could separate the case of Spain from the course of the ideal Western modernity has resulted in a process of exclusion in which components such as religion have been systematically erased from narratives of Spanish cultural modernity.

The task of scholars implicitly became to honour the modern, liberal, and secular cultural tradition that was silenced and effaced by the anti-modern, authoritarian, and religious-based Franco regime. Without minimizing the achievements of this liberal-secular tradition within a hostile context, I would like to call attention to the manner in which liberal-secular premises have become naturalized in the scholarship on modern Spanish culture. This secularist angle from which Peninsular studies, along with other disciplines, tacitly operate is, as Michael Kaufmann asserts in relation to American literary studies, "normative, if not entirely neutral" (43). We make claims from a specific secularist tradition that moulds our hypotheses and dictates the notions and categories we employ in our interpretative frameworks.[15] But we do not feel obliged to make a disclaimer about it. It is simply the standard, naturalized position for humanities inquiry, which is governed, as political theorist Wendy Brown notes, by "the presumptive secularism of critique" ("Introduction" 8). Our interpretation of the cultural production of the late Franco period and beyond is shaped by our unexamined normative secularism that makes religion intrinsically incompatible with modernity. In doing so, I am afraid that we are somewhat imposing our political assumptions over our objects of study.

The picture gets even more intricate when we consider that the engineers of the modernization process – the technocrats appointed in the late 1950s – contributed a great deal to the narrative of secularization that continues to frame our discussions of modernity in Spain. The technocrats replaced the religious self-validation of the regime, anchored in the myths of "eternal Spain" and the rhetoric of the messianic nation, with a conceptual agenda that stressed economic development and rational thinking. The regime's new political cadre instilled in public discourse what Raymond Carr and Juan Pablo Fusi termed a "semantic revolution": a new vocabulary that, drawing on the language of international business, worshipped the logic of rationalization (54). This new vocabulary operated as the discursive wrap to the series of fast-paced socioeconomic transformations that Spain underwent from around 1960 until the mid-1970s. These transformations began with the 1959 Stabilization Plan (*Plan de estabilización*), which was implemented to accelerate the process of industrialization and to develop a market economy that would supersede two decades of economic isolation. On the verge of bankruptcy, Spain could no longer utilize only its own resources and needed to be open to international trade. The action of the technocrats crystallized in a series of development plans that had an immediate impact. The Spanish economy grew from 1960 to 1974 at "an average of 6.6 percent overall, 9.4 percent in the industrial sector" (Shubert 207). Most historians and social analysts agree that these impressive figures resulted from the combined force of three factors. First, the increase in foreign investments into Spain, from $40 million in 1960 to $697 million by 1970, permitted the acquisition of new technology to help the industrial sector. Second, the so-called economic miracle owing to the explosion of tourism, which registered an increase of visitors from 6 million in 1960 to 30 million in 1975, leaving an estimated profit of $3 billion (Riquer i Permanyer 260). The third major source of capital came from the remittances sent by emigrants working abroad, calculated in 1965 at $362 million and at $1.1 billion in 1973 (Shubert 209).

The favourable macroeconomic indicators and the overall improvement in social welfare gave the regime's administration the chance to uphold its authority by emphasizing a new type of political legitimacy. Recalling the framework of political domination outlined by Max Weber in *Economy and Society*, we can characterize this new legitimacy sought by the technocrats as one resting on rational-legal grounds. Weber argued that the stability and durability of any ruling power depend not so much on exercising sheer power as on its ability to secure legitimacy. Any established order tries to convince social groups of its right to exercise that authority. If it succeeds, populations will obey enthusiastically. Weber distinguished three types of legitimate domination that have historically existed as "ideal types": 1) charismatic legitimacy, the most archaic form of domination, which rests on "devotion to the exceptional sanctity, heroism or exemplary character of an individual person"; 2) traditional legitimacy, the trust in the inviolability of foundational principles and traditions, and in the rightfulness of those who exercise the authority under those principles; and 3) rational legitimacy, the most modern form, when authority does not reside in persons or traditions, but in the belief in the suitable enactment of impersonal rules and norms that prompt obedience (215).

Charismatic and traditional authority prevailed until the late 1950s. The devotion to Franco's sanctity was fundamental in securing legitimacy. Franco's collaborators fabricated a charismatic image of a sovereign who only had to "answer before God and before history" – Franco dixit – for the way he governed.[16] But Franco's charisma was never appealing enough to secure the legitimacy of an administration that established itself in power through a coup d'état leading to a civil war. Hence the regime emphasized his duty of making sure that traditional values were revamped. The self-perceived historic mission to spread the Spanish Catholic essence around the world was the main tradition invoked to justify the regime's actions. In this way, the overturning of the legitimate democratic government of the Second Republic was repackaged as a religious crusade against the atheist threat of communism. Iconic figures such as El Cid, the Reyes Católicos, and Teresa de Ávila were accordingly reinvented to serve as historical models of that crusade spirit. Thus, Spanish national identity was redefined, pivoting on a political theology that upheld a notion of sovereignty with exclusionary implications. Drawing on Giorgio Agamben's theory of sovereign power, William Viestenz argues that Spanish national identity under Franco "came to resemble an exceptional sacred cult" (6), since the metaphysical substance of the nation – the traditional type of legitimacy in Weber's paradigm – depended on scapegoating elements unwelcome to that sacred essence, which Franco conceptualized as the "Anti-España."[17] But, as Viestenz contends, the "*Anti-España*" was crucial to the regime's political theology and "could never be eradicated" (71). The traditional legitimacy of the regime rested on the biopolitical production of bare life, on the inclusive exclusion of the "*Anti-España*" that assured the stability of Franco's sovereignty.

As time went on, the charismatic and traditional grounds for authority needed to be invigorated. New generations of Spaniards did not have the same connection with the symbolic meaning of the Civil War as a religious crusade. Similarly, charismatic legitimacy was bound to wane with time, especially as Franco started to show signs of aging. This is why the new technocratic cadres had to switch the focus to underscoring the achievements of their administration. Those achievements included the economic growth and the improved welfare of Spaniards. Therefore, the "semantic revolution" of the technocratic administration was a necessary step to diminish the traditional ideological components of the official language so that citizens would show loyalty to the efficiency of the regime's administration. However, the traditional and charismatic types of legitimacy did not disappear completely, but rather started to be strategically deployed, as Paloma Aguilar notes, "in a kind of alternating preeminence" (37). The new rational form of legitimacy was intended to support the regime, not to weaken its bases, so the administration could not jettison traditional and charismatic authority altogether.

While it is true that in the 1960s the technocrats, in seeking to strengthen the rational-legal legitimacy of the regime, put religious integrity and spiritual notions of national essence on the symbolic back burner to fabricate the image of a modern, efficient, and peaceful government (Crumbaugh 9; Pavlović, *The Mobile* 1), this does not mean that the "gospel of business efficiency" (Carr and Fusi 81) erased the Catholic gospel from the governmental structure and from political thought. In highlighting the regime's switch of self-representational tactics, cultural critics have overemphasized the displacement of religion and the Church from public affairs. Peninsularists have equated the increasing rationalization in the management of the public domain with the complete social differentiation of spheres. As James Beckford argues, it is plausible for a society to become rationalized, in the sense of "the methodical pursuit of efficient relations between means and ends" – something that the technocrats made a priority in Spain – without being fully differentiated (47). As I show in detail in the next section, religious considerations and a Catholic-infused economic ethos still had a substantial function in shaping the new configuration of the regime's administration and economic policies.

The Spirit of Catholic Capitalism

In his analysis of the technocratic phase of the regime, Justin Crumbaugh complicates the familiar story that posits Franco's Spain as the anti-modern political exception in Western Europe. Using tourism as the signpost of a modern form of governance, Crumbaugh shows how the regime began to practise what Michel Foucault referred to as the "governmentalization of the State" in modern Western societies. By that, Foucault meant the development of an amalgamation of institutions, procedures, calculations, tactics, and reflections aimed at the welfare of the population and which has "as its principal form of knowledge political economy" (102). This governmentalization of the state is, according to Foucault, a necessary step that allows the state to survive, since it shifts the focus away from the act of governing itself – and from the figure of the sovereign – to the well-being of the populace (100). In this way, the sovereign leader is no longer the pivotal figure in the political game; rather, meticulous economic planning and careful management of resources take centre stage, as what Foucault calls "the art of government" becomes an abstract, non-subjective "political science" (101).[18]

In his examination of the aesthetic dimension of this "art of governing" in Franco's Spain in the 1960s, Crumbaugh argues that the regime deployed the "spectacle of tourism" to fabricate the image of a country that provided "access to or at least identification with the newfound economic and social opportunities that were said to accompany modernization." Tourism became a strategy of self-representation through which Francoism exercised a modern form of power not based on violent means of coercion to enforce traditional values but on co-opting narratives of development that were typically associated with modern liberal democracies (20). Crumbaugh's suggestion to focus less on the regime's exceptionality and more on its similarities with Western liberal democracies has been furthered by other critics, most notably by Tatjana Pavlović, who analyses the role of the burgeoning consumer culture in fostering the regime's shift to a modern self-image that "ceased to be metaphysical and became more frankly material" (*The Mobile* 1). For both scholars, a similar process of disavowing or of downplaying Spain's exceptional location in relation to modern European democracies entails not accepting "at face value Francoism's attempts to associate itself with a rarefied past of imperial glory and religious crusade, or its claims to spiritual or cultural superiority" (Crumbaugh 19). These views suggest that the regime's spiritual justifications were discursive strategies that framed its first two decades. The very process of framing the image of a nation chosen by God would seem, from this perspective, more important than the actual "Catholicization" of Spanish society. There is, however, an important caveat to this interpretation: the actual practices linked to the discourse. The sacralization of Spanish society influenced policy-making, transformed the educational system, and shaped social norms and mores. In this sense, a plausible question arises: Why do we have to "de-Catholicize" technocratic Spain in order to wrap our heads around the modernization in the management style?

The technocrats introduced a modern outlook in their governance techniques, but this mutation involved more than simply pragmatic administration, since religion was still a key part of the mix. After all, a number of the leading technocrats were members of the religious organization Opus Dei. The Opus Dei technocrats, if anything, were complying with Opus Dei's spiritual mission. For José Casanova, "the Opus Dei ethic" is behind the modernization of Spanish economy. By that he means, in a Weberian sense, "the practical impulses for action which are founded in the psychological and pragmatic contexts of religion" ("The Opus Dei" 53). In Opus Dei's case, the practical impulses for action were those related to the doctrine of "the sanctification of the secular world" (Payne 190). For Escrivá de Balaguer, being holy, following and living the Opus Dei spirit, consists of a threefold task: "to sanctify work itself, to sanctify oneself in work and to sanctify others with work" (*Conversaciones* 25). In following this directive, Opus Dei members developed a work ethic as a way of achieving personal sanctification and of carrying out the duties of the apostolate. Members of Opus Dei occupying public positions acted according to the secular spirituality that the Institute instilled in them, as they took to heart their religious calling to perfection, the complete devotion to excellence in work. The disciplined rationalization of the individual and collective conduct of Opus Dei members was suitable for the process of bureaucratic and economic rationalization that Spain underwent during the development years.

The Opus Dei technocrats revised Spanish traditionalism, incorporating the "instrumental" rationality that for Max Weber was central to the development of Western modernity. They envisioned the modernization process by strategically emphasizing, in Weberian terms, "instrumental rationality," even if "substantive rationality" was still a key component. Substantive rationality refers for Weber to the "constellation of values toward which action is oriented" (Kalberg 45), which in Spain's case meant the Catholic principles that are essential to Spain's history; "instrumental" rationality implies decision-making according to rational objectives and based on technical solutions instead of on the absolute value of religious and ethical beliefs (Weber, *Economy and Society* 12–26). The business-savvy Opus Dei technocrats applied the criteria of instrumental rationality in implementing their reform of the Spanish economy and administration. But in Laureano López Rodó's development plan, outlined in his books *Política y desarrollo* (1970) and *Nuevo horizonte del desarrollo* (1972), generating economic development also entailed taking into consideration substantive rationality. López Rodó, known as "the technocrat *par excellence*" (Carr and Fusi 35), always argued that the horizon of the development plan went beyond rational calculations about the economy; it should also be a platform of social development based on the idea of solidarity (*Política* 75). When presenting the third development plan, López Rodó still insisted that development is not about "tosco materialismo" (coarse materialism) and mere possessions; rather, it should be put to the service of spiritual values and be subordinated to the "supremos ideales de la Patria y del hombre" (supreme ideals of the fatherland and of man) (*Nuevo horizonte* 10).

The main notion we can extrapolate from López Rodó's "development literature" is that Spain's *desarrollismo* was not an abstract application of a Western model of bureaucratic rationalization. Max Weber had already claimed that the rationalization process is a developmental sequence that should be thought of as an "ideal type" that can have "quite considerable heuristic value" (*The Methodology* 101). For Weber, "ideal types" should be used for "comparison with empirical reality in order to establish its divergences and similarities" (43), as conceptual constructs that are ideal in the sense of being abstractions from concrete social reality. Therefore, they may serve as analytical tools that identify general sociohistorical patterns that need to be compared and contrasted with specific empirical cases. In Spain's case, the rationalization of the economy during the development years cannot be understood without reference to non-economic considerations: the "irrational" tradition that had thus far defined "Spanishness" for the regime. However, these traditional Catholic principles did not appear in López Rodó's model of development as a pompous metaphysical self-justification of the regime, as it happened in the first years of Francoism, but in the form of secularized ideals of social justice.

This explains why the Opus Dei ministers constantly mixed the technical and the moral planes in their public remarks. For instance, Mariano Navarro Rubio ended his term as finance minister (1957–65) by suggesting that his successor should go by the following recipe: "Levantar a Dios muy alto en España" (To elevate God very high in Spain) (Ynfante 208). Alberto Ullastres, minister of economy, consistently asserted that his economic reforms had a religious keystone, or better yet, that the economic and the moral went hand-in-hand. Ullastres often expressed his notion of development and progress as this moral-economic interface through biblical metaphors: "La justicia social, sí; pero a ras de tierra, acordándonos de aquello de que todos estamos sumidos en el pecado original" (We need social justice, but at the ground level, we must remember that we are all marked by original sin) (quoted in Hermet, *Los católicos I* 119).[19] As these examples drawn from "technocratic literature" showcase, substantive rationality still mattered to the Opus Dei technocrats.

Ironically enough, the Opus Dei ministers' worst intellectual nightmare might have come out of their own camp. In particular, Gonzalo Fernández de la Mora's *El crepúsculo de las ideologías* (1965) created the myth of depoliticized technocrats for whom governing was equivalent to running a factory, an exercise of mere technical expertise (122). This book became an instant classic of the theoretical discourse on technocratic ruling. Fernández de la Mora's most famous proposition pertained to the need for a scientific type of administration carried out by experts, not ideologues (14). Ideology is passé, a sign of underdevelopment that generates social tensions leading to class struggles (20), so it should be replaced by technical and economic planning (16). This is not, he further argued, a new ideology but an "ideocracy," which he defined as a politics of rationalized ideas (145). This "ideocracy" entailed a superintellectualization of politics (23–4), so that the "ideocrats," the experts in management, would make all the political decisions. Moreover, this necessary rationalization and technification of the state would join hands with a general political apathy on the part of the satisfied population (57–9). Far from being a sign of a crisis of the political model, this political apathy would be instead the proof of its good health (57).

In its rigid technocratic doctrinarianism, Fernández de la Mora's book deviated to a certain extent from the way López Rodó envisioned the development process. For the latter, economic development was a means of legitimizing the regime. The development plan had to serve the spirit of the fundamental principles of the Movement and comprise a Catholic notion of development. Fernández de la Mora was on the López Rodó side of the political spectrum as a fellow traditionalist and monarchist, and as an Opus Dei–friendly figure – though not a member of the religious organization. But in *El crepúsculo de las ideologías* he got carried away by the modernization theory and the technocratic model. Although he claimed that his "ideocracy" was not a depoliticized system, but only de-ideologized (119), his extreme technification and rationalization of the government would entail the eradication of any non-scientific knowledge and expertise. Weber would call Fernández de la Mora's ideocracy a "normative ideal" in the sense of a moral imperative that "assumes the dominance of pure economic interests and precludes the operation of political and other non-economic considerations" (*The Methodology* 44). It would involve a relocation of the public role of religion. For Fernández de la Mora, the twilight of ideology did not mean the twilight of religious principles (133–7), but rather their privatization (126). He thus assumed a secularized notion of history in which "progress" was associated with the rationalization of the public sphere. This supremacy of instrumental rationality entailed a break from the political theology that had characterized the Spanish traditionalist intellectuals. The extreme rationalization of political life would annul the religious validation of the regime's political system, and it would make Franco's role as the sovereign superfluous. Evidently, this was a radical proposition in a confessional state. Putting into practice the twilight of ideology as envisioned by Fernández de la Mora would involve the twilight of the Franco regime as it existed. It would definitely imply the end of the marriage between throne and altar, the end of the confessional status of Spain. This is why his theoretical model was ultimately unfeasible under the prevailing political structures of the regime.

Cultural critics have taken Fernández de la Mora's post-ideological society as the conceptual paradigm to evaluate the model of development that the technocrats implemented in Spain. And, perhaps unintentionally, they have made it a technocratic "normative ideal" in the Weberian sense, when it was only an expedient "ideal type" to be measured against the actual course that the process of development took.

This is probably why they have tended to overstress the secularization process during the development years, understood not only as the decline in religious beliefs and practices but also as the disappearance of the sacred from the public sphere. However, we know things did not work out exactly that way. It was López Rodó's model of "technocracy *à la española*" as a combination of rational management of the economy and observance of Spain's spiritual mission that prevailed in practice, if only for a few more years.

Both Franco and the Opus Dei technocrats still counted on the Church's endorsement to implement their project of modernization without political modernity. If only the Vatican II Council had never taken place. The tense atmosphere after the Second Vatican Council (1962–5) made religion a highly politicized issue with a crucial impact on Spanish society. As historian Stanley Payne asserts, "[i]n no Catholic society did the dramatic new doctrines of Vatican Council II have such a marked effect as in Spain" (195). Vatican II sought to renew the structures of the Catholic Church as well as to address the social, political, cultural, economic, and technological changes brought by modernity. The Church hoped to make its message more accessible for everyone and more influential in its coeval society; ultimately, the goal was to stay in business amid the escalating trend towards secularization (Brassloff 12). Several of the declarations, constitutions, and decrees of the council were received by the hardline factions as frontal attacks on the regime, since they supported human rights, required religious liberty, and advocated for political pluralism (Lannon, "Catholicism" 279). The Constitution *Gaudium et Spes* (1965) sanctioned a model of society radically different from Franco's Spain: one grounded in civil sovereignty, in the division of political powers, and in the autonomy of the Church.[20]

This is why the Opus Dei technocrats increasingly clashed with other sides of the Francoist political spectrum, especially the *aperturista* faction of Manuel Fraga, who took a stand in favour of Vatican II recommendations. He envisioned political development as the proper administering of the economy that would also operate as a mechanism of subject formation and, ultimately, as a way of reaching social consensus once the Spanish population reformulated their own "understanding of selfhood and government" and began "to govern themselves and others" (Crumbaugh 9, 20). A heretofore unnoticed religious component also underpinned his notion of "political development." In *Horizonte español*, Fraga conceived his modern form of governance as a "tercera vía" (third way), an alternative to both liberal capitalism and communism (197). This third way entailed implementing Vatican recommendations for development as stipulated by the papal encyclicals *Mater et Magistra* (1961) and *Pacem in terris* (1963). Quoting from the first one, Fraga contended that economic development involved private initiative controlled by the state with the main goal of generating social progress and equal distribution of wealth (*Horizonte* 198). Fraga explained at length the religious basis of this "third way" in *El desarrollo político*. He argued that the political order needed to be based upon a moral order (197). Equally, the economy was not an autonomous sphere, but one guided by religious and ethical principles (119). For Fraga, religion was not only a private matter whose public dimension was confined to the temple; rather, religion should guide economic development, as corporations should adhere to a corporate morality (136–7). Drawing again from *Mater et Magistra,* Fraga assigned the Church the task of leading the process of improving the people's welfare to achieve a superior goal: spiritual perfection through material profits. Scientific-economic progress per se was not enough; progress should serve a religious ethic, and the Church's post-conciliar acceptance of progress via its new social doctrine had showed the path to do so (140). According to Fraga, the main lesson from the Vatican II Council was the Church's changing attitude towards intervening in temporal matters and towards reconfiguring the modern world with a Christian ethos (120).

Three entire chapters of *El desarrollo político* were devoted to the interface between religion and the modernization of the political-economic system. Fraga's *aperturismo* could be described as an attempt to implement the spirit of the conciliar *aggiornamento,* the Vatican II mandate to catch up with modernity, in the Spanish political sphere. This open endorsement of conciliar recommendations increasingly put Fraga at odds with the Opus Dei technocrats. While the latter also believed in the rationalization of the economy, they did not share Fraga's conviction to do so via the terms recommended by the Council. One of the innovative ideas of *Gaudium et Spes* was the concept of the Church as a "community" that intervenes in the world to demand social justice (sections 23–32). This directive could not be assimilated by Opus Dei members, whose concept of the Church was that of a patriarchal family with a corporate hierarchical structure (with Escrivá de Balaguer at the top of the ladder). The Opus Dei technocrats wanted to modernize the economy without changing the authoritarian political basis of the regime. In addition, Opus Dei rejected the idea of direct action of the Church in temporal matters, and instead proposed indirect intervention through the professional achievements of lay people and their sanctification of the world through their work. The traditionalist Opus Dei technocrats also rejected the Vatican II call to come to terms with all aspects of modernity in society. This is why they resented Fraga's press law (1966) and feared "the negative social impacts of tourism" (Pack 107). The main point of dispute between the two factions was therefore not their overall agreement on economic policy but their substantial disagreements about their differing notions of a religious-based political development. Both Fraga and López Rodó argued for a model of development beyond pure rational planning to achieve social justice. But the paths to that desired development were quite different; one took the direction signalled by Vatican II and the other skipped it.

Modernization and Economic Theology

The case of Spain during the development years should thus be grasped by considering approaches to modern politics through the prism of religion.[21] Among them, I am going to highlight Giorgio Agamben's *The Kingdom and the Glory*, the third instalment of his *homo sacer* saga. Agamben traces a theological genealogy of economy and government – what Foucault called "governmentality" – from the medieval Christian notion of providence until the present time to claim that religious concepts are still "at the center of the political apparatuses of contemporary democracies," as they have been throughout Western history. On the surface, this may seem like mere paraphrasing of the famous proposition underpinning Carl Schmitt's *Political Theology* (1922): "All significant concepts of the modern theory of the state are secularized theological concepts" (36). Similar to Schmitt, Agamben sees theological notions re-emerging in secular political discourse. However, if for Schmitt sovereignty is the pivotal concept that links theology and politics, Agamben poses the centrality of the "economy," conceived as an *oikonomia*, an internal organization of both the divine and human reigns that comprises economy and government (*The Kingdom* 1). For Schmitt, the sovereign is "he who decides on the exception," the one who has absolute power as an embodiment of the divine, just as the legal exception that the sovereign decides "is analogous to the miracle in theology" (5); Agamben reacts to this excessive concentration of power in the sovereign and instead argues that power now adopts the form of an "economy" in the sense of manifesting itself through governance and proper management.[22]

While Agamben aligns with Foucault in seeking an alternative paradigm to the limitations of political theology, the difference is that for Agamben both paradigms of power – political theology and economic theology – originate in Christian theology and have coexisted in time, in diverse degrees depending on the historical moment. While Foucault locates "governmentality" as a defining feature of the modern period, Agamben extends it throughout the history of Western rule. Strikingly, Agamben faults Foucault for not realizing that his paradigm of governmentality harks back to God, as seen in the trinitarian paradigm, which is the very origin of the differentiation of spheres typical of modern political systems (*The Kingdom* 110–11). Agamben contends that the divine reign already reflected a split between absolute rule (God) and governmental functions – performed by the angels with administrative vocation, the "angel-functionaries" (166). Therefore, the "providential *gubernatio* of the world," its economy, is in itself "nothing but a reformulation and development of the theological *oikonomia*" (141–2). The repercussion of this scenario is that the mundane world reflects the same hierarchical organization as the divine one, which allows us to understand the relationship between sovereignty and economy – between political theology and economic theology.

For Agamben, the key to bringing together both modes of power is the concept of "glory," understood as external practices such as liturgy, prayer, art, and architecture, among others, that typify God's workings in the world and that are similar to the angels' worshipping of the Lord in the celestial realm (*The Kingdom* 193). The role of the Church and its relationship with that celestial realm is intrinsically political, because it imitates the angels and partakes in the glorification of God through acclamations as a way of achieving "full celestial citizenship." This is what Agamben calls the "angelic vocation" of human beings, of the angelic bureaucrats (147). One may argue that some of the paraphernalia of this glory has evaporated in modernity, but Agamben claims, again drawing on Schmitt, that it resurfaces in other shapes in modern Western democracies, such as in the form of public opinion and in the role of media (255). What is truly innovative in Agamben is his cross-reading of Schmitt and Guy Debord (*The Society of Spectacle*) to argue that democratic consensus is now reached through modern forms of acclamation – Schmitt's notion of public opinion – that, like capital itself, "assume the mediatic form of the image" as a collection of spectacles (255). The function of glory that used to take centre stage in the political arena, and which was previously enacted in liturgy and ceremonials, now becomes embedded in media discourse, and from there penetrates all aspects of life and society, both the public and private spheres. Thus, for Agamben liberal democracies and their modern form of biopolitics are "entirely founded upon glory," on the productive use of acclamation that is "multiplied and disseminated by the media beyond imagination" (256).

Agamben's paradigm poses a radical critique of modern democracies and also helps us understand the last phase of Francoism, one in which the shift from an autarkic to a technocratic system can be read as a move from a political-theological paradigm of sovereign power – one that rested in the figure of the *caudillo* by the grace of God, as William Viestenz aptly put it – towards an economic-theological paradigm that came close to that of modern Western democracies. In this shift, the improvement of the welfare of citizens became the regime's main goal, and the political function of glory, while still present, was reformulated and disseminated in new ways. The difference with respect to contemporary democracies lies in the fact that the logic of economy during the development years still retained an explicit transcendental point of reference, whereas in contemporary liberal democracies the level of the government becomes so preponderant – through the spectacular magic of media to generate consensus – that economy and glory become somewhat impossible to tell apart.

Liturgies and ceremonies performing the political function of glory did not disappear during the technocratic phase of the regime. Two prominent examples of those glorious ceremonies will in fact be relevant to two of the films discussed in subsequent chapters. The first one was the official celebration of the fourth centenary of the reform of the Discalced Carmelites. The commemoration included a plethora of events related to the journey of the relic of Teresa de Ávila's incorrupt left arm across the country from August 1962 to August 1963.[23] The second grandiose ceremony was the celebration in 1964 of the "Twenty-Five Years of Peace," a huge propaganda campaign orchestrated by Manuel Fraga to honour the silver anniversary of the regime. The purpose of the campaign was the pursuit of a new form of legitimacy for the regime based on rational grounds: the celebration of the peace and prosperity achieved under Franco's rule. However, the events of this celebration – including the feature-length film *Franco, ese hombre* that I will analyse in chapter 1 – served to reinforce Franco as a saint and the sacred origin of the confessional state. Both the "Twenty-Five Years of Peace" and the fourth centenary of Carmelites' reform functioned as glorious ceremonies to performatively wield sovereign power. As liturgies and ceremonies were increasingly less used, the acclamatory aspects of power were reconfigured through media discourses that infiltrated all aspects of social life to achieve social consensus. During his term as minister of information and tourism from 1962 to 1969, Manuel Fraga became a master in using media for greater efficiency of the political system, as he prioritized "a conscious repoliticization of society through the symbolic channels made available by Spain's emergent information age" (Crumbaugh 42). Fraga saw the importance of the tourism boom and of the growing mass culture both as profitable industries and as means of fabricating a modernized image of Spain. Media discourses helped produce a discursive framework to shape a new national subject who would embrace the economic liberalization and would actively take part in its management while still being comfortable without democratic participation.

With *Confessional Cinema* I want to propose that cinema acted as a cogent medium channelling, sometimes with a critical edge, the political function of "glory" in late-Franco Spain. I examine a significant corpus of religious films (over fifty) that engaged the shift from political theology to economic theology in the regime's administration. Many of them were popular and profitable films (some with more than two and three million spectators) that on the surface seemed to endorse pro-regime agendas. They had a crucial role in advertising the image of economic modernization in synchrony with Spain's Catholic kernel and in promoting social consensus. In this sense, these pro-regime films generally operated with what Jacques Rancière calls the logic of consensus, a particular way to conceptualize and represent the political community as "the sum of the parts of the social body" (42) that coexist in an idyllic place – the peace and prosperity secured by the Francoist regime in the development years. But confessional films did more than echo the regime's new political discourse regarding modernization; they actively contributed to that discourse by praising some its tenets (industrialization, economic growth, the emergence of a thriving consumer culture) while simultaneously exposing, however unconsciously, its contradictions. As examples of what Sally Faulkner termed the "cinema of contradiction" of the development years, Spanish confessional cinema of the 1960s (and early 1970s in my account) encapsulated, often in conflicting ways, conservative and dissident values (*A Cinema* 1–3).

The key point is that these films did not merely reflect or replicate political messages that existed prior to them but also embodied, sometimes with a disruptive effect, the tensions and incongruities in that evolving political discourse. As I explained before, in the shift from political theology to economic theology, Francoist propaganda toned down its exaltation of essential truths as the repository of Spanish national identity and the legitimacy of its leader invested with divine power. Instead of metaphysical justifications of Spanishness, which ultimately hinged on violence and a discriminatory sacred cult, the emphasis shifted to a rational discourse that highlighted the achievements of the efficient administration of the regime in providing wealth and safety for all Spaniards. But during that process, religion became a factor of dissent that complicated the function and meaning of confessional cinema. In particular, some religious films increasingly made it apparent that the authoritarian political system of Francoism was at odds with the renewed values of post–Vatican II Catholicism. The films that were expected to epitomize the achievements of the regime's administration revealed the cracks in the wall of the political discourse of late Francoism: the more that these films began to embrace the main tenets of post–Vatican II Catholicism (religious freedom, civil sovereignty, and political pluralism), the more they put forward religion as a dissident factor.

Once conciliar recommendations began to be implemented, reformist factions of the Spanish Church started to promote modern democracy as the ideal form of governance, and ceased being the ideological partner of Francoism. The rupture of the coalition between throne and altar was not a strategy of Francoism (or of the technocrats in charge of the administration) to perpetuate itself in power; on the contrary, it was the Church that grew tired of an alliance with a reigning power that contravened its renewed pastoral mission. For Alfonso Botti, Francoism wanted to preserve *Nacional-Catolicismo*, even if dressed in technocratic garments (131). What the regime could not predict was that the majority of the Church would develop an aversion to the confessional status of Spain. In fact, as Rafael Gómez contends, it was the opposition to the regime that turned "confessional," since political defiance was exercised in the name of religion (287). Therefore, the link between religion and politics became even stronger in the last years of the regime. The difference is that, instead of an instrument to legitimize the ruling order, religion became by the early 1970s a destabilizing factor that strengthened resistance to the regime and promoted the transition to a modern democracy as the inevitable course of action for Spanish society.

The Spanish film industry took seriously this public dimension of religion in the last phase of the regime. This included both mainstream popular films and the acclaimed pictures of the leftist auteurs such as Luis Buñuel and the young directors of the *Nuevo Cine Español*. As Elizabeth Scarlett rightly points out, "[c]onflicted Catholicism stretches across both kinds of filmmakers" (5). As I will show, though, commercial cinema astonishingly engaged the renewed role of religion in the Spanish public sphere of the late-Franco period more than most of the dissident directors. For the latter, and with the exception of the late works of Luis Buñuel, religion tended to be inextricably associated with the memory of the Civil War and the early Francoist period. The young auteurs of the *Nuevo Cine Español* perceived the public dimension of religion through the prism of the 1940s, as a repressive and anti-modern force, and overlooked its transformed public function at the twilight of the regime.

In the remaining chapters I examine how the Spanish film industry engaged, and at times questioned, the home-grown model of technocracy that combined rational management of the economy with the preservation of Spain's Catholic backbone. Chapter 1 delves into the upsurge of hagiographic films that praise the life of saints and religious heroes and heroines as a "hinge film genre" in the first half of the 1960s, when the transition from the autarkic to the technocratic phase of the regime was taking place. Focusing on the use of the technology of lighting, I call attention to the manner in which films such as *Teresa de Jesús* (Juan de Orduña, 1961), *Rosa de Lima* (José María Elorrieta, 1961), and *Fray Escoba* (Ramón Torrado, 1961) constructed an idealized image of female sainthood with racial implications in an attempt to reinvigorate traditional values underpinning the regime. These films constituted cinematic responses to the challenges that emerged because of the modernization process, for they provided some sort of reassurance to Catholic spectators who were grappling with the rapid changes that seemed to agitate the stability of traditional values. Other hagiographic films reflected ongoing tensions that ensued from the regime's attempt to switch the grounds for political legitimacy. *Franco, ese hombre* (José Luis Sáenz de Heredia, 1964), supposedly made to endorse a new type of legitimacy based on rational-legal grounds, ultimately tried to reinforce Franco's charismatic authority in the Spanish political imagination. Finally, I discuss how *El señor de La Salle* (Luis César Amadori, 1965) disrupted the typical connotations of high-key and low-key approaches to lighting in commercial cinema. This visual treatment was deployed in this film to present emergent social values about the role that religion and the Church should play in the modern world. The religious hero of *El señor* stands as a model of modern sainthood that suggested that the Church should intervene in worldly matters as an independent organization seeking social justice and, thereby, untied to platforms of power.

In the second half of the 1960s, the most common manifestation of confessional cinema shifted to comedies that addressed the impact of the development plans and Vatican II recommendations on Spanish society. Chapter 2 examines a sub-type, the "comedia del desarrollismo," post–Vatican II comedies such as *Fray Torero* (José Luis Sáenz de Heredia, 1966), *El padre Manolo, El padre Coplillas* (Ramón Comas, 1969), and *Sor Citröen* that featured clergy who eagerly implemented conciliar recommendations and adapted to the dynamics of capitalist modernization. Working through the tension between tradition and modernity, most of these films celebrated economic liberalization and the prosperity of the new consumer society. Post–Vatican II comedies constituted cinematic configurations of the discursive framework of the regime in its technocratic phase. Through the analysis of key aspects of their composition, editing, and iconography, I will show how post–Vatican II comedies also accommodated competing views on these issues. Towards the end of the chapter, I analyse how the film *Sor Citröen* left room for a reading that reveals the contradictions behind the official developmental triumphalism, while José Luis Sáenz de Heredia's *¡Se armó el belén!* argued for a return to a focus on the figure of the sovereign, the dictator Franco, instead of on economic development.

Chapter 3 highlights "nun films" that represented how women religious negotiated the changes within the Catholic Church due to the Vatican II Council. I pay attention to the way the celluloid nuns undertook their renewed mission and responsibilities, showing along the way the internal tensions within the Church triggered by the conciliar recommendations. Surprisingly, though, nun films were used more to comment on other pressing social issues than to offer a thorough account of the condition of Spanish nuns in the 1960s. Above all, nun films engaged the shifting condition of women in the developing Spanish society. Women's incorporation into the job market in the 1960s allowed them a certain degree of financial independence and social mobility, which generated anxiety over threatening models of modern womanhood. Nun films such as *Sor Ye-Yé* and *La novicia rebelde* (Luis Lucia, 1971) responded to those anxieties by promoting traditional gender roles through the deployment of certain genre conventions of the romantic comedy and the musical. Popular pro-regime films, just like the Church, embraced certain modern values but kept a reactionary position with regard to gender and sexuality.

In the last chapter, "Narratives of Suspicion," I turn to the young directors associated with the *Nuevo Cine Español*. In the first part, I focus on Basilio Martín Patino's *Canciones para después de una guerra* and *Caudillo*, and on Carlos Saura's *La prima Angélica*. I show how these films, drawing on Luis Buñuel's anti-clerical film legacy, engaged religion filtered through the memory of the Civil War to denounce the alliance between the Church and the political authorities of the regime. Disruptive visual and aural elements, discontinuity editing, and framing and lighting patterns were deployed to present narratives that contest the official triumphalism over the national state of affairs and, above all, to suggest a link of Catholicism to confinement and repression. In the second part, I analyse three other films that also approached the topic of religion with suspicion by zooming in on the links of religious organizations to platforms of power, but in these three cases beyond the framework of the crusade church. Concretely, I draw attention to how *El buen amor* (Francisco Regueiro, 1963), *La casa sin fronteras* (Pedro Olea, 1972), and *La trastienda* (Jordi Grau, 1975) represented the role of the Opus Dei spirituality and economic ethos in the social and economic fabric of Spain's development years.

A word about the case studies selected and the ones discarded for in-depth analysis. Beginning with the latter, although I make references to Luis Buñuel throughout the book, and I begin chapter 4 by commenting on the significance of *Nazarín* and *Viridiana*, I have not included a separate chapter analysing the prominent role of religion in Buñuel's other important films of this period such as *El ángel exterminador*, *Simón del desierto*, *La Voie Lactée*, and *Tristana*. I am aware that such a chapter would have complemented chapter 4 as a noteworthy counter-example to most of the pro-regime confessional films I discuss in chapters 1, 2, and 3. I feel compelled to clarify why I have decided not to do so. First of all, from the above list, only *Viridiana* and *Tristana* were Spanish productions; actually both of them were co-productions, of Spain / Mexico and France / Italy / Spain, respectively. The other ones belong to Buñuel's Mexican and French exile periods and, if we use a strict notion of national cinema, do not belong to the history of Spanish cinema. More than that, I have decided not to focus on Buñuel because there is already a vast corpus of scholarship on his oeuvre, including detailed analyses of the significance of religion in his most acclaimed films.[24]

The selected case studies include an array of films and directors, ranging from high-profile pro-regime filmmakers such as José Luis Sáenz de Heredia and Juan de Orduña, who enjoyed official recognition and prestige among the regime elites, to commercially successful directors such as Ramón Fernández, Luis Lucia, Pedro Lazaga, and Ramón Torrado. From the oppositional camp associated with the *Nuevo Cine Español,* I address films by Basilio Martín Patino, Pedro Olea, and Carlos Saura. I have chosen to analyse a variety of films that best represent and engage with the issues I want to explore. Most of them were highly popular and commercial; others were influential because of the patronage and publicity they received from the regime's official platforms, such as José Luis Sáenz de Heredia's *Franco, ese hombre* and Juan de Orduña's *Teresa de Jesús;* films in a third group were prominent because of public controversies they spurred, as in the case of Pedro Olea's *La casa sin fronteras,* Carlos Saura's *La prima Angélica,* and Jordi Grau's *La trastienda.* Seen collectively, they illustrate the complex and far from monolithic approaches of the Spanish film industry to the role that religion and the Catholic Church played in the late Franco period.

Chapter One

Lighting Sainthood in the Time of Technocracy

Hagiographic films, that is, films that venerate the lives of saints or other models of piety, became pervasive in Spanish cinema in the early 1960s. These stories of visions, miraculous powers, redemptive suffering, and unbreakable devotion delivered an uplifting effect for viewers in need of emotional and spiritual solace. Since these stories tend to extol a traditional, and sometimes atavistic, mentality, they do not fit comfortably within the standard understanding of the development of Spanish cinema in the 1960s as closely related to the modernization process during the last part of the Franco regime. Elisa Chuliá argues that Catholic presence in society after 1957 took a different shape both in public discourse and in cultural production, since "[s]tories of saints, of blessed, pious young people and charitable women gave way to stories of men and women who were moving up the social scale and overcoming the problems they faced through work" (172). However, as I pointed out in the introduction, cinema proved to be a recalcitrant counter-example to these types of blanket statements regarding cultural production during the period of *desarrollismo*.

When Luis Lucia made *Molokai* (1959), a saccharine depiction of the Belgian missionary Saint Damien of Veuster (1840–1889), there was no indication that the hagiographic film was a worn-out genre in the Spanish film industry. This film was a box-office success and launched the acting career of Javier Escrivá.[1] It also received ample official support and prestigious awards: Premio Especial del Sindicato, several awards by the Círculo de Escritores Cinematográficos and the magazines *Revista Internacional del Cine* and *Fotogramas*. Moreover, as Joaquín de Prada sarcastically noted in his review of the film for *Cinema Universitario*, hagiographic films seemed to retain an aura of national significance: "'Molokai' ha alcanzado un carácter cuasi oficial de res pública, un interés nacional que la hace intocable" ("Molokai" has achieved a quasi-official status of *res publica,* a national interest that makes it untouchable) (64). Time proved Joaquín de Prada right, and, much to his disappointment, the early 1960s constituted the peak years of hagiographic films with titles such as *Rosa de Lima, Fray Escoba, Teresa de Jesús, Isidro, el Labrador* (Rafael Salvia, 1964), *Aquella joven de blanco* (León Klimovsky, 1965), *El señor de La Salle,* and *Cotolay* (Juan Antonio Nieves Conde, 1966). Along with these films, the highly publicized documentary *Franco, ese hombre* cast Francisco Franco as the saint who saved Spain from Communism in the Civil War.

Scholars of Spanish film under Franco have either ignored this heavy traffic of saints in the Spanish cinema or have mentioned them in passing as mere remnants of the previous decade.[2] It seems that Spanish film scholars cannot accept that the hagiographic film, a genre associated with comforting platitudes rather than with promoting social change, could gain so much currency at a time when Spain was promoting its affinities with the more modernized European countries. So they simply erased it from the map. As remnants of the declining presence of the Catholic Church in the film industry, hagiographic films are seen on the whole as anachronistic and extraneous to the larger narrative of modernization that frames conceptualizations of Spanish cinema and the broader development of Spanish culture and society in the 1960s. In terms of Raymond Williams's framework of "epochal analysis" of cultural processes, hagiographic films are perceived, along with other cultural expressions that contain traditional religious messages, as manifestations of "the archaic," as "that which is wholly recognized as an element of the past" and no longer active and effective in the present (122). The larger aversion to popular genre cinema of the Franco era as aesthetically poor further fuels Spanish film critics' lack of interest in hagiographic films.

Given their prevalence in the 1960s, hagiographic films deserve a closer examination instead of being contrasted, along with other popular genres deemed equally worthless and complicit with the political status quo, to more prestigious forms of filmmaking. Hagiographic films were not mere instruments of social control, even if the hagiography, as a genre, has often lent itself to all kinds of political appropriation in all its forms since its manifestations in late antiquity and the medieval era (Ashbrook Harvey 616). In fact, Spanish hagiographic films of the 1960s deviated from the anti-communist hagiographies of the 1950s such as *La señora de Fátima* (Rafael Gil) and *Cerca del cielo* (Domingo Viladomat, 1951), in which the cult of saints was a means of transmitting messages that were supposedly religious, but in reality political, of obedience to the existing sociopolitical order. As I will show, the visual styles of these hagiographic films also had ideological strings, but these were not necessarily as blatant and one-dimensional as in their precursors. My goal in this chapter is to show that these films acted as a "hinge film genre" for the history of Spanish cinema. By that I mean that hagiographic films were a genre in between two epistemic moments, as they denoted the transition from the autarkic to the technocratic period that was deemed by economists the "hinge decade" (*decenio bisagra*). This term aptly encapsulated "the shift from post-war insistence on moderation, restrictions, hoarding or rationing" to an economic and social discourse that promoted adopting consumer culture and embracing modern values (Pavlović, *The Mobile* 2). Through the analysis of their different visual styles and, especially, of their uses of the technology of lighting, I will show how some hagiographic films supported the sacred imagining of Spanish national identity that was pivotal in the autarkic period of the regime (*Fray Escoba*, *Teresa de Jesús*, and *Rosa de Lima*), while others (*El señor de La Salle* and in part *Aquella joven de blanco*) presented views that were more in tune with a post–Vatican II understanding of society and the role of religion in that modern society. If Michel de Certeau claimed that literary hagiographies are a "discourse" that exists "on the outer edge of historiography, as its temptation and betrayal" (269), I would like to suggest here that Spanish hagiographic films in the 1960s existed on the outer edge of the official rhetoric of the regime, sometimes endorsing its foundational tenets – traditional and charismatic types of legitimacy – and providing a contrasting foil to modernity, while at other times embracing evolving modern values that clashed with the concurrently developing political discourse of the regime.

Pamela Grace describes hagiographic films as a separate genre, which she calls "hagiopic," that is related but not identical to the biopics about notable historical figures. Working with a wide corpus of American and European films, she identifies two main differences that illustrate the hagiopic's individuality: 1) the hagiopic is specifically interested in the connection of the religious hero(ine), who has been chosen as such by God, with the sacred; and 2) hagiopics depict a unique fictional world that audiences would not find in any other genre, one full of miracles, heavenly apparitions, and the ubiquitous presence of an ever-benevolent God that predetermines the narrative (1–2). Grace grants to this distinctive cinematic universe of hagiopics the status of a narrative chronotope – in the Bakhtinian sense – that she cleverly calls "miracle-time," a time-space configuration in which "the blind and the lame can be cured; lowly peasants can be honored with divine visitors; the relentless march of chronological time can be stopped, and there is a sense that the fullness of time will eventually arrive" (5). This means that hagiopics operate with a sacred temporality that eschews the course of linear historiography and is ritualistic in nature.

Spanish hagiopics in the 1960s embraced this "miracle-time" chronotope and also deployed a set of recurring and distinctive technical devices. Among these devices, two stood out. The first one was the importance of sound devices and a ceremonial and often melodramatic musical score to announce divine apparitions. For example, in León Klimovsky's *Aquella joven de blanco* the Virgin's apparitions are heralded by whirling wind sounds and the heroine's miraculous actions are punctuated by liturgically infused music. This is a Spanish version of the life of the French mystic and saint Bernadette Subirous (1844–1879), a young peasant from Lourdes, a small town in Southern France, who claimed to have seen the image of the Virgin Mary incarnated in a young lady dressed in white in 1858.[3] Another sound device typical of hagiopics that this film deploys to convey its pious message is the use of two voice-overs, one as a prologue and another one as an epilogue. While we see footage of sick pilgrims arriving at the train station in Lourdes, a female off-screen voice explains that those visitors are seeking to benefit from the curative effects of the waters of Lourdes. A shot of the preserved dead body of Bernadette, introduced as the saintly figure who miraculously intervenes to relieve the pain of the gathered crowd, leaves no room for the spectators' imagination. No suspense or surprises await us, only an exemplary story. But this documentary-style preface is more than an informative spoiler; it also establishes the premises of the type of hagiography we are about to watch: a consoling film. Just as the crowds arrive in Lourdes eager to hold on to their faith in the soothing effects of the miraculous site, viewers willing to bear the predictable plot might be rewarded with the consolation and redemption that the off-screen voice promises. Whatever their sufferings, sticking to their belief is the right thing to do. And it will pay off. The epilogue spells out that reward and brings the narrative back full circle by transporting us from the fictional to the documentary, from the nineteenth century to the 1960s, and from the particular to the universal.

The second technical element that devotees of the genre expected to find in the cinematic lexicon of a Spanish hagiopic was the use of celestial light, or a special lighting treatment to draw attention to the saintly figures. In a general sense, light is of paramount importance in film, even though it is often taken for granted and relegated to a narrowly mechanical function (Handley 120; Millerson 15). Charles Handley aptly summarized this relevance by stating that cinema is a medium of light, since "the visual part of the illusion we call motion picture is nothing but the accurate control of light" (120). However, lighting typically goes unnoticed, since viewers tend to focus on other aspects such as acting or narrative. This is why Gerald Millerson talks about "the intangibility of lighting" to refer to the fact that lighting tends to fly under the viewers' radar, even if they are deeply influenced by its effect (236). If appropriate use of light technology is indispensable in any type of filmmaking, it is even more imperative in religious pictures because of the rich meanings that light has in the Christian cultural tradition. From the Genesis 1:3, where the Old Testament records God stating "Let there be light," the difference between light and darkness is a fundamental distinction with moral implications (such as good versus evil). Throughout the scriptures, Christianity is referred to as light and the references to God as being "light" or "bringing light" to the world are ubiquitous. Candles, lamps, and flames typically signify the visible manifestation of God as the light of the world and are therefore powerful symbols for Christian believers.

Since Spanish hagiopics screened the lives of saints and martyrs as edifying models to follow, the light thrown at these extraordinary subjects had to be equally remarkable to distinguish them from regular characters. But this stylistic convention varied significantly from film to film in terms of degree, frequency of use, and narrative importance. In *Teresa de Jesús, Fray Escoba,* and *Aquella joven de blanco,* celestial light illuminates the saints when they communicate with Christ figures or Marian apparitions. In the latter film, the change of light in the Marian apparition scenes bordered the ridiculous, as reviews pointed out (Arroita 322). In *Rosa de Lima,* the use of special light on the saint's face and hair appears in just about every other shot of Rosa. Close inspection of the use of light is indeed crucial to understanding the types of messages these hagiopics intended to produce. Lighting in these films cannot be explained only in technological terms. It is also a matter of aesthetics, an aesthetic technology, which in turn has social and cultural implications. I will devote a good portion of the chapter to showcase how the analysis of the uses of lighting helps us gauge the diverse responses hagiographic films offered to the challenges posed by the modernizing developments in the 1960s. The divergent, and at times astonishingly unexpected, lighting treatments of Spanish hagiopics both projected and embodied the tensions generated by the changing role of religion and the Church in the Spanish public sphere as well as by the transition from political theology to the paradigm of economic theology in the regime's political imagination.

In the next section ("Constructing Gendered Sainthood"), I pay attention to the use of light to construct an ideal image of female sainthood that presented the figures of saints in a manner that was tolerable to the Spanish society of the early 1960s. This entailed leaving out the controversial aspects of those saints' profiles and, thereby, an exercise of historical omission. In the second section ("The Light of Empire"), I tackle the racial implications of that idealized image of female sainthood in hagiopics that served to justify Spain's colonialist project at a time when the regime was under international pressure to forsake its last colonial possessions. The third section ("The Light of the Living Dead") focuses on the striking use of lighting and other visual techniques in the closing interview of the film *Franco, ese hombre* to dramatize the anxieties intrinsic in the regime's attempt to negotiate the tensions arising from its own internal development. In particular, the visual presentation of Franco reveals fears that ensued from the regime's need to achieve social consent on rational grounds instead of on charismatic and traditional grounds. In the final section ("The Light of the Modern Church"), I analyse how the cinematic style in *El señor de La Salle* differed from previous Spanish hagiopics. My argument there is that the film subverts the usual meanings that high-key and low-key approaches to lighting typically take in mainstream cinema. This visual treatment is used to represent the shifting ground of religion in Spain in light of the changes brought by the Vatican II Council and to embrace the implementation of modern values in society.

Constructing Gendered Sainthood

The corporeal image of celluloid saints and, related to that, the way they were lit was extremely important considering the Christian theological tradition of incarnation. The embodiment of God in flesh by assuming a human nature through the body of Christ is a central doctrine of Catholicism. The depiction of the body thus occupies a focal position in Catholic iconography, as it is seen in a long-standing tradition of visual representations of the body of Christ and the Virgin Mary, as well as of saints and martyrs, in painting, sculptures, photography, television, and, of course, cinema. An important point in the fixation of Catholicism on the body, especially on the body of Christ, is that it contains a soul that is not really part of it. The body/soul dichotomy has given rise to the "prison metaphor" that is prevalent in Western culture: the idea that the body is not only inferior to the soul, but also the soul's prison (Schrader 88). There is actually a productive tension in Christian theology between emphasis on incarnation (corporeal humanity, physical suffering) and the body/soul dichotomy. Christ and the Virgin Mary transcended this dualistic scheme and escaped the prison of the body, so they became most worthy of imitation. As Richard Dyer recapitulates, these two figures inspired gender ideals ensuing from the special relations of their respective bodies to the soul: "Mary is a vessel for the spirit; she does nothing and indeed has no carnal knowledge, but is filled with God," while Christ is simultaneously "fully divine and fully human." The ideals of female and male behaviour derived from this are well known: passivity, receptivity, and maternal instincts for women; the conflict between mind and body for males, as attested by "suffering as the supreme expression of both spiritual and physical striving" (*White* 16–17).

Two Spanish hagiopics made in 1961, *Teresa de Jesús* and *Rosa de Lima,* depicted exemplary human beings who excelled at imitating these gendered ideals of transcendence of the body/soul dichotomy. Both Teresa de Jesús and Rosa de Lima were saints with powerful symbolic projections related to national identity. Since the 1920s, Teresa was celebrated in Spain as the "patron saint of the Spanish race" (Rowe 227), while Saint Rosa de Lima was regarded as the patron saint of America, since she was America's first saint, and one who had a "meteroric elevation to the altar" (Morgan 14).[4] As models of female sainthood, the cinematic Rosa and Teresa needed to match the highest ideal of femininity, the Virgin Mary. This meant that the actresses playing their roles had to give an impression of virtue and purity. The first key step was to carry out an appropriate casting. In *Rosa de Lima,* Elorrieta made the right choice with María Mahor, whose angelic face fitted the physical profile of the ever-holy character and had the approval of the Catholic-oriented media. The second issue of *Cinestudio* included a short note announcing the forthcoming release of *Rosa de Lima* and praising the casting of María Mahor for the role as "la persona ideal para encarnar este personaje: una artista de gran temperamento emocional, de delicada belleza y con la juventud casi de la adolescencia" (the ideal person for this role: an artist with a strong personality, delicate beauty, and quasi-adolescent youth) ("La mística"). For Teresa, Juan de Orduña called on his long-time muse, Aurora Bautista, whose acclaimed roles as the embodiment of national womanhood in the historical costume dramas *Locura de amor* (1948) and *Agustina de Aragón* (1950) made her a safe bet. This casting paid off with a decent commercial run of seventy days of showings in Madrid theatres (Camporesi 124). This was a good choice for a strong female figure such as Teresa de Jesús, since Bautista had made a name for herself in those costume dramas with "her unrelenting physical mobility and powerful voice projection" (Labanyi, "Feminizing" 168). But it also meant that Orduña had to somehow mitigate Bautista's acting energy, and her excessive "theatricality" (Nieto Jiménez 489), to depict the image of ethereal purity. This is where the relevance of lighting, along with other elements of the mise-en-scène such as costume and make-up, came into the picture.

Richard Dyer has argued that lighting as an aesthetic technology has been deployed to draw attention to gender differentiation in cinema. A trend in filmmaking since the classic Hollywood era has been to use more light to illuminate the faces of white women, depicted as an extreme, idealized representation of virtue and goodness (*White* 127). This gendered (and racial) pattern of lighting is particularly conspicuous in the case of hagiographic films. Since the medieval hagiographies, representations of piety have been indistinguishably mixed with representations of ideal femininity. Codes of holiness are bound by different gendered expectations to the extent that, as Gail Ashton claims, "what it means to be a female saint is not quite the same as what it means to be a male saint" (2). Mainstream cinema has generally followed these gender distinctions when lighting female celluloid saints to ensure the idealized image of purity that Dyer noted. In the cases of *Rosa de Lima* and *Teresa de Jesús*, the idealized image of purity was delivered by consistently using a high-key approach on the female lead roles. This entailed a balanced use of the three-point lighting system that was customary for classic Hollywood cinema. The three basic positions for lighting are a key light (the primary source of illumination focused on the character and creating the strongest shadows), a fill light (a less intense source of light that comes from around the camera and serves to reduce or eliminate the shadows created by the key light), and a back light (which comes from behind and above the figure and serves to separate the subject from the background and, simultaneously, to balance the intensity of the key light) (Bordwell and Thompson 181; Hayward 209; Millerson 74; Villarejo 33). The balanced combination of these three sources of light, and especially the right amount of fill and back light, reduced or eliminated any shadows on the faces of the cinematic Rosa and Teresa in most of the shots of both films.

Like the supreme model of femininity in the Catholic tradition, the Virgin Mary, these celluloid saints needed to look ethereal rather than physically attractive. The goal was to achieve an angelic look that glowed rather than shone. "Shine," as Dyer points out, "is the mirror effect of sweat, itself connoting physicality, the emissions of the body and unladylike labour" (*White* 122). By association with the dirt of the body, shine could imply a sexual activity that would be absolutely incompatible with the context of female sainthood. The lighting treatment in combination with the appropriate make-up assured that Rosa and Teresa showed no signs of shining. Modifications of the quality of light, hard when a higher concentration of light on their faces was required or soft in the opposite cases, and the direction – front, back, side, or under – further ensured the glow of these two female saints. A prominent example appears in *Rosa de Lima* when Rosa tells a priest in confession that she has decided to take the sacred vows. While Rosa is kneeling down in the confessional booth, we see a medium close-up of her face turned three-quarters to the right. A hard key and back light combines with the soft fill light to differentiate her angelic face from the dimly illuminated surroundings below it, while avoiding any trace of shadows on her facial features. Even though this approach is rather unnaturalistic, especially by comparison with the unattractive shadows covering the confessor's face framed in the same shots, it falls within the lighting conventions of cinematic female sainthood.

To enhance the image of the angelically glowing female saint, the contrast with other characters, and, above all, with the male ones who posed a sexual threat, was crucial. When the young Teresa de Jesús interacts with men who aspire to her love, the disparity in the lighting treatment is noticeable: her body is rimmed with light while the male figures appear darker and shadows are cast on their faces. Screening female characters lighter and whiter than their male counterparts is a prevalent convention in mainstream cinema to construct heterosexual relationships, which typically carries "the connotations of dark desire for the light" (Dyer, *White* 134). In those romantic situations, as the male character approaches the female angelic image, the light tends to grow gradually stronger on him, as if he is illuminated by her light and, implicitly, by her chasteness. However, Orduña's film is not about heterosexual desire but about praising the virtues of the female saint, so no such lighting convergence takes place. Light and darkness, purity and sexual desire must remain separated.

This contrast is pushed to the extreme in *Rosa de Lima*. In a ball for the high society of Lima where Rosa's parents hope she will accept Don Carlos (Antonio Almorós) as her fiancé, Rosa appears in the ballroom dressed in white from head to toe. Both the long dress resembling bridal wear – and hence signposting her virginity – and the white bonnet, along with the hard key light and the abundant make-up, make her facial skin look extremely white. The interactions of Rosa with Carlos and with Gil de Cepeda, a heartless Spanish *hidalgo* played by the American actor Frank Latimore, are shot with a sharp lighting contrast between the angelically whitened Rosa and the desiring men in a much darker tone. Especially exaggerated is the use of a hard back light to make Rosa's light brown hair look blonde, which further accentuates the glow of the angelic woman. In her thorough study of fairy tales, Marina Warner maps out a long-standing cultural tradition that links blondeness to lightness – in the sense of whiteness – with the connotations of pure, clean, and good. Particularly, Warner singles out "the identification of blondes with heavenly effulgence" in the Christian metaphysics of light in such a way that blondeness "appears to reflect solar radiance, the totality of the spectrum, the flooding wholeness of light which Dante finds grows more and more sizzling as he rises in Paradise" (366). Blondness contributes to make Rosa's skin look more pale, which suggests two things: lack of exposure to the sun – which was a sign of working-class women – and, even more importantly in terms of sexuality, lack of exposure to the desiring gaze of the male.

Through the interactions of the aesthetic technology of lighting with other elements of the mise-en-scène, particularly make-up and costume, these Spanish hagiopics thus constructed an idealized image of female sainthood. *Construct*, indeed, is a key term here, since these two saints' stories encompassed ingredients that were ambivalent and susceptible to unorthodox readings. Recent scholarship on the significance of literary hagiographies contends that saints' stories do not afford simple explanations (Ashton, Boisvert, DuPont, Kleinberg, Morgan). Teresa de Ávila may well be the quintessential example of that. Although Francoism refashioned her figure as a passive, submissive, and eternally pious woman (Graham 184), and Juan de Orduña's film portrayed

1.1 The glow of the angelic white woman in *Rosa de Lima* (1961). Permission to reproduce the still from EGEDA.

her as an angelic woman, Teresa de Ávila's complexity as a historical figure goes beyond these straightforward characterizations. Teresa's rebellious mindset and relentless activity as a religious reformer deflate attempts to cast her as submissive. Also, in Teresa's life and writings scholars have seen examples of a (proto)feminist consciousness that contradicts representations overemphasizing her domestic virtues (Barbeito Carneiro, Mujica, Simerka, Alison Weber). As Denise DuPont aptly put it, Teresa's "power as a symbol" is precisely "her lack of fixity, manifested as a resistance to definitive identification with any political or social agenda" (29). Juan de Orduña's film downplays Teresa's intellectual contributions to literature and theology. We only see her writing letters in two brief moments (minutes 58 and 90). This choice matches the reassignment of female virtues to Teresa in the early Francoist period. New biographies of the saint, such as the one written by Silverio de Santa Teresa in 1939, spread the notion that Teresa preferred the needle and the thread to the pen (207).[5]

Equally toned down are Teresa's personal relationships with men. Bárbara Mujica documents how some biographies of Teresa have described a youthful affair with her cousin prior to taking her vows, and have even claimed that she had lost her virginity as a result of that affair (26). In the film, this is softened as innocent flirtation with two young men: her cousin Pedro and Álvaro de Osorio. As soon as Teresa's father (Roberto Rey) becomes aware of it, he sends her to a convent to safeguard her chastity. In this way, Juan de Orduña frames one of the most controversial episodes of Teresa's biography, and one potentially damaging to her profile as the patron saint of the Spanish race, as innocent play that in the end serves to reinforce patriarchal authority as well as to certify Teresa's purity. And the magic of lighting does the rest.

Similarly, Elorrieta bypasses any aspect of Rosa de Lima's life that could appear unorthodox. First, there is not a single scene or mention of Rosa's intellectual activity. Although Teodoro Hampe Martínez claims that Rosa de Lima did not follow the model of the "monja escritora" (nun writer) (8), she did in fact leave behind a good deal of writing, including letters, poetry, and spiritual notebooks. Rosa's texts echo patterns and ideas of mystical writing developed by both Teresa de Ávila and San Juan de la Cruz, and display a paradox similar to those of Teresa: "she is a woman writing under obedience to a confessor but who claims authority for her own mystical experience" (Myers 36). Yet, Elorrieta's film only offers her penances and miracles, which fit better into the acceptable models of female sanctity under Franco. Interestingly enough, Rosa's severe penitential exercises constituted one of the most controversial elements of her profile, and one that had to be downplayed in her canonization processes. The Counter-Reformation had toughened up regulations of saintly practices in order to keep spiritual practices under control and minimize heretical conduct. Highly individual spiritual trajectories, while taken as models of piety, could also threaten the Church's authority if left unsupervised (Myers 14). Rosa de Lima's case is even thornier than Teresa de Ávila's, because, unlike the Spanish mystic, Rosa hardly followed the Counter-Reformation guidelines for acceptable forms of sanctity. Her extreme penitential practices sidestepped the mandate to moderate penances, and her decision not to join a convent also deviated from the Tridentine efforts to cloister religious women (Myers 16). Rosa entered the Dominican Order as a third-order nun and took the vows of poverty, chastity, and obedience, but she chose not to live in the cloister. Thus, she continued to be a holy free spirit and did not follow the Church's determination to ensure absolute orthodoxy.

This exercise of editing the threatening aspects of the saints' profiles exemplifies Fredric Jameson's "strategies of containment." Jameson uses this concept to refer to the framing of stories to make them digestible for a specific culture and historical moment. These strategies involve not only the outright excision of certain aspects but also a form of repression "beneath the later formalized surface" of content that is packaged in fictional form to conceal what would be unacceptable as a historical account (213). These Spanish hagiopics offered what we can term, borrowing from Roland Barthes (himself borrowing from Oscar Wilde), a fiction that dares not to speak its name.[6] Biographical narratives, hagiographic or otherwise, always entail an act of invention, of selecting materials and excluding others (Backscheider 18). Fiction permeates these filmic stories of holy heroines because events are represented toeing the line of the official reconstruction their lives, and that entailed downplaying certain events and silencing others outright. Complying with a hallmark that Ronald Bergan grants to all biopics, these films asked the audience not so much to suspend their disbelief as to suspend their prior knowledge of the subject (22). They are hybrid narratives that comprise historical representation and fictional construction, offering what Michel de Certeau deems distinctive of literary hagiographies: "a poetics of meaning that cannot be reduced to an exactitude of facts," one whose value is not "'authenticity' or 'historical value'" (274, 270). In *Rosa de Lima* and *Teresa de Jesús*, though, the poetics becomes a gender politics enacted by the persuasive uses of the technology of lighting to naturalize acceptable models of female virtue.

The Light of Empire

The construction of the angelically glowing woman also had significant racial implications. By obsessively equating virtue and goodness with whiteness through the use of lighting, make-up, and costume, Spanish hagiopics conflated the descriptive functions of colour with its symbolic cultural uses. In so doing, these films adhered to what Richard Dyer identifies as a common trend in the Western cultural tradition, a slippage between three separate uses of "whiteness" that in theory do not need to overlap: white as a hue, as skin, and as symbol (*White* 64). Focusing specifically on the ideological effects of lighting, Dyer points out how cinema from its early days has employed the technology of lighting, in combination with the use of film stock and make-up, to privilege white people as the norm (90–1). Although a survey of the history of the practice of artificial light in the film industry would reveal different cycles, some of them ostensibly recurring (Handley 120), one trend has remained stable until the present day: lighting in cinema has been a white-centric aesthetic technology that privileges the white face and, more importantly, constructs it as its benchmark (Dyer, *White* 97). Non-white faces, in contrast, have been confined to the shadows, both literally and metaphorically, hard to be seen as autonomous individuals (102). This pattern is of course not entirely sacrosanct, but it is widespread enough to go virtually unnoticed. This naturalized image in motion pictures is linked to broader racial dynamics in the Western world – namely, the "invisibility of whiteness as a racial position in dominant discourses" (3) – so that white people think of themselves as just people and only non-white people appear as racialized subjects (1). The most insidious aspect of this dynamic is that it becomes attached to moral codes in the sense that white people become inherently identified with good qualities while people of colour tend to inhabit the territory of evil in motion pictures.

The points raised by Dyer are very useful in fathoming the ideological uses of the technology of lighting in Spanish hagiopics set overseas. In *Molokai*, the arrival of Father Damian on the island damned by leprosy is presented through high-contrast lighting effects typical of horror movies. A hard key light exposes the figure of the priest, dressed in a white cassock, while fill light is significantly lessened, thus creating a chiaroscuro effect with sinister connotations punctuated by the distressing musical beats that can be heard as background. A male voiceover draws attention to the sombre air of the scene to highlight the whiteness of the figure of the priest, interpreted as the bearer of peace and love, in comparison with the darkness of the people around the leprosy village, to whom he refers as "alimañas" ("vermin" or figuratively bad people, "scoundrel" in English). Throughout the film, the moral judgment appended to the contrast between light and whiteness on the one hand and dark shadows on the other also bears a racial and racist connotation, since many of the subjects cast in shadows are people of colour.

Along these lines, in *Rosa de Lima* there is a blatant discrepancy between the lighting treatment of all the actors playing white female characters – not just Rosa – and the ones playing the roles of indigenous natives of the Viceroyalty of Peru. In all the scenes that take place in Rosa's family house, each shot framing the parents makes the aforementioned gendered distinction by having the loving mother, played by Lina Yegros, look significantly lighter and whiter than the father (Pastor Serrador). This is somewhat predictable, given the symbolic role of motherhood as the repository of the moral values of the family and the nation during Francoism.[7] But the same lighting and make-up treatment shockingly appears in the case of Lucía (Isa Paz), the owner of a tavern originally from Cádiz. Lucía inherited the tavern from a man with whom we suppose she was sexually involved, and she seems to welcome Gil de Cepeda's predatory flirtation. Clearly, she is hardly the archetype of female chastity venerated by this hagiopic. However, she appears in carefully lit medium close-ups in which the use of a hard back light ensures that her hair has the blonde glare of the angelic woman. A very different lighting arrangement illuminates Magdalena (played by Spanish actress Paula Martel, who is "indigenized" by brown make-up), a native Peruvian who has to farm and work in a tavern to survive. In a dramatic scene in which Magdalena is rejected (and spat on) by her husband Dimas (played by Virgilio Teixeira, equally "indigenized" by make-up), a close-up in high angle of Magdalena reveals a shiny face full of shadows. If we recall Dyer's comments about the implications of the contrast between shine and glow, "shine connotes sweat, something inappropriate to ladies, that is, really white women," since the origin of the sweat could be all kinds of physical work, including sexual activity (*White* 78). It is clear, then, that the lighting in *Rosa de Lima* hierarchizes characters not necessarily in terms of holiness and purity, as we would expect in a hagiographic film, but rather in terms of class and race.

Fray Escoba is perhaps the most glaring example of these racial codes at stake in Spanish hagiopics. This film screens the holy life of Saint Martín de Porres (1579–1639), the first mulatto saint of America, and was a commercial hit with seventy days of showings in the Gran Vía Theatre in Madrid (Camporesi 123). On a narrative level, both Martín (played by Cuban actor René Muñoz) and his mother Ana (Esther Zulema) are depicted as morally flawless, matching the qualities of holiness that other Spanish hagiopics assign to saints and maternal figures. Nevertheless, the lighting suggests otherwise. Both have dark skin that appears with shiny highlights and unflattering sweat throughout the film. It is important to emphasize that the sweat on their skin is not only the figurative consequence of shine that Dyer theorized (shine connoting sweat and body's dirt) but also physically perceptible sweat. The scene of Ana in her deathbed is especially prominent because of the parallels of the mise-en-scène with almost identical scenes in *Rosa de*

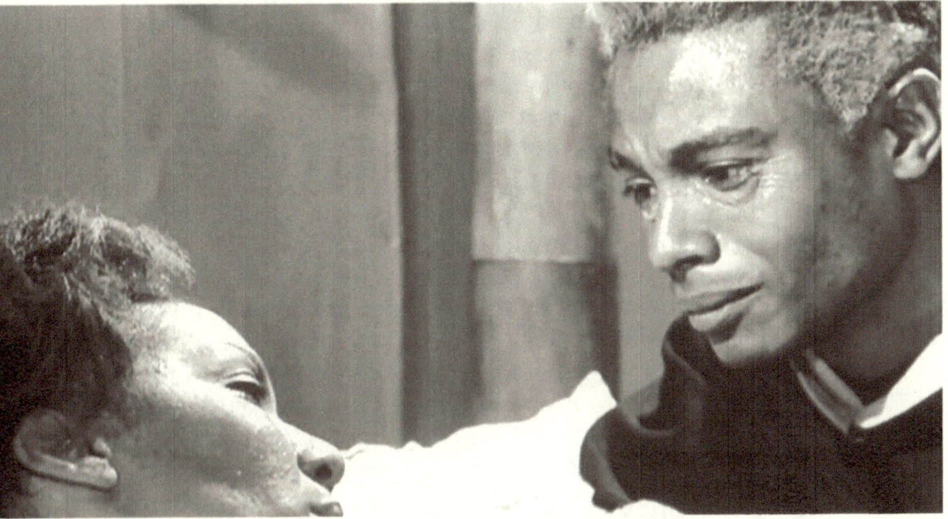

1.2 The shine and sweat of non-white subjects in *Fray Escoba* (1961). Permission to reproduce the still from EGEDA.

Lima and *Teresa de Jesús*. The virtuous women lie in bed surrounded by family members and close friends, with their white clothes and the white bed sheets denoting "whiteness" (with all the corresponding moral connotations of cleanliness and goodness), and a noticeable crucifix mounted above the headboard. But there is a noteworthy difference: Rosa and Teresa appear with an almost ethereal tranquillity that is visually reinforced through the use of sufficient fill light to offset the hard key light, and the appropriate make-up to remove any shadows or shine from their faces. A shot that frames both the moribund Ana and Martín evinces that Ana and Martín are not afforded the same lighting privileges. While in *Rosa de Lima* and *Teresa de Jesús* the signs of the saints' corporeality vanish under the light, in *Fray Escoba* the skin of René Muñoz and his mother shines and sweats profusely.

One may attribute this to the overall deficient technical production of the film. *Fray Escoba* was shot entirely in Ávila with a mediocre mise-en-scène hardly resembling colonial Lima, including, as José Luis Castro de Paz and Jaime Pena Pérez point out, "ambientación limeña de cartón pedra e carnavalesco vestuario" (cardboard setting and carnivalesque costume) (75).[8] But a brief, and apparently inconsequential, scene midway through the film dispels any doubts about the deliberate (mis)use of lighting conventions. After mediating in a street fight, Martín is heading back to the convent and accidentally bumps into two nuns. One of them is a young nun, named Rosa, who enthusiastically recognizes Fray Escoba, already a celebrity in Lima. While they chat, there is a medium close-up of Martín in which the only visible source of light is the natural reflection of the sun, which gives him shiny highlights on the left side of his face while the right side is covered with a shadow. There is no additional fill light to counterweigh the effect of the natural side-lighting or to reduce the visible sweat on his face – in this case directly caused by the physical activity of being involved in a fight. The reverse shot of Rosa is, technically speaking, diametrically opposed. It is almost a textbook example of dexterous use of the three-point lighting system to properly light a face in an outdoor scenario. The balanced use of the key, fill, and back lights illuminates Rosa's face while removing any shadows from her facial features or around her figure. The back light neatly distinguishes her figure in the foreground from a white wall with sun reflection in the background. The make-up on her face further whitens her completion and neutralizes any shine. By now, the pattern is familiar: this is another prototypical representation of the angelically glowing white woman.

This idealized representation of the young nun is a clue for viewers to identify her as Saint Rosa de Lima, who was contemporaneous with Martín de Porres. This scene probably generated some cinematic delight in followers of hagiopics, who would recognize the cameo appearance, as they would Martín's own cameo in several moments of Elorrieta's *Rosa de Lima*. But it also makes all the more apparent the ideological implications of the lighting treatment. The carefully lit reverse shots of Rosa in *Fray Escoba* expose that the lighting treatment on the non-white characters of this film, including the celebrated mulatto saint, is a conscious choice to make them appear shiny and sweaty, to partner shininess – with all its connotations of dirt and impurity, in both a physical and a spiritual sense – with non-white people.

The interesting part of this lighting treatment is that it contradicts the political message the film tries to deliver. *Fray Escoba* distils a tribute to the Francoist defence of Spanish colonialism that drew on the myth of *Hispanidad*. As is well known, that discourse relied on the benevolence of the religiously oriented Spanish colonial project because it fostered cultural fraternization. Unlike other European colonial projects, allegedly oriented towards accumulation of wealth and based on a racist hierarchy that precluded miscegenation, the Spanish one claimed to be founded on the Christian ideal that all human beings are equal in God's eyes (Maeztu 73). The conceptual framework of *Hispanidad* rested on the conviction that miscegenation was not an unplanned collateral effect of Spain's colonial presence but rather was its main prop or, as Ernesto Giménez Caballero argued, "its mysticism," since Catholicism united all Spanish-speaking countries in universal fraternity (5). *Fray Escoba* activates the rhetoric of *Hispanidad* by underscoring that Martín's skin colour is not a barrier to becoming a religious hero. He is admitted into the Dominican community as a tertiary, and the narrative emphasizes that it is Martín's decision – and not the racist barriers within the Catholic Church – to stay that way and not become a regular lay brother of the religious order.[9] When his father (Alfredo Mayo) pushes to have his son become a regular member, a position more appropriate to his Spanish lineage, the prior of the convent makes clear that it is Martín who refuses to do so based on his humility. What the film does not explain is that there were colonial laws that tried to prevent natives and black people from making profession in a religious order, even if it was at the discretion of priors to break those laws (García Rivera 4). When they finally convince Martín to become a lay brother, the prior explains during the ceremony that for the Dominican Order races do not exist. The film is saturated with moments like this one to convey the message that the Church – and the Spanish colonial authorities by extension – treated the American natives as spiritually equal. However, as noted before, the message implied by the film's dialogue and narrative diegesis is belied by the lighting.

The lighting treatment in *Rosa de Lima* inscribes a similar discourse of colonial relations. Given her strong symbolic projection, Rosa de Lima was a pious figure claimed by a variety of stakeholders. The *criollos* claimed her as the "patron saint of America," as the representative of the emergent creole identity in the Americas. Historian Teodoro Hampe Martínez has shown how the creole elites played a crucial role in the success of her beatification process and in her subsequent canonization in 1671 (11). Rosa de Lima was also venerated by the Spanish crown as a religious heroine who proved the establishment of Catholic beliefs over native paganism in the New World, as a testament of the success of a "new type of conquistador" – a virgin warrior – in the evangelizing endeavours of the motherland (Myers 29). The virgin warrior was also a central image in Orduña's *Teresa de Jesús*. One of the promotional posters of the film shows an aggrandized image of the saint holding a sword. The poster refers to one of the key scenes in the narrative. Midway through the film, Teresa is visited by a missionary friar who brings her a family sword with which Teresa's brother, Antonio, fought and heroically died in the Spanish colonies as "a good Spaniard and a good Christian." Teresa embraces the sword to conceptualize the expansion of her reform as a spiritual Reconquest. She then kisses the hilt – shaped like a cross – and the films cuts to a close-up of the hilt of the sword, placed in the cart that will take Teresa in her journey to set up new convents. This scene encapsulates an ideological manoeuvre that was ubiquitous during Francoism: the glorification of religious saints as military heroes and, conversely, of civil authorities as saints – for example, the "hagiographication" of the *caudillo* that I will shortly examine in *Franco, ese hombre*. Teresa is presented as a warrior of God, driven by the struggle against the spread of Protestantism and the concern over the need to convert to Catholicism the indigenous natives in the American colonies.

In *Rosa de Lima*, by lighting the virgin warrior as a glowing angelic white woman, Elorrieta incites viewers to see her as a white Spaniard, as a converter of pagans and guardian of Catholic orthodoxy instead of as a symbol of the shaping of creole identity. This ideological apropriation of the figure of Rosa through the technology of light draws a parallel with the metaphorical implications of Rosa's name and holy activity in relation to the Spanish colonial spiritual mission. Hagiographers of the saint reported that, although born Isabel Flores de Oliva, her name was changed to Rosa "when a servant saw the baby's face transformed into a rose, a symbol of a European flower transplanted to the New World" (Myers 25). Borrowing from Rosa's hagiographers, Elorrieta's film dwells on this trope of the transplantation of the rose. As Frank Graziano has explained, all the different versions of the trope have in common the conceptualization of the Americas as a savage indigenous realm of paganism turned into a "divine garden" that is laboriously tended by the Dominican missionaries. Missionary labourers cultivated "the good plants (virtues)" and removed "the weeds (vices)." With suitable gardening work, "the weeds themselves could be metamorphosed into flowers" (75). Elorrieta's film persistently refers to Rosa's role in helping "weeds" to transform into "flowers." Upon dying, her only wish for her Dominican sisters is to take care of her garden: "Sembrad muchas rosas a su alrededor" (plant many roses around it). Rosa symbolically appears as the gardener of the edenic transformation of the Americas under the tutelage of the Dominican friars and, ultimately, of the Spanish evangelizing enterprise. This film thus associates the Spanish colonial project with the evangelizing activity of missionaries to convert the natives and not with the rapacious spirit of conquistadors and their fortune-hunters.

Seen together, *Fray Escoba, Rosa de Lima,* and *Teresa de Jesús* offered cinematic excursions into Counter-Reformation Spain and the Spanish colonies in the late sixteenth century to highlight edifying models of sainthood that called attention to an inherent identification between Catholic faith and Spain's national essence. Although far from the overtly propagandistic hagiopics of the previous decade, these films vicariously helped to convey a justification of the regime based on traditional grounds. Showcasing their saintly heroes as religious-political icons, these three films extolled Spain's messianic mission to lead the Counter-Reformation at home and to propagate Catholicism in the colonies. But what has drawn my attention here is that these films inscribed race and gender as central components of that ethno-religious notion of Spanishness. Eva Woods Peiró argues in her book *White Gypsies* that cinema has had a pivotal – and understudied – role in the racialization of Spanish culture throughout the twentieth century (xi), which has often been connected to the expansion and reenactment of the Spanish imperialist discourse (11). Tied to Francoism's (futile) attempt to relocate Spain to an influential geopolitical position in the world order, the narratives of these hagiopics went the extra mile to present a benevolent face of the Spanish colonial enterprise as one resting on a spiritual notion of the Spanish race – *Hispanidad* – that brought together Spain and its former colonies by means of their shared language and religion. However, my analysis has exposed that elements of their mise-en-scène such as costume, make-up, and, above all, lighting linked the eulogized spiritual concept of the Spanish race, of which these celluloid saints were revered representatives, to biological notions that had exclusionary and racist ramifications. As Susan Martin-Márquez has aptly shown, "from the early modern era on, notions of blood legacies have always circulated throughout Spanish cultural discourse" (*Disorientations* 50). The aesthetic technology of lighting in these hagiopics was a persuasive tool to construct models of sainthood to embody a unitary concept of national identity that discarded racial otherness, even if disguised in religious messages of Catholic fraternity.

The question that arises is why Spanish cinema reactivates the idealized image of the glowingly pure white woman glued to colonial aspirations at a time when both the social role of women and Spain's colonial involvement were changing in a completely different direction. According to Richard Dyer, this is not only logical but in fact wholly predictable. The angelically glowing white woman is "an extreme representation," in the sense that it is an idealization that in the Anglo-American context "reached its apogee towards the end of the nineteenth century and especially in situations of heightened perceived threat to the hegemony of whiteness" (*White* 127). He singled out the Indian Mutiny of 1857 and the Jamaican revolt of 1865 against the British Empire, and the defeat of the South and, hence, the end of slavery in the United States, as key historical moments in which ideological concern with racial imagery increased. These examples show that the revival of the representation of glowingly angelic women should almost automatically compel us to identify the historical crossroads or the social current exemplified by this idealized representation.

In the case of Spain in the early 1960s, these hagiopics may be indicative of the need to find new justifications for Spain's colonial enterprises in the face of international pressure to accelerate decolonization processes. Spain's entry into the United Nations coincided with the end of the protectorate in Morocco in 1956, but control over Equatorial Guinea and the Western Sahara still put Spain in the international spotlight for not complying with UN recommendations. This reading makes even more sense if we consider that two years later Ramón Torrado transplanted René Muñoz and Jesús Tordesillas to the context of Equatorial Guinea to make *Cristo negro,* a missionary film that idealizes the proselytizing basis of the Spanish colonial project, this time in Africa. José Luis Castro de Paz and Jaime Pena Pérez consider *Cristo negro* a sequel to *Fray Escoba,* since it featured the same artistic and technical crew (76). Susan Martin-Márquez has analysed *Cristo negro* along these lines to note that it not only praises the spiritual mission of Spain in Guinea but also casts doubts on Guinea's ability to be independent ("De *Cristo negro*" 59). The goal, of course, was to excuse the delay in forsaking colonial possessions. Even if not set in Africa, I believe that the three hagiopics I have analysed could be read as a colonial litany in response to the imminent decolonizing process in Equatorial Guinea. The sixteenth century is the channel, but not the subject matter, of these three films. They are not heritage films, as they do not aspire to represent the time period with authenticity and historical accuracy – to the contrary, they are full of factual errors – but rather they use the colonial past to draw an allegory of contemporary issues. They revitalize the ideological framework of *Hispanidad* to revisit the colonial past at a time when Spain's colonial project – in the present and in Africa – was again a pressing issue.[10] In this way, these three hagiopics proved the significant role that religion played well into the 1960s to provide a justification for the legitimacy of the regime's political system and, in this case, of its imperialist aspirations. Spanish cinema channelled that justification in these hagiopics through the idealized image of the glowingly angelic woman that the technology of lighting offered as a national model of white sanctity.

The Light of the Living Dead: Saénz de Heredia's *Franco, ese hombre*

The visual apparatuses of the three hagiopics I have analysed so far constructed models of sanctity that were expedient to normative agendas of the regime. However, as with any representation, filmic or otherwise, what might appear to be a closed system of fixed meanings – and hagiographies are particularly liable to this cataloguing, among other reasons because their narratives are rather formulaic – "might also be a place where meanings are contested or resisted" (Ashton 2). The purpose of this section is to show how even a hagiographic film like José Luis Sáenz de Heredia's *Franco, ese hombre,* which was produced by the political elite with the intention of worshipping the figure of the dictator as a saint while at the same time celebrating the new official image of the regime, contains contradictions in its message. Existing analyses of *Franco, ese hombre* have focused on the ideological function of this hagiopic to provide a renewed image of a regime that had surpassed the autarkic period (Berthier, "José Luis"; Quintana, "Y el Caudillo"; Tranche and Sánchez-Biosca). But they have surprisingly overlooked the final segment of the film, a four-minute interview with Francisco Franco himself. In my view, this closing interview makes evident the discrepancies between the intended message and the final product of *Franco, ese hombre* and, in so doing, constitutes a salient testament of the anxieties emerging within pro-regime cultural platforms over the pursuit of a rationalization of the legitimacy of the regime. Through the analysis of the lighting treatment, the framing, and the camera angles chosen for this closing interview, I will show that the visual presentation of Franco as a saintly hero is, at best, bizarre. The closing interview perversely depicts Franco as zombie-like, an almost mindless, politically brain-dead figure out of touch with the evolving times. This shocking visual presentation reveals incipient fears about the shift the regime was taking from the political-theological paradigm of sovereign power to the economic-providential paradigm.

The origin of *Franco, ese hombre* was the commemoration of the "Twenty-Five Years of Peace" devised by Manuel Fraga. The massive celebration included abundant publicity exhibited all over the country, the release of a series of fourteen stamps (with four million copies), an extraordinary National Lottery draw, medals from the Casa de la Moneda, and a plethora of official publications and competitions "organised for poetry, novels, cinema journalism, radio and television" (Paloma Aguilar 115–16). Along with the touristic slogan "Spain Is Different," Fraga choreographed a sharp-witted campaign using the mass media to portray an updated image of the regime. Fraga's move involved replacing the rhetoric of the religious crusade with a more conciliatory message of peace and prosperity that tried not to alienate those Spaniards who sided with the vanquished of the war. The architects of the campaign sought to capitalize on the symbolic meaning of "peace" as the real victory of the regime by associating it with the material prosperity that Spaniards were beginning to enjoy. The focal marketing hook was that the prosperity of Spain during the development years was as much the outcome of Franco's adeptness at maintaining social order as it was the result of the new economic policies.[11] As part of this campaign, seasoned director José Luis Sáenz de Heredia was commissioned to create a film venerating the figure of Franco. He accepted the job with the condition of getting the stamp of approval to produce a feature-length film instead of a short documentary (García Escudero, "La imagen" 170). Given his credentials, his petition was granted. Sáenz de Heredia had previously directed *Raza* (1942), based on a story written by Franco himself under the pseudonym of Jaime de Andrade. The success of that war film, which lived up to Franco's expectations, seemed to be enough warranty. Sáenz de Heredia wanted to stage a reverential image of the dictator, so he made a documentary hagiography, since Franco is depicted as the heroic saint responsible for saving Spain from Communism.

Like any conventional hagiographic narrative, the hero's trajectory is organized with a cause-and-effect logic: early deeds and skills anticipate later accomplishments; each experience in the young Franco's life is a logical step towards his rise to heroic eminence. The choice of the hagiographic narrative frame was no coincidence. At the heyday of the popularity of hagiopics, Sáenz de Heredia probably thought that manufacturing Franco's biography in the form of a saint's life would be an easy sell. It was the perfect pattern to emphasize the supernatural qualities of the charismatic ruler. The film was indeed a bigger box-office success than expected for a documentary, with eighty-three days of showings in the Palacio de la Música and Fuencarral Theatres in Madrid (Camporesi 123), thanks to the ample publicity campaign on television during the month of November 1964 (Quintana, "Y el

Caudillo" 179). But Franco himself did not like it because there were too many military parades (Preston 715). Franco's assessment summarizes what in my view is conspicuous: the perverse effects by which the final product turned away from the intended outcome.

This impression begins with the title. Sáenz de Heredia justified it as an attempt to deliver the message that the film was not a political pamphlet, but one that focused on the humanity of the figure (Castro 377). As a matter of fact, the credits appear over images of a humane Franco involved in non-official tasks such as interacting with family members, hunting, fishing, and playing board games. A total of twenty-three photographs offer an overview of some of Franco's hobbies. But the promise of an intimate portrait of the dictator soon vanishes, as Sáenz de Heredia opens the film with seven minutes of footage of the grandiose military parade commemorating the "Twenty-Five Years of Peace," and the rest of the film is a narration in flashback that focuses on Franco's military career. His triumphs leading the colonial army in Morocco are explained in full detail. However, there is no more news about his personal hobbies until the last ten minutes of the film, when Franco's passions for sailing, hunting, fishing, painting, and reading are briefly mentioned, this time over a montage of moving images. But the film quickly circles back to the military parade with which it began. One gets the feeling that the film should have been titled "Franco, ese militar." For a documentary financed by a campaign intending to cash in on the meaning of peace, *Franco, ese hombre* has not only too many military parades but also too much footage of battles and violence.

The urgent need for a new discursive coating to strengthen the legitimacy of the regime was largely due to the growing anxiety over the physical deterioration of the *caudillo*. Franco was seventy-two years old and, despite the efforts to disguise it in media coverage, he showed increasing, even if sporadic, signs of advancing Parkinson's disease (Preston 719–20, 729). Sáenz de Heredia took great pride in the closing interview of *Franco, ese hombre*, which turned out to be a missed opportunity to stage a filmic rejuvenation surgery.[12] In fact, the interview reinforces Franco's decline. It begins with an eerie long shot of Franco seated in the dark after watching the footage of the documentary. Instead of Spain's guiding light, Franco appears in dark shadow; instead of a benevolent saint, one might be tempted to associate him with evil. When the lights of the Palacio del Pardo's screening room are turned on, a medium long shot shows José Luis Sáenz de Heredia walking towards Franco until he stands in front of the seated dictator to ask him some questions. When it is Franco's turn to answer, the camera zooms in to give us a closer look at the leader, who provides highly rehearsed answers. The rest of the conversation is filmed with a shot/reverse shot structure that oscillates between medium close-ups of Franco and medium shots of Sáenz de Heredia in low angle. The camera then zooms out to bring circularity to the whole scene by returning to the initial medium long shot.

Some of the medium close-ups of Franco are not symmetrically framed, so Franco appears, ironically enough, on the far left side of the frame. This is rather surprising in the context of a hagiographic film. A more congruent framing of a subject that a film invests with divine qualities would be a symmetrical, closed-frame shot of the full figure in a central position, which is the selected framing for the reverse shots in medium close-up of Sáenz de Heredia. Even more surprising is that the key light illuminating Franco's face is significantly softer than the one illuminating Sáenz de Heredia. Most embarrassingly, the vertical angle of the lamp that provides the key light seems too steep, and there is not enough fill light to diffuse the shadows cast by this wrongly angled primary source of light. This emphasizes the size of Franco's forehead and his baldness, and, above all, it gives him bags under his sunken eyes and long vertical nose shadows. The overall effect is rather unflattering to Franco, as it highlights his aging appearance. Instead of the work of an established professional such as Sáenz de Heredia, the lighting treatment appears amateurish. In addition, although the idea behind the seated versus standing arrangement was probably to establish a visual hierarchy between the national saint and the filmmaker serving as mere messenger, it has the reverse effect. The shots of Sáenz de Heredia somewhat aggrandize his figure by the recurrent use of heroic low-angle shots, while conversely diminishing Franco's. If anything, these shots might reveal anxiety to conceal Franco's diminished stature.

Given the blatant contrast between the framing, the camera angles, and the lighting used to represent Franco and Sáenz de Heredia, one cannot help but wonder if the poor visual treatment of the admired saintly hero is merely the result of incompetent planning. One is tempted to interpret it instead as unconscious display of the director's ego. It is as if, in his meticulous concern to frame and light himself properly, Sáenz de Heredia had lost sight – both literally and metaphorically – of the figure of Franco, which became reduced to a visual afterthought in reverse shot. Or even more perversely, though this is very unlikely, it may be the director's conscious statement of self-sacralization as a demiurge-like figure responsible for fashioning the universe of this film. Speculation about motives aside, the effect is that the visual treatment of the figure of Franco in this closing interview does not match the deferential verbal treatment he receives from his interviewer, who addresses the dictator by repeating, almost obsessively, the formula "Su Excelencia" (Your Excellency). Nor does it correspond to what a spectator could expect from a director with three decades of filmmaking experience.

A close scrutiny of the interview sequence reveals another odd detail that emphasizes Franco's physical deterioration. Since Franco has to completely turn his head to his left to be able to look at the standing film director, it is plausible to wonder if Franco's odd – and uncomfortably rigid – position in his seat was a flaw in the preparation for the shooting or an improvised solution because the dictator was physically unable to stand for the duration of the interview. Furthermore, the post-interview footage calls even more attention to the dictator's physical appearance, although this time in a futile attempt to look at him through rose-coloured glasses. Once the interview is over, the two men shake hands, and Franco leaves the room. A tracking shot offers a close-up of Franco's feet and legs as he walks back to his office. Almost a wicked intertextual reference to Luis Buñuel's fetishizing fascination with feet, these shots of Franco's walk are used to comment on his "paso firme," that is, as a metaphor of the leader's determination and unbending convictions. Also, these concluding shots bring the documentary back full circle to the hagiographic framework, as Sáenz de Heredia comments: "Le deseamos para el bien de España que Dios siga guiando como hasta ahora el acierto de sus pasos" (We wish for Spain's sake that God continues guiding his steps). Yet, in the context of Franco's increasing difficulty in hiding the signs of his developing Parkinson's – whose main symptoms are "a rigid stance, an unsure walk and a vacant, open-mouthed facial expression" (Preston 720) – and in combination with the initial creepy shot of Franco in the dark, the shots of his rigid gait end up appearing to a contemporary viewer like shots from *The Walking Dead*.

The lighting treatment of this final segment underlines this (un)intentionally parodic presentation of Franco as a zombie-like figure. After shaking hands with Sáenz de Heredia and prior to the close-up of his legs, Franco walks towards a door. The camera remains on a stationary support but pans to the left to scan the space horizontally and show Franco reaching the door. He turns robotically to his right to initiate his walk through the corridors of the palace. A chandelier hanging on the ceiling by the door profusely illuminates the area behind the door to such an extent that Franco's figure, dressed as he is in a dark-coloured suit, appears as a dark silhouette. The very last shot of the film further highlights this presentation. Once Franco reaches the end of the corridor and turns left to cross into another room, the camera stops but tilts slightly to scan the space vertically and show the dictator walking towards the end of the room. The more Franco walks, the more his figure appears as a silhouette against a lit background. Eventually, the monster fades into the dark.

As Gerald Millerson points out, the sihouette treatment in cinema lighting serves to concentrate on a subject's outline and to suppress all surface details. Shooting an unlit subject against a lit background is typically used "for dramatic, mysterious, and decorative effects" (238). In the overall eerie atmosphere of this sequence, it only reinforces the zombie-like presentation of Franco, as a mere silhouette devoid of any details or features normally visible in human beings. Zombies are undead creatures, typically depicted as non-thinking entitites, human corpses whose bodies have been revived but who are "effectively brain-dread, so that everything that made them individual – memories, language, aspirations, sense of identity and independent thought – is cancelled out" (Felix 192). Since the lighting treatment in this segment neutralizes any individual feature of Franco's figure, one is drawn to entertain the thought that instead of the guiding light of the Spanish nation, what we see here is the light of the living dead. Historians and cultural analysts have called attention to the fact that Franco, as he aged, became a figurehead of the regime who did not truly understand the policies and reforms his administration was implementing in the 1960s. Testimonies of his political collaborators seemed to substantiate the hypothesis that Franco was politically brain-dead in the last phase of his regime. For instance, Paul Preston documents that López Rodó allegedly said that they had "to 'furnish Franco's head with ideas'" (695). It is as if this film were metaphorically presenting a subject who was already dead (politically speaking), but who was reanimated, like a zombie, by this campaign of the "Twenty-Five Years of Peace" to come back to satisfy his hunger for human flesh. In fact, despite his multiple health issues, Franco came back to sign execution orders.[13]

This was not the only time that Franco was depicted by media discourses as a partially non-human entity. Most famously, as Francisco LaRubia-Prado has shown, the shocking picture published by *La Revista del Mundo* in 1984 presented Franco on his deathbed full of medical and surgical devices to keep him alive and, thereby, "as a cyborg, a partially organic and partially mechanistic entity" (135). Drawing on the concept of cyborg as a metaphor for ontological hybridity, LaRubia-Prado interprets this photograph as a compelling symbol of Franco's ambiguous political career as a hybrid creature with inconsistent political ideas; or better yet, with a political identity assembled by the official rhetoric. The constructedness and ambiguity of Franco's political trajectory can be extended to the macro-level "of a regime that, while preaching *ad nauseam* an organic, nationalist ideology, was nevertheless desperate for technological advances that would assure its own survival" (137). From this view, Spain appears as a cyborg-state, a hybrid creature that dislodged itself from its organic origins – an inherently Catholic nation – to embrace "the logic of the capitalist technological devil" (150) necessary for the process of modernization that brought Spain closer to modern Western European countries.

Although I do not share the idea that the regime had to strip itself of its Catholic values to embrace modernization, the parallels of the image of Franco as a cyborg that LaRubia-Prado analyses with the depiction of Franco as a zombie in Sáenz de Heredia's film prove rather striking. In an insightful article that compares cyborgs and zombies in popular mythologies, Jonathan Paul Marshall notes that a common feature of both figures is their ambivalent nature, as they are both bordering life and death, the organic and the inorganic (124). Also, I would add, their liminality makes them act both as subjects and objects, and to be feared as a monstruous entities that are similar to yet different from us, since they are neither truly living (or organic in the case of the cyborg) nor dead (or mechanistic). Like cyborgs, zombies as metaphors are prevalent in popular culture, in academic discourse and theory, and even in discussions about the state of academia itself (Whelan, Walker, and Moore). A particular aspect of the zombie as a cinematic trope makes it appealing to conceptualize the depiction of Franco in Sáenz de Heredia's film beyond an opportunistic impulse to draw on what has been called the "zombie renaissance" in contemporary popular culture and society (Hubner, Leaning, and Manning). Zombies in cinema characteristically gesture towards the arrival of apocalypse, as the symptom and dreadful embodiment of dubious social currents that in all probability will bring society's downfall (Pagano 75). As with the image of the glowingly angelic female saint that I analysed in the previous section, the deployment of Franco as a zombie figure in this film should prompt us to identify specific shifting elements of Spanish society in the 1960s which this zombie figure may indicate. Among them, we could regard Franco-as-a-zombie as symptomatic of the sharp changes brought by the capitalist modernization of Spain during the development years, which was implemented by the technocrats despite Franco's scepticism.

Zombie figures as metaphors or as a means of sociopolitical critique abound in the history of cinema. A pioneering example of this is the zombie classic *King of the Zombies* (Jean Yarbrough, 1941), a political parable of the apocalyptic fears caused by the Second World War and the hazardous use of scientific innovation. Zombies as tropes of pressing sociopolitical issues seem to surface, as Jean Comaroff and John Comaroff have argued, in times of crisis triggered by acute shifts related to capitalist development (782–3). The quintessential example of this may well be the American-Italian production *Dawn of the Dead* (1978), directed by George A. Romero, in which the zombie metaphor is adopted to critically evaluate the impact of consumer capitalism. Like Franco, Sáenz de Heredia was sceptical about the radical changes implemented by the new political cadres of the regime. As some of his later films will indicate, he feared a zombification of Spanish society in the sense of its becoming a multitude of brainless consumers who may lose their cultural identity. Interestingly enough, he channels this fear by visualizing Franco (instead of the average Spanish citizen) as a zombie-like figure in *Franco, ese hombre*. The dialogue heard during the zombie-like presentation of Franco stipulates the formula to resist this process of zombification: reinforcing the sacred foundation of Spain's national identity and using military resources to carry out Spain's spiritual mission in the world. Franco invokes the crusade spirit of the Civil War and asks Spanish citizens to keep up their sacrifices for the sake of Spain's high mission. In case two and a half decades of the same rhetoric did not suffice, Franco proceeds to clarify the terms of such a mission: Spain continues to be the spiritual reserve of the Western world.

Earlier in the film, this crusade spirit is linked to a nostalgic remembrance of the lost empire. A shot of a world map highlights in (bloody) red – never mind the aspiration to exalt peace – Spain's imperial possessions in the sixteenth century, and subsequent shots enumerate the chronological loss of every colony. To top it off, the voice-over narrator provides specific data about the dates of each colonial loss as well as numbers of vassals and kilometres of land lost. The data used does not support the new rational logic of the Spanish economy, which was in vogue in the public discourse of the new hordes of technocrats taking over the regime's administration. Instead, it makes more vivid the pathetic staging of Spain's colonial disasters as a lost paradise. The recalcitrant insistence on the old rhetoric of the traditional type of legitimacy for the regime not only is rather anachronistic but also contradicts the overall spirit of the "Twenty-Five Years of Peace" campaign that funded this film. As I explained before, the campaign was intended to recognize the points of reference underpinning the regime's legitimacy, but by adapting them to the changing conditions of the 1960s. Economic growth and the resulting overall improvement in the level of wealth and quality of life of Spaniards constituted the perfect opportunity to advertise the expansion of the regime's legitimacy to rational grounds: the effective management of the country's resources. Ultimately, the goal was to reinforce the authority of the regime and, thereby, to assure its continuation, by counteracting the expected waning of charismatic and traditional authority due to Franco's inevitable aging process and to the weakening of traditional values in the face of modernity.

As a fellow combatant in the Nationalist faction of the war, Sáenz de Heredia had too much admiration for the legionnaire Franco and was too attached to "el espíritu del 18 de Julio" (the spirit of July 18, 1936). Putting victory and peace in the same sentence did not resonate with Sáenz de Heredia, but the victory of war did. This reveals that commissioning Sáenz de Heredia was probably the only mistake that Fraga made in his otherwise masterful planning of the "Twenty-Five Years of Peace." Nancy Berthier argues that the images of the military parade throughout the film focus more on the new generations, symbolically attached to "peace." For her, *Franco, ese hombre* is structured around binary poles of past/present, war/peace, older generations/newer generations in such a way that the first elements of the binaries – past, war, older generations – serve to justify the second ones – present time, peace, newer generations – and, conversely, the new elements that symbolize the ideal present confirm the validity of the past ones ("José Luis" 210). In my view, the film had the opposite effect, emphasizing that the diverse factions of the administration were advancing at different velocities in the 1960s. The old guard led by Franco and President Carrero Blanco, the so-called *inmovilistas*, were out of sync with the vision and action of the young technocrats. The former take centre stage in *Franco, ese hombre* through every act of their saintly hero; the latter are only mentioned in passing, as observers at the military parade, and introduced as "modernos colaboradores en las tareas de gobierno" (modern collaborators in governing tasks), that is, demoted to mere independent contractors of the Franco administration. The former cling to the victory of war and to spiritual justifications of the regime; the latter want to resemanticize victory as the peace leading to material prosperity, even if that prosperity still rests on a Catholic-infused cosmovision. This hagiopic explains Franco's military triumphs as the miraculous actions of a saintly figure and, thereby, reinscribes the early regime's interpretation of the Civil War and its self-validation in terms of a religious crusade. Although meant as a cultural intervention to complement the new official image of a regime in tune with the times, *Franco, ese hombre* instead portrays how certain sectors of the regime still interacted with the challenges of those new times through a 1930s lens.[14]

As I will show in the next chapter, Sáenz de Heredia's later film *¡Se armó el belén!* (1969) took his fears about the changes in the regime to another level by openly lambasting the new logic of economic rationalization and consumerism that became prevalent in all spheres of Spanish society in the late 1960s. While not as blatantly, the visual treatment of Franco in the closing interview of *Franco, ese hombre* already reveals the filmmaker's anxiety about a state of zombification of the *Generalísimo* and Spain during the development years if the administration kept departing from the crusade spirit that underpinned the regime in the first place. As Rowena Harper notes, there is always an unsettling change in the classic zombie story: "There has been a death, signaled by a rotten corpse, which confronts us with the fact that something we have long held dear … just isn't what it used to be" (30). In this case, the traditional values underpinning the regime seem under attack, as embodied by the less-than-vigorous physical image of the (un)charismatic leader. Although this film was made prior to the zombie mania generated by George A. Romero's classic, *Night of the Living Dead* (1968), the visual presentation of Franco in the closing interview, and particularly the aforementioned lighting treatment of the saintly hero, certainly appears for a contemporary viewer as the light of the living dead.

The Light of the Modern Church: Conciliar Saints and the Church of the Poor

Hagiographic films gradually started to engage more critically with the confessional status of Spain, the shifting relations between the Church and the state, and the Church's internal transformations owing to the ongoing Vatican II Council. Films such as Rafael Salvia's *Isidro, el Labrador* and León Klimovsky's *Aquella joven de blanco* featured members of the Church who aligned with peasant believers against the town's political and economic elite, thus undoing the expected association between throne and altar. These two hagiopics invited the audience to identify with the humble believers and to oppose community leaders and secular sceptics who negate the power of religion to shape public life. They conferred a redemptive value on Catholic faith at a time when the stability of the Church and its appropriate place in society were under scrutiny. Also, the emphasis of both films on poverty and social disparity brought to the fore an uncomfortable issue for films that were supposedly complicit with the ruling administration: the shortcomings of the "economic miracle" in making the necessary social reforms "such as the expansion of the Welfare State and the redistribution of national wealth" (Townson 13), since rural areas and some regions remained significantly behind (Buchanan 91). Although these films spoke about past epochs, they still broke the "developmental decorum" of pro-regime films in the 1960s: it was not appropriate to show misery.

Poverty, advocacy for the working class, and antagonism towards the elite, especially the Church elite, feature prominently in *El señor de La Salle*, the film I want to highlight in this section. This film narrates the life of the French priest and educational reformer St John Baptist de La Salle (1651–1719), and was inspired by the historical novel *Master of Mischief Makers* (1952), a fictional account of La Salle's life by Leo Charles Burkhard. Director Luis César Amadori worked with a superb cast of male stars, including Hollywood celebrity Mel Ferrer and Spanish icons such as Fernando Rey and Alfredo Mayo. As Amadori admitted in an interview published by *Cinestudio*, he managed a considerable budget that shows in the good production values of the film (Julián Alonso 37) and in the decent commercial run in Spain with 911,893 tickets sold and fifty-six days of showings at the Palacio de la Música theatre in Madrid (Camporesi 125). In typical hagiographic fashion, *El señor* offers the drama of trial, suffering, and redemption that the protagonist undergoes. The film narrative focuses on John Baptist of La Salle (Mel Ferrer), a priest of a distinguished and affluent family, who is made canon of the Cathedral Chapter at Rheims, but immediately thereafter has an accidental episode that causes him to have an epiphany: he realizes that he has turned his back on the problems of the poor all his life. John initiates his holy mission: providing free schooling for the poor. Inevitably, this brings John opposition from the ecclesiastical authorities, who in seventeenth-century France were in charge of education, and eventually from secular ones, who accuse him of misappropriation of funds.

As expected in a hagiopic, John will endure all these trials and tribulations and will finally make his ultimate wish come true: to make his network of schools a religious order, the Institute of the Brothers of the Christian Schools. However, the film's visual style significantly departs from previous Spanish hagiopics, as do the overall spectatorial identifications the film generates. The big budget allowed Amadori to plan an elaborate mise-en-scène. This resulted in a less formulaic narrative that did not have to depend on the usual suspects of hagiopics' cinematic conventions, such as flashy celestial light, overdramatic ceremonial music, and rudimentary sound devices. Some salient elements of the mise-en-scène of *El señor de La Salle* such as setting, costume, make-up, and lighting work together with framing devices and a carefully planned composition to deliver a message that deviates from prior Spanish hagiopics. The life of a French saint in the second half of the seventeenth century is used here to carry a message that is relevant in the context of the mid-1960s in Spain. Although *El señor de La Salle* focuses on a critique of the Church's scandalous wealth and connections with political power during the Bourbon dynasty in France, the message is also persuasive in the context of the turmoil within the Spanish Church caused by the Vatican II Council.

In opposition to the cardboard settings in *Fray Escoba* and *Rosa de Lima*, Amadori could afford to portray the film's period with a certain degree of historical verisimilitude. The ability to shoot on existing locations offered a more or less credible epochal rendering, even though those locations did not match the fictional places. For example, the scenes outside and inside the Cathedral of Rheims were shot in the Cathedral of Toledo, and the outdoor scenes in Paris were shot in Salamanca. Other elements of the mise-en-scène such as costume, props, and make-up had a similar function. Characters from the royal family, the aristocracy, and the Church's hierarchy wear lavish costumes in terms of their colour, fabric, and attention to detail. Costume props such as showy jewellery and expensive-looking handkerchiefs complete their opulent looks. By contrast, John Baptist and his collaborators wear modest black gowns and caps with no other ornaments. Two specific costume props have a major narrative function to mark class differences in the stratified society of France under Louis XIV. The first one is the hair arrangements. Male characters from the upper and upper-middle classes wear large wigs – even if not powdered as was in fashion at that time – while women wear a coiffure supplemented by artificial hair. La Salle's entourage and all the characters of low origins wear no chic hairpieces, only their natural hair. Also, a distinctive trait of the Brothers' outfit is the loose sleeves of their gowns, which resemble the usual gear of peasants. Make-up contributes to emphasize class divisions, as wealthy characters such as the Cardinal Noailles (Rafael Rivelles) are frequently shown touching up their faces with white powder to maintain a trendy appearance.

Costume, hair, and make-up thus function beyond providing historical accuracy to convey fundamental narrative messages and build our perceptions of the characters. And so does the dexterous use of lighting. Traditional hagiopics like *Teresa de Jesús* and *Rosa de Lima* are known for their use of celestial light to illuminate the saintly figures and differentiate them from regular characters. The unique profile of the religious hero of *El señor de La Salle,* whose sainthood ensues from mundane deeds and not from miraculous acts, does not prompt such lighting conventions. La Salle's sanctity was not linked to divine apparitions or supernatural events, so overstated celestial lights are out of order. Instead, his moral and intellectual authority over other characters is rendered through framing devices such as medium shots and medium close-ups in heroic low angles that magnify his already imposing figure (Mel Ferrer was noticeably taller than most of the other actors in the film). The opening sequence sets the tone for the rest of the film. A long shot in low angle displays La Salle approaching the camera riding a horse. The camera pans to the left to follow his motion as a competent equestrian. An editing cut takes us to the entrance of a building. La Salle dismounts, and, after another cut, the camera frames the character from below in a medium close-up that displays his elegant figure and suggests his high social rank. From that moment, framing becomes a powerful motif in the film through the repetition of heroic low-angle shots in association with La Salle's distinction, but later in relation to his moral grandeur instead of his class status.

Although departing from the conventions of traditional hagiopics, cinematographer Antonio Macasoli skilfully used lighting to further direct attention to the social hierarchies the film calls into question. Notably, the film relies on a contrast between high-key lighting in the scenes portraying the settings of wealthy characters and low-key lighting creating shadows when screening the world of the lower classes. All scenes in John Baptist's family mansion, in the Versailles Palace, and in the Cardinal's residence are presented in high-key. An extreme instance of this high-key approach takes place in the ballroom scenes in La Salle's family mansion. These are all brightly lit, with few (if any) shadows and a perfect equilibrium of the quality, source, and direction of the light so as not to prioritize any space or subject in the frame. From left to right, from front to back, all characters and spaces are displayed under the same balanced light. This is a rather unnatural effect, typical in musicals and comedies (Monaco 166). Also, as Gerald Millerson notes, an excessive amount of fill light in high-key lighting situations "conveys an impression of 'openness' and space" but can simultaneously suggest an overall flat effect, even a "lifeless" one (77–8). In the most extreme cases, which Millerson calls "very high-key," the picture becomes "full of light-gray to white tones" that may convey a feeling of triviality (239). All those effects are perceptible in these scenes of *El señor de La Salle*. The strong fill light evokes the artificiality of the universe of the aristocratic classes, who live turning their backs on the real lights of society, including the hard edges and shadows.

These scenes presented with high-key technique are cleverly edited to appear in radical contrast with the scenes treated with a low-key approach. In the latter, the key light does not dominate and the lighting is mostly dark and, at times, shadowy, hiding details of the figures. These are the scenes that take place in settings such as the tavern where La Salle goes to recruit teachers, the first school he founds, and the prison where he visits his former traitor Clement (Manuel Gil). The most extreme example of low-key lighting appears in the poor underworld where La Salle goes to chase Andrés (Marc Michel), who has stolen his necklace. A soft key light coming diagonally illuminates the figure of the priest and Bernarda (Nuria Torray), but the other characters – Bernarda's parents and some beggars – and the background of the scene are rendered in almost complete darkness. The gloomy overhead tonal areas seem to weigh down on the characters and elicit a feeling of captivity. The shadow of a barred window behind the characters further evokes the situation of confinement in which these marginalized characters live. The music also gestures towards the shadowy underworld by changing to tunes conveying suspense and distress. Low-key lighting is frequently applied to mysterious or gloomy scenes that denote fear and evil. Paradoxically, La Salle experiences an epiphany through this contact with the sombre underworld and decides to change his life. This epiphany becomes a narrative turning point, propelling the protagonist's renewed life project to help the poor and the marginalized. The bright light of his wealthy existence blinded his vision of what his apostolic mission should be; the darkness of the underworld ironically enables him to see that mission clearly.

Later in the narrative, Andrés pays a visit to La Salle to return the stolen necklace and express his willingness to join the priest's educational project as a teacher. Apart from the low-key illumination, this scene also includes high-contrast lighting effects. Generally known as chiaroscuro and typical of film noir and horror movies, this technique creates sharp contrasts between light and shadows through the absence of fill light (Hayward 210). After an argument with his collaborators, who express their discomfort with the vows of poverty La Salle wants them to take, La Salle appears overwhelmed, with his face and arms on the dining table, as if conceding defeat. A strange sound alerts him and he goes to check on it at the school's entrance. Suddenly a shadowy silhouette crosses the door against a softly lit background. An editing cut to a close-up of La Salle's face – one of the very few in the film – lit from the left side and with no light on the wall reveals his unease about the unannounced visitor. Since La Salle is mostly photographed through medium shots and medium close-ups throughout the film, the few close-ups like this one have substantial force. Fill and back lights are almost absent, thus creating very sharp shadows and an extreme contrast with the hard key light. The visitor, Andrés, walks towards the lit area of the scene – a hard key light coming diagonally and from below – and his face is exposed to La Salle and the viewers. The character who was formerly living in the shadows of the underworld walks into the healing light to join La Salle's holy mission.

This is another narrative turning point in the film signifying the solidification, not the defeat, of La Salle's dream. But the interesting part from a cinematic point of view is that it epitomizes, along with the scene in the poor underworld discussed above, an overall lighting logic in the film that subverts the viewers' expectations of the meaning of lighting: low-key lighting and darkness are not indicative of sinister aspects. Mainstream cinema predictably follows what Richard Dyer calls the "technical-epistemological configuration" of Western culture, which consists of the standard association of light with knowledge (*White* 110).[15] But lighting, or any other element of the mise-en-scène and of a film's visual style, does not carry absolute meanings, and the specific context of each film determines the function of those technical qualities. *El señor de La Salle* is a cogent example of the uniqueness of individual films, including mainstream commercial films, to offset expectations about the meaning of technical conventions. *El señor* turns around the lighting tradition described by Dyer that associates light with knowledge, since the characters living in darkness are the ones who eventually shed light on society's shortcomings. Reversing the epistemology of light in Western culture, shadowy characters turn out to be the enlightened ones, while the bright light of the wealthy appears as a screen blinding their intellect. La Salle and his collaborators come out from the shadows to become pioneers of modern education by implementing two major innovations. The first one is the adoption of the vernacular French instead of Latin for reading; the second one has to do with logistics and methodology: La Salle establishes a fixed schedule of classes and also an adaptation of a "simultaneous method" of teaching, in which a large group of students would be instructed at the same time, instead of the individual lessons used thus far. Although this simultaneous method had already been used by the Jesuits in their colleges, John Baptist was the first one to adapt it and popularize it in the context of elementary education (Battersby 80).

Furthermore, the composition and the camera angles work in tandem with lighting to signpost the film's dissident potential. Closed frames and symmetrical compositions of the saintly protagonist with his collaborators constitute cinematographic techniques that point towards the democratic values this film privileges. La Salle resigns as a canon and disposes of his wealth by distributing it among the poor people of Rheims. He realizes that to be able to teach and catechize the poor, he needs to live and suffer like one of them. When La Salle makes his last visit to his house to remove all valuables for sale, his uncle (Tomás Blanco) reprimands him for getting rid of his wealth. The framing and composition of that scene is crucial. The camera pans to the left, accompanying La Salle's own movement to position himself in front of his uncle. As he walks towards his uncle, the focal length of the camera is modified by means of a zoom-in that magnifies not only La Salle's figure but also Pedro's (Pepe Rubio) and Andrés's, while the uncle's figure appears out of focus. Pedro and Andrés are situated at the back, on either side of La Salle's figure, looking at the uncle over La Salle's shoulder in a perfectly symmetrical composition that emphasizes the words La Salle is pronouncing regarding social equality: "Si conseguimos que el pobre mire cara a cara al poderoso, si podemos igualarlos en el saber, el mundo se convertirá en algo luminoso, más cerca de la paz, más cerca de la fraternidad humana" (If we get the poor to meet face to face with the powerful, if we can make them equal in knowledge, the world will become a brighter place, closer to peace, closer to human fraternity).[16] La Salle's speech dwells on the aforementioned sacred tradition that mobilizes metaphors connecting light with knowledge, here meaning peace, equality, and human fraternity. One more detail in this frame is conspicuous. Pedro and Andrés are situated on either side of La Salle's figure and also on either side of the borders of a painting with geometrical motifs of a rhomboid shape. Rhomboids are parallelograms with unequal adjacent sides, and in the context of this scene they

1.3 Symmetrical composition connoting social equality in *El señor de La Salle* (1965). Permission to reproduce the still from EGEDA.

connote the unequal social relations La Salle is discussing. In addition, the rhomboid pattern in the background painting may also suggest the condition of confinement in which people like his uncle who are dominated by material possessions live. La Salle has seen the light and has therefore set himself free from that material incarceration by sharing his wealth with the poor. This is visually reinforced by his walking out of the frame, again accompanied by Pedro and Andrés, while his uncle remains onscreen, and trapped by the symbolic rhomboid-like pattern in the background.

The careful planning of the composition and the framing thus emphasizes the meaning of a crucial scene that encapsulates the social message of the film. If read in its historical matrix, this universal message of the film carries more significance. Released in 1965 when the Vatican II Council was wrapping up its sessions, *El señor* incorporates the spirit of several of the conciliar documents that shook the foundation of the Catholic Church. In particular, La Salle's determination to detach himself from riches as an imperative step towards the Christian perfection that he required of his followers seems to echo *Perfectae Caritatis,* a decree on the adaptation and renewal of religious life. This decree mandated that clergy should practise "voluntary poverty." Religious communities should use their resources "for other needs of the Church and the support of the poor whom all religious should love after the example of Christ" and, therefore, "should avoid every appearance of luxury, excessive wealth and the accumulation of goods" (Vatican). The film takes sides in the intense debates and divisions in the Church by allegorically favouring those willing to live diligently according to Vatican II recommendations, rather than the ecclesiastical hierarchy, reluctant to renounce their privileges. John Baptist of La Salle, the pioneer of modern education and a man ahead of his time, is an edifying example who carries the banner for the new "Church of the poor," the one willing to intervene in temporal matters and to seek social justice, in opposition to the "crusade Church" that underpinned National-Catholicism and alienated working classes and the vanquished of the war. This is the first religious film of my corpus that implicitly embraces the Vatican II renovation of the Church and also the first film in which religion openly becomes a dissenting factor.

The innovative visual style of *El señor de La Salle* and its different message with respect to previous hagiopics illustrate that scholars cannot continue to lump together all hagiographic films as aesthetically worthless and brainwashing instruments that pro-regime cultural platforms employed to indoctrinate the Spanish masses in the early 1960s. Some of them looked to the past for edifying stories of religious hero(in)es that allegorically served as a way to reactivate the traditional values that underpinned the regime in its first two decades (*Teresa de Jesús, Rosa de Lima,* and *Fray Escoba*). Deeply consoling and nostalgic, these films provided comfort to Catholic audiences as they tried to grasp the nature of the transformations taking place in Spain that seemed to put traditional values under attack. *Franco, ese hombre,* while apparently made to project a new rational-legal type of legitimacy for the regime, ended up reinforcing the residual role of the sacred in the Spanish political imagination of the mid-1960s to exercise sovereign power. The final product, though, had the perverse effect of presenting Franco as a zombie-like figure instead of a sovereign invested with divine qualities. Finally, *El señor de La Salle* made room for emergent values concerning the role that the Catholic Church should take in the modern world. Framed within the context of the recommendations of Vatican II, this film implied through the example of its Conciliar-like saint that the Church had a duty to intervene in temporal matters as an independent institution concerned with social justice instead of with power ambitions.

El señor de La Salle marked the twilight of the hagiographic film cycle, but not the twilight of the Spanish film industry's interest in the role of religion in Spanish society and in the state of flux of the Catholic Church in the post–Vatican II context.[17] Other subgenres of religious films emerged in response to those fluctuating circumstances. In the next chapter, I will examine the most popular of those subgenres among Spanish audiences, the post–Vatican II comedies of development, which were deployed as mass culture articulations of the regime's technocratic discursive framework during the 1960s and early 1970s. By pointing out that capitalist modernization and Catholicism were perfectly compatible within the authoritarian system, these comedies served to naturalize the economic-providential paradigm of governance that the regime implemented as the path to modernity in the development years. Simultaneously, by endorsing the council's values, post–Vatican II comedies followed the lead of *El señor de La Salle* in becoming channels for staging cultural criticism and, in particular, the Church's increasing ideological detachment from the regime's administration.

Chapter Two

Praying for Development in Post–Vatican II Comedies

The most common configuration of confessional cinema shifted in the second part of the 1960s in response to evolving historical circumstances. Instead of hagiographic films that often held on to traditional values in the face of the modernization, post–Vatican II comedies that spotlighted the modernization process took centre stage. These films were a sub-type of the "comedia del desarrollismo" (comedies of development), a Spanish cinematic genre that enjoyed extensive popular support in the 1960s and early 1970s. Like their broader template, post–Vatican II comedies accommodated an optimistic version of socioeconomic developments, but they added to the mix a focus on the religion-modernity interface and on the council's impact on Spanish society. Featuring clergy who enthusiastically adopted conciliar recommendations and clashed with factors of conservative containment within the Church, post–Vatican II comedies tended to celebrate the renewal of the Church's pastoral mission as much as the advent of consumer society and the material prosperity enjoyed under the patronage of Franco.

The purpose of this chapter is to identify and evaluate the niche that was occupied by post–Vatican II comedies in the landscape of the Spanish film industry of the late 1960s and early 1970s. They emerged connected to the tradition of Spanish comedies, especially the comedy of development, but inscribed stylistic – mainly related to composition and editing – and thematic features that distinguished them. Genre is thus a useful analytical tool here, as long as it is understood as discursive, mutable, and, above all, culturally and historically specific. Post–Vatican II comedies became a subgeneric cycle in their own right with massive commercial appeal because they engaged pressing social and political issues: secularization, the renewal of the Church, and the changing relations between throne and altar. I set out to test the straightforward hypothesis that post–Vatican II comedies contained a meta-theoretical discourse, in the sense that they comprised a justification of the shift the regime took from political theology to economic theology. While I highlight that the regime's mutations were proportionate to those of Western modernity, post–Vatican II comedies also typically rounded off their stories by reminding spectators that Spain could be modern without abandoning its Catholic core. In this way, post–Vatican II comedies contributed to the development discourse – hence their meta-theoretical edge – by adding an important nuance to Manuel Fraga's (in)famous slogan. Borrowing from Tom Buchanan, we could say that post–Vatican II comedies advocated that "instead of 'Spain is different,' the true message should have been 'Spain – the same but different'" (95).

My point is that post–Vatican II comedies of development played a key role, especially because of their massive appeal among Spanish audiences, in the glorious apparatus that was instrumental for the proper functioning of the new paradigm of economic theology in the 1960s. Formerly confined to the sphere of liturgy and official ceremonials, these forms of public acclamation did not evaporate with modernization, but shifted to the domain of public opinion to generate consensus. As I explained in the introduction, Giorgio Agamben considers that modern forms of ruling, including contemporary democracies, depend on the function of glory disseminated by media discourses that have an impact in every space of the public and private spheres (*The Kingdom* 256). These forms of acclamation, channelled through media discourses, retain from liturgy and ceremonials their ritualistic nature. They are structured and repetitive acts detached from the routines of everyday life through which a community can symbolically express shared values. They can operate similarly to Émile Durkheim's notion of religious rituals: ritualized acts of a particular religious group that "unite its adherents in a single moral community called church" (46). Religion is not just about beliefs experienced on an individual basis; religion links individuals to each other through its symbolic dimension to stimulate feelings of collective belonging. Therefore, media rituals performing the function of glory during the development years were, just like religious rituals, a tool to validate social coherence.

What I am suggesting is that the massively consumed post–Vatican II comedies had a ritualized dimension performing the function of glory in the new paradigm of economic theology supporting the regime. Apart from the ritualistic dimension embedded in the practices of cinema going, post–Vatican II comedies deployed a recurrent set of stylistic elements that I will explain in the next section (the use of the zoom lens, framing devices, synergical crosscutting, and iconography) to reiterate that the socioeconomic modernization of Spanish society was compatible with, and indeed contingent upon, safeguarding Catholic values. The directive use of these repeated visual cues went hand-in-hand with formulaic narratives that delivered a festive tribute to this home-grown model of Catholic modernity. Audiences could recognize these visual and narrative cues as repetitive elements expressing shared societal values and, thereby, arousing their sense of belonging and participation in the social wholeness.

But since the grounds of Spanish Catholicism and its institutional links to the regime started to shift drastically in the mid-1960s as a result of Vatican II, this added a layer of complexity to these comedies that needs to be taken into consideration. Political changes fostered by Vatican II recommendations took effect almost immediately with the Law of Religious Liberty in June 1967, which in theory abolished the old Spanish fundamentalism regarding religious beliefs, although in reality it was more a law of religious tolerance than of religious freedom (Feliciano Montero 110).[1] But this law symbolically produced a domino effect: the Spanish Church began to accept that the secularization process was a reality, and also that its role was to strengthen Catholic beliefs in society as a free choice and not by imposing them from above. The advancement of the reformist factions of the Church – despite fierce resistance from conservative sectors – clearly identified the inevitable path towards separation between ecclesiastical and civil powers, as it made the 1953 *Concordato* with the Vatican an anachronistic document. This concordat represented, as Manuel Tuñón de Lara observed, the spirit of the Council of Trent in the times of the Second Vatican Council (159). It was an obsolete document that put the Franco administration in the spotlight, since authoritarian regimes were not exactly the model of Catholic society that the new face of the Church envisioned. From being a document that assured the marriage between throne and altar, it had become a "Discordato" (Gómez Pérez 8), creating discrepancy and dispute. In 1966 the Episcopal Conference promulgated that the Church was predisposed to forsake all government concessions and, especially, tax exemptions and privileges. According to Norman Cooper, "[i]t was becoming gradually clear to the bishops that the time was approaching when it would be difficult for them to reconcile post-conciliar papal policy with close ties with Francoism" (65).[2] In the last few years of the regime, religion gradually became a factor of dissidence instead of the main ideological pillar of the authoritarian regime; the "Crusade Church" gave way to a "Church of contestation" (Blázquez, *La traición* 119). Given that post–Vatican II comedies generally praised the conciliar reforms, this complicated their ideological adherences and at times even generated stimulating counter-readings. But not all of them followed the same ideological pattern. Towards the end of the chapter I will examine José Luis Sáenz de Heredia's *¡Se armó el belén!* (1969) as a counter-example that presented the post-conciliar context in negative terms, thus warning us against simple approaches to this subgenre.

The Look of a Subgenre

The comedy of *desarrollismo* encapsulated a wide corpus of films created in one of the most fertile and commercially successful periods of cinematic production in Spain.[3] The label "comedia del desarrollismo" was first coined by Javier Hernández Ruiz and Pablo Pérez Rubio to designate a *cine artesanal* shaped by three main influences: the Spanish folkloric cultural tradition, the Italian comedy of the early 1950s, and Hollywood genres (313). The protean and multiform nature of this genre produced varying manifestations within a unified look (316). These heterogeneous materials were crafted by collaborative teams that echoed, albeit on a reduced scale, the specialized production system of the Hollywood studios. These teams manufactured a type of comedy which, unlike earlier *comedias costumbristas* of the 1940s and 1950s, did not offer the image of a poor society that struggled to survive with the aid of its uncontaminated spiritual values, but "una visión rosa, exaltadora del desarrollismo y del modo de vida de las clases favorecidas" (a rosy vision of the development years and of the lifestyle of privileged social classes) (314). For Hernández Ruiz and Pérez Rubio, the comedy of *desarrollismo* was a genre formula that ran parallel to, or better yet constituted, the filmic correlative of *desarrollismo* in the 1960s, since it praised its tenets and achievements.

Until recently, the comedy of development has received scant critical attention, as it has been considered aesthetically worthless and ideologically reactionary.[4] For example, Casimiro Torreiro mentions it under the rubric "comedias 'a la española'" as part of the "filones subgenéricos, ficciones construidas con los materiales de deshecho de los géneros clásicos" (the subgeneric gold mine, fictions constructed with the leftovers of the classical genres) ("¿Una dictadura liberal?" 312). By seeing comedies of development as leftovers of the classical comedy, Torreiro presupposes the existence of pure generic formulas and, moreover, prescribes the quality of any given genre film in terms of its capacity to operate within its generic boundaries and resist adulteration. This is a rather traditional view of film genres that has been soundly contested in genre studies following the lead of, for example, Jacques Derrida. In his well-known article "La loi du genre / The Law of Genre," Derrida concluded that "[e]very text participates in one or several genres, there is no genreless text; there is always a genre and genres, yet such participation never amounts to belonging" (212). Since films often engage in or contain elements of multiple genres, one could in fact argue that generic mixing is the norm rather than the exception. While Derrida's critique of generic purity is applicable to the discussion of any genre, it is especially relevant to the film comedy, a genre that is remarkably prone to hybridization. Film comedy stands out for its formal diversity, which allows for multiple sub-types, and for its capacity both to borrow conventions from other genres and to lend itself to participation in other generic contexts. For Steve Neale and Frank Krutnik, this is "in large part because the local forms responsible for producing laughter can be inserted at some point into most other generic contexts without disturbing their conventions" (18). This means that trying to operate with a single standardized definition or methodology to pin down such a variety of forms would prove insufficient.

Although a lengthy articulation of a theory of film comedy surpasses the scope of my goals for this chapter, suffice it to say that there are at least two reasons why following Derrida's proposition and detaching our critical examination from the view of genre as belonging would be a more productive approach to post–Vatican II comedies. First of all, understanding a genre as a closed and static set of textual structures fails to recognize the industrial dimension that is central to the development of film genres. Scholars such as Steve Neale (*Genre and Hollywood*) and Rick Altman (*Film/Genre*) have convincingly argued that we need to expand our understanding of genres beyond the texts to also account for the role of the industry that manufactures and sells them and the audiences that ultimately consume and make sense of them. For Altman, the process that he calls "genrification," that is, the concrete process of formation and redefinition of film genres over time, entails an elaborate set of relationships among producers, publicists, distribution platforms, the film texts, and the spectators. The negotiation among all the different agents of this process occurs in such a way that new elements are constantly added to established genres until a new genre cycle is created. Although Neale and Altman limit their discussions to Hollywood films, their point is no less valid for other cinematic contexts such as Spain. Post–Vatican II comedies added elements of previous confessional films to the formula of the comedy of development to create a customized subgenre that spoke to Spanish audiences in the late 1960s and early 1970s.

By way of example, *Este cura* (Enrique Carreras, 1968) borrowed from the hagiographic films of the early 1960s the lighting pattern of the glowing white saint to light its female lead. Each time Soledad (Evangelina Salazar) becomes visible, the lighting tonality changes so that a high-key approach in combination with the make-up gives her a dazzling appearance devoid of shadows or sweat. Hard back lighting creates a halo effect over her head and underscores her blondeness and whiteness. The point was to give her a Virgin-like ethereal, noncorporeal quality in close-ups of her face and in medium close-ups in which she appears with her baby in her arms. This lighting treatment thus adds a conservative message in terms of gender to the pattern of the comedy of development. The film takes a stand in favour of breaking with certain traditional structures of society and promoting the modernization of the social fabric, but this is still a patriarchal community in which a woman's role is to be a repository of spiritual values. This lighting treatment was not a uniform feature of the visual styles of all post–Vatican II comedies, however. As I will show in my analyses, each post–Vatican II comedy mixed the religious elements and messages in a way that was not necessarily identical to the one chosen by other films, consequently creating specific meanings worth examining to get a nuanced picture of the whole cycle. In addition, some of them incorporated elements of other generic or subgeneric patterns, such as noir, melodrama, and the musical (*El padre Manolo* and *El padre Coplillas*); slapstick comedy (*Sor Citröen*); and slapstick and the musical (*La novicia rebelde*). Their "participation," to borrow again from Derrida, in the post–Vatican II comedy cycle means that they employed enough conventions of that subgenre that one cannot understand them without reference to it; at the same time, they did not exist only as post–Vatican II comedies, for they also participated in or mixed elements of other generic templates.

The key to this notion of genre as a discursive category that transforms over time is not so much, as Jay Beck and Vicente Rodríguez Ortega argue, a matter of "what representational templates are mobilized but how this combinatory process alters its different components" (13). The meanings created by this art of generic mixing also depend, apart from the industrial practices and the evolution of cinematic forms, on aspects of social and cultural history that affect the way viewers consume and interpret films. It is in this sense that Altman contends that the textual structures of films cannot be dislodged "from the institutions and social habits that frame them and lend them the appearance of making meaning on their own" (*Film/Genre* 211). In the specific case of post–Vatican II comedies, their commercial success owed a great deal to the remarkable public interest in religion in the late 1960s due to the impact of Vatican II that I explained above. Publications about religious topics, and especially about the crisis within the Catholic Church and about its changing relationship with the state, became top sellers in Spain. In fact, as Frances Lannon notes, it would be hard "to catalogue all the books, symposia, lectures, questionnaires, and special issues of ecclesiastical journals" devoted to the impact of Vatican II in Spain between 1968 and 1975 (*Privilege* 115). Simply put, religion was a hot topic in post–Vatican II Spain, and the film industry did not miss the opportunity to partake in and to profit from that public conversation. The demand for post–Vatican II comedies was thus created by the industry, but in response and as a way of contributing to the debates on relevant social issues.

Followers of this cycle could expect a functional visual style that resorted to a few foreseeable technical conventions. But this functionality is not to be confused with the minimalist style that, as I explained in the introduction, Paul Schrader termed "transcendental style" in a systematic attempt to theorize a style of religious films. By contrast, the few technical conventions recurrently deployed by post–Vatican II comedies had a directive function to impel viewers towards a particular interpretation of their messages in relation to the modernity-religion interface in post–Vatican II Spain. The Church's detour to come to terms with the modern world was visually signalled by adopting technical devices such as the zoom lens that were considered modern at that time. Used to manipulate the focal length and to alter perspective relations and the apparent size of people and objects shown in the image, the zoom lens became a trendy technique in Hollywood cinema in the late 1950s thanks to the improved portability of cameras (Bordwell and

Thompson 219). This zooming trend reached the Spanish film industry in the 1960s and became one of the visual trademarks of the comedies of development. It was an inexpensive technical device that added dynamism and fast execution of cinematic movement. Post–Vatican II comedies often employed this modern technique self-reflectively to identify, and sometimes magnify, the figure of a character struggling with adjustments to modernity. For example, in *¡Se armó el belén!*, the priest don Mariano, played by Paco Martínez Soria, is sent to visit a new church led by a young priest to learn modern techniques of apostolate. A bird's-eye view from the top of the modern church shows a minuscule figure dressed in a black soutane, as if he were a vulnerable ant that could be crushed by the pace of modernity. By zooming in, the camera takes us close to the figure in black, don Mariano, whose face shows signs of feeling overwhelmed, almost scared by the magnitude of the megastar church.

Self-reflective allusions to modernity were also flagged by the repetition of certain iconographic places and buildings associated with Spanish modernity in film after film. One of them is the RTVE (Spanish public television) building. Many post–Vatican II comedies include a scene in which an ecclesiastical figure visits the RTVE building, often shown in a magnifying low-angle long shot, to raise funds for his parish, whether it is by performing live on television himself (*El padre Manolo, El padre Coplillas*), by convincing someone else there to raise funds on his behalf (*Un curita cañón* [Luis María Delgado, 1974]), or by having his parish featured on a television program that would bring them fame and recognition (*¡Se armó el belén!*). Another icon of modernity in post–Vatican II comedies is the almost customary long shot of a modern medical centre, often the Hospital Universitario La Paz in Madrid. Opened in 1964 as the first large hospital in Spain, La Paz appears in scenes that dramatize that religion and the advances of modern science are perfectly compatible (*Sor Citröen* and *¡Se armó el belén!*).

Two more stylistic features related to the comedies' composition and editing were particularly salient. One was the use of framing as a categorizing motif in moral and spiritual terms. Low angulation was deployed to ennoble characters of a high moral stature (especially male religious figures such as priests and friars), while high-angle shots usually announced characters representing evil, corrupted forces, or those who were spiritually empty. Although this angulation pattern is a widespread convention in cinema, what made it noteworthy in post–Vatican II comedies was its systematic and cross-referential practice.

This afforded audiences an automatic insight into characters' qualities and moral conflicts. The pattern was so painstakingly applied that when it was broken, typically towards the resolution of narrative conflicts, it indicated the moral redemption of characters formerly associated with malevolent or immoral forces (as we will see in the analyses of *Fray Torero, El padre Manolo,* and *¡Se armó el belén!*).

The last stylistic feature of these films I want to highlight is the use of a distinct type of crosscutting editing. In general, crosscutting is a form of editing used to indicate temporal simultaneity; that is, to present narrative actions that are happening in several places at approximately the same time. In quite a few of the post–Vatican II comedies, it was used to unite actions that epitomized the collaboration of modern advances (technological, mechanical, medical, and so on) with the providential intervention of heavenly elements. *Este cura* can be taken as a paradigmatic example to illustrate this point. The film opens with an extreme long shot of a plane landing at the Barajas airport in Madrid. Editing cuts take viewers to a woman having a baby in a hospital, then back to the airport, where an airline worker announces the arrival of a flight from Rome, and back to the hospital, where the new mother rests with her baby in a room with a big crucifix mounted above the headboard. An additional cut back to the airport shows representatives of the Spanish Church being received as celebrities after their participation in the Vatican II Council. Apart from connecting two lines of action, the crosscutting editing here is used to prompt spectators to make from the onset the visual association between modernity and the renewed, post–Vatican II Catholic Church, which will be the main narrative thread throughout the film. Reminiscent of the doctrine of "synergism," a crucial piece of the salvation theology of Catholicism that teaches that salvation is the result of the cooperation of human effort with divine grace, what I would like to call "synergical crosscutting" reminds the late 1960s audiences that the development miracle of Spain was as much facilitated by divine intervention as by human-driven scientific and rational innovation. The spectators who saw this film on the big screen (788,750 tickets sold) could grasp, if they were devotees of the cycle, the function of this editing device almost automatically, since previous comedies such as *Sor Citröen* and *Sor Ye-Yé* also deployed synergical crosscutting to convey that scientific innovation, modernity, and Catholicism are not mutually exclusive discourses.

As we can see, these directive visual elements constantly drew attention to the ubiquitous dialectic between tradition and modernity underlying these comedies. Surprisingly, most of the authors of the otherwise sound project *El "cine de barrio" tardofranquista*, edited by Miguel Ángel Huerta Floriano and Ernesto Pérez Morán, assume in their conclusions that comedies of development ultimately took a stand to defend the conservative side of this dialectic: a reaction against modernity. In what follows, I wish to provide a corrective to this somewhat simplistic rendering of the core messages of this subgenre. Many comedies of development, and certainly most post–Vatican II comedies, extolled the "miracle" of *desarrollismo* and embraced certain aspects of cultural modernity. Of course, this meant that the shift to modernity should take place by negotiating a balance with traditional values, including Catholic precepts and a patriarchal view of society. A closer inspection of these comedies' stylistic and thematic specificities will reveal a variety of resolutions to the tradition versus modernity conflict, thus preventing one from making any kind of blanket statement about this subgenre.

Embracing Catholic Modernity

The always business-savvy Cesáreo González was one of the first film producers to exploit the public interest in the impact of Vatican II on Spanish society. He convinced José Luis Sáenz de Heredia to direct *Fray Torero* (1966), a film that employed the tried and tested formula of mixing bullfighting with religion. This formula had been popularized by the different versions of *El niño de las monjas* (in 1925 directed by José Calvache Walken; in 1935 by José Buchs; and in 1959 by Ignacio Iquino), the story of a baby abandoned at a convent door who is educated by nuns until he decides to become a bullfighter. Inspired by a similar story, the play *Los Gabrieles*, written by Ramón Peña and Ramón López Montenegro and premiered at the Infanta Isabel Theatre in Madrid in 1916, it was adapted by Sáenz de Heredia to fit the mould of the comedy of *desarrollismo*. González and Sáenz de Heredia relied in *Fray Torero* on the appeal of the bullfighter Paco Camino, at that time at the peak of his popularity. Sáenz de Heredia always regretted having directed this film (Abajo de Pablo 138), and critical reviews of the film upon its release were generally negative. For example, the review published in *Cartelera Turia* considered the film "infrapopular y ajeno a cualquier conciencia artística" (below popular taste and lacking any artistic awareness) (Pastor). However, the film was a commercial success, and Cesáreo González proved once again that he had a keen eye for the market, as it sold 1,294,950 tickets.

The film pivots both thematically and ideologically on binary oppositions (rural / urban, tradition / modernity). The action takes place in a small town near Madrid in which eight friars and a young postulant, Francisco, who becomes a bullfighter (Paco Camino), live off alms in a fifteenth-century convent. The convent becomes the object of desire of the town's officials, because its location coincides with the spot that a development project has designated for building a gas station with adjacent facilities on the side of a new highway. The resolution of the film offers a compromise to end the tension not by getting rid of tradition (forcing the convent to disappear) but by having the friars manage the gas station and benefit from its profits. A couple of foreign tourists stop by the new station and are taken aback when they realize that the gas station worker is a friar. One of them enthusiastically asserts, "Yes, España es diferente" (Yes, Spain is different). The unrealistic and humorous finale condenses the message of this comedy of development, which promotes a form of moderate *aperturismo* to reconfigure Spanish "difference" without abandoning it. Economic liberalization, the promotion of consumerism, and the exploitation of difference as a commodity are the means to preserve that difference and not to tear it down.

The symbolic roles of the ritualistic practices of bullfighting and Catholicism in this resolution of the tradition versus modernity conflict are crucial. Both practices involve collective rites that reconfigure time-honoured Spanish cultural traditions. Both are "invented traditions" in the sense articulated by Eric Hobsbawm, as "a set of practices, normally governed by overtly or tacitly accepted rules and of a ritual or symbolic nature, which seek to inculcate certain values and norms of behavior by repetition, which automatically implies continuity with the past" (1). But the key is that these rites are re-elaborated by the community in a dynamic negotiation between tradition and innovation. Bullfighting involves the reenactment of an old cultural manifestation, but it is not the opposite of modernity. And, as this film suggests, neither is religion. The old popular practices of spontaneous play with and sacrifice of the bull became subjected to rules and professionalized from the end of the eighteenth century onward until they became enclosed in the limits of a bullring and elevated to the category of a modern art form that keeps its ties to popular festive origins (Colón Perales 41). Bullfighting, as we know it today, has a double modality, aesthetic and festive, since it is both an aesthetic experience and a collective popular ritual involving a sacrifice with real blood (Martín Arias 55). As an "invented tradition," bullfighting employs old materials with a ritualistic language elaborated in a process of symbolic syncretism. This means that bullfighting went through "a process of formalization and ritualization, characterized by reference to the past, if only by imposing repetition" (Hobsbawm 4).

Bullfighting in this film is presented as a modern spectacle in which "un actor-artista (heredero del sacerdote del ritual estatal-religioso) es capaz de ejercer sus acciones en pos de la producción de una emoción especial, la estética, trasunto de la experiencia religiosa" (an actor-artist, who is an heir of the priest in the religious-state ritual, is able produce a special emotion, the aesthetic one, which is a reflection of the religious experience) (Martín Arias 55). The identification between the bullfighter and the religious leader is made apparent in a comical scene early in the film in which Francisco helps the bullfighter Manuel (Antonio Garisa) to put on the jacket of his *traje de luces*, and Manuel comments, foreshadowing the course of events of the film, that he might exchange it for Francisco's habit. This identification is not merely a gag to provide comic relief, but the cinematic articulation of the deeper symbolic ties between bullfighting and Catholic rituals. In its modern construction, or "invention," to return to Hobsbawm's notion, bullfighting was subjected to the same principle of universalization that gave rise to the modern Catholic Mass: the abstraction of diverse rites and myths that were equivalent or at least somewhat compatible. In this sense, the perception of the matador as the priest of a community of worshippers is well documented among aficionados and experts. The matador is assisted by *banderilleros* and *peones de brega* just as the priest is surrounded by altar boys. Also like the priest, the matador possesses a mysterious gift that enables him to carry out a sacred action, the sacrifice. Yet, to get to that point he needs to go through a tough learning process, part of an enclosed and hierarchical system that matches that of the Catholic Church. Finally, comparisons between bullfighting and Catholic rituals are further reinforced by the symbolic parallelism between the bullfighting ring as a temple of worship and the Catholic churches (Delgado Ruiz 197–9).

With this in mind, in *Fray Torero* the ritualistic practices of bullfighting and Catholicism appear as invented traditions with at least two overlapping functions. First of all, they symbolize, especially in the final sequence that I will shortly analyse, social cohesion and group belonging, presented as critical to coping with the speed of change in the development years. Related to that, they serve to legitimize the renewed institutional structures of the post–Vatican II Catholic Church represented here by the friars as well as the equally transformed way of governing in the technocratic era of Francoism. *Fray Torero* emphasizes that bullfighting is an aesthetic-festive spectacle that resembles a religious ritual and has the function of enabling a modern community to strengthen its identity and mitigate the anxiety created by the socio-economic transformations of the development era. Francisco's character embodies this form of Catholic modernity in which Spanish cultural difference could coexist in harmony with the course of modernization. He is a flawless religious hero whose skills and hard work fighting the bulls attract the kind of popularity and financial success necessary to help keep the convent afloat. Visually, Sáenz de Heredia marks the importance of his spiritual mission by recurrently framing him, along with other model clerical characters, with heroic low-angle shots that enlarge their moral figure over secular characters. Fray Torero's example typifies the prospects for upward mobility in the evolving Spanish society; more importantly, he epitomizes (national) spiritual superiority over rampant materialism. The latter is embodied by the rich but morally decayed Mirta (Angélica María), who seduces him and tries to divert him from his morally irreproachable path. Fray Torero ignores the allure of fame and sex, sticks to his Catholic beliefs, and requests to be ordained as a lay brother of the convent.

The film closes with the religious ceremony in which Fray Torero is ordained with the whole town in attendance, including the formerly sceptical town officials. From a formal point of view, framing devices and the meticulous choice of camera angles are again the straightforward visual techniques Sáenz de Heredia employs to signal the ideological agenda of the film sealed by this happy ending. A series of medium close-ups of each character that has had a significant role in the film serves almost as a head count to prove that everyone in the town has showed up to participate in the ceremony. Interestingly, these individual shots are framed in a low angle, a technique thus far limited mostly to framing clerical characters. The use of low-angle shots in this final sequence to frame characters formerly depicted as malicious, and in some cases criminal, flags their moral redemption. An editing cut takes viewers to an extreme long shot from the back of the church that frames the ceremony from a high angle and from the rear. This abrupt change in camera distance and angle delivers one of the few extreme long shots of the film and shifts the focus from an individual to a collective plane. Because of the substantial distance of the camera, human figures are barely visible. The function of this broad view is precisely to highlight the symbolic function of the religious ritual in amalgamating the community. Religion unites the previously divided town that celebrates the development miracle as a consensual party of a happy community for which spiritual victories are as important as material ones. Characters representing traditional Spanishness (especially the friars) internalize the state's new economic agenda and rhetoric, while characters that perform the role of the modern technocratic state embrace the Catholic backbone that supports the development miracle. With the example of *Fray Torero*, Sáenz de Heredia seems to endorse the Catholic-infused development discourse: development is not mere rational calculation, but a political program put to the service of the highest national values, and among those Spain's spiritual mission still looms large.

Fray Torero therefore stages an idyllic example of the functioning of the economic-providential paradigm of power to which Francoism shifted in the 1960s. Economic modernization is presented as the inevitable course of action that is carried out by the collective action of the whole population – including rural areas such as the fictional town of this film – an action that internalizes the plans and devices to exercise the rational management of the resources that the technocrats put in place at the state level. From the onset, Sáenz de Heredia seeks spectatorial identification with this paradigm shift, which is visually marked, as in the resolution, by the use of a long shot that carries significant meaning. The film opens with the failed visit of the major (José María Prada) and his assistant Bernardo (Agustín González) to the convent, for they are unable to convince the friars to agree to move the convent to a different location. In their car, Bernardo and the major complain about the friars' resistance to progress. The car, a symbol of the very progress they encourage, gets stuck, and Bernardo has to push it from behind so that the major can start the engine. The adept planning of the sequence includes a long shot of the stuck car with the vast, desert-like scenery in the background. The message suggested by this long shot is clear: progress is necessary to overcome stagnation – what Alex Longhurst theorized as the "developmental cul-de-sac" that Spain faced in the late 1950s (18) – and to transform the desolate Castilian region from wasteland to productive landscape.

By the end of the film, both the secular townspeople and the friars deploy the development strategies – and utter its rhetoric – in their pursuit of financial improvement. Their plans for development appear as a small-scale model of the wide-ranging socioeconomic planning of the government, thereby fictionalizing the feasibility of a type of modern, decentred power in which sovereignty becomes non-subjective and assumes the form of the proper administration of assets and the increase of opportunities for wealth for the population at large. Moreover, this modernization of the economy does not necessarily lead to disavowing cultural difference, in this case the town's pride in their convent and their Catholic traditions; to the contrary, it relies heavily on selling it. Building the gas station, with the potential appeal of tourism, augurs material prosperity and a reassertion of their tradition and identity. That tradition is put on display for tourists who are willing to pay extra money for their gas – on top of buying the friars' holy cards – in exchange for the unique cultural experience of being serviced by clergy. In this way, *Fray Torero* resembles *El turismo es un gran invento* (Pedro Lazaga, 1968), another comedy of *desarrollismo* that stages how townspeople learn to adopt the development strategies, and, especially, the invention of tourism, as their own. This involvement of the population in the manufacturing and selling of their own cultural difference entails, as Justin Crumbaugh argues in relation to Lazaga's film (22), learning to associate with tourism as a discourse in which townspeople are both objects and agents of the invention.

The new element that *Fray Torero* adds to the formula mastered by Lazaga is the crucial mediation of providence. An accidental short-circuit sets the convent on fire, but Bernardo, who was planning to burn the convent to facilitate the gas station project, interprets it as a sign from God, and redeems himself by acting heroically in the rescue operations. He then lobbies to have the town's officials accept the compromise solution offered by the friars. At the beginning of the film, secular town officials and the friars appear to be in separate and mutually exclusive camps, but the religious mediation solves this clash and elicits a happy ending in which both camps reconcile. Secular authorities, led by the born-again Catholic Bernardo, embrace the belief that development and progress still have to be put to the service of the spiritual values of traditionalist Spain: orthodox Catholicism and authoritarian rule. The film tackles the religious substratum underpinning the modern form of power implemented in the development years of Francoism, guided by both instrumental and substantive rationality. Conversely, in the aftermath of Vatican II, the friars take the conciliar recommendation to find the path to a more productive encounter with modernity quite literally. They become entrepreneurs who enthusiastically participate in capitalist development. In addition, their determination garners them national fame to the extent that they make it into a NO-DO newsreel, which further increases their profit by providing free advertising. If, as I contended at the beginning of this chapter, post–Vatican II comedies could be interpreted as filmic channels to endorse the economic-providential paradigm of power, then the reference to the NO-DO highlights how the political function of glory, no longer exclusively performed in liturgy and ceremonies, becomes inserted in media discourses, and from there infiltrates other spheres of society.

In putting to work the symbolic functions of the "invented traditions" of bullfighting and Catholicism to endorse the new image of the regime, *Fray Torero* simultaneously made apparent the constructedness embedded in that discourse. This becomes all the more evident in the film through the performances of secondary characters whose comic voices parody the development discourse. These include, for example, the city councillors who discuss the inopportune glitch in their plans to build the gas station. Their conversation is packed with "development rhetoric," since they talk about the town as "un enclave estratégico" (a strategic site) and the incorporation of society into the development plan as a necessary step to join the "Mercado Común" (Common Market) so that Spain can sell the surplus of its production. This is a comical scene, in which the humour derives from these rural characters' attempt to co-opt the language of the technocrats in the government – who themselves copy the language of international business. Bernardo takes the lead in the conversation by stating the need to take baby steps so that Spain will someday become part of the Common Market. This echoes a historical occurrence: the Spanish government's unsuccessful efforts to have the European Economic Community (EEC) accept Spain as a member. Spain first reached out to the EEC in 1962 to express its intention to become a member but received a categorically negative reaction that prevented a formal petition to join.[5] Bernardo sounds like a pragmatic politician, well aware of the need to plant a seed. Spain needed to make the necessary economic reforms so that it could join the European market some day. Bernardo's speech seems to emulate less that of a gold digger and more that of a long-term planner, since he speaks like a technocrat in his own right. Except that his performance, with his histrionic arm movements, produces a comic effect. This is a signature physical trait of the actor Agustín González, one of the great *cómicos* of Spanish cinema, who made a living with his exaggerated arm movements and his perpetually raised tone of voice. Also, almost every time he appears on screen, he is smoking and drinking an alcoholic beverage, which further undermines his image of managerial efficiency.

Beyond entrance into the European market, the comical conversation of the council members stages other pillars of the technocrats' development discourse. For instance, they discuss tourism as the best source of capital. Within the overall sentiment that industrialization and foreign investments were the motors of economic growth, tourism became the crown jewel of that discourse, not only as the main source of recapitalization of the economy but also as a compelling instrument to project a renewed image of Spain on the international stage. Along with transforming the economy by reducing the market restrictions imposed by the autarkic system in order to attract foreign investments and to open up to the circuits of foreign trade, the goal was to refashion national identity to emphasize similarities to neighbouring Western democracies. The "peaceful invasion" of European tourists (Pack) was the best symbolic engine to project the desired Europeanization of the country, a political instrument to reinvent Spain's difference and make it look more similar to Western democracies, even if maintaining its non-democratic structures (Crumbaugh). Interestingly, the exaggerated enunciation of this development propaganda by characters that provide comic relief creates a parody that ends up having a boomerang effect. Bernardo mimics the language of the technocrats, but since his words produce comical effects, he degrades that discourse to triviality.

Even more prominent is the mocking performance of Antonio Garisa as Manuel "El Mellizo," a bullfighter by necessity. Garisa is another actor renowned for the comic physicality of his performances. In the tribute written in *El País* upon his death, Casimiro Torreiro described among Garisa's branded physical traits "su cara de *bulldog* amable, irónico y socarrón, a su bigotillo y a sus impágables ojeras" (his bulldog face, nice, ironic and sarcastic, his little moustache and his priceless eye bags) ("Murió"). In *Fray Torero*, his comic physicality extends beyond his peculiar facial attributes to his whole body. Several laughable moments in the film have to do with his obesity, which curtails his ability to run in front of a bull, and with his speech impediments. In scenes that require seriousness, as when he interacts with the superiors of the convent, Garisa slurs his words together and often makes no sense. Every time Garisa appears on screen, his gestures, his movements, and his words are excessively comical. He embodies two of the central discourses of the film, bullfighting and Catholicism, but with his comic performance he parodies the solemnity of both.

Antonio Garisa's parodic performance needs to be considered in relation to the tradition of *cómicos* in popular Spanish cinema that Steven Marsh discusses as conforming to Bakhtin's depiction of carnivalesque clowns (23–40). In his well-known essay "Forms of Time and Chronotope in the Novel," in the book *The Dialogic Imagination*, Bakhtin argues that the figures he identifies as clowns, fools, and rogues "create around themselves their own little world, their own chronotope" that consists of passing for others, in their condition of "life's maskers" who mimic others' form of existence and discourses. This makes them laughable figures, "laughed at by others, and themselves as well," but also confers on them "their own special rights and privileges" (159). These privileges pertain to their freedom to say what others would not dare and, thereby, to expose the fabrication that lies behind accepted truths and the gaps in authorized ideological claims, or as Bakhtin puts it, "the right not to understand, the right to confuse, to tease, to hyperbolize life" (163). Garisa plays the role of the carnivalesque clown who, as Marsh argues in relation to Manolo Morán's comic acting in Miguel Mihura's films, relativizes and decentres officially sanctioned discourses "not by intellectual rebuttal but in performance" (27). This post–Vatican II comedy reinscribes national traditions – bullfighting and Catholic rituals – to uphold the paradigm shift from political theology to economic theology. Yet, it concurrently offers, through comic inversion, the potential to question the grounds of the appropriation of those national traditions for political purposes.

Through the use of popular traditions with potential for dissident reception in *Fray Torero*, Sáenz de Heredia operates within a more complex ideological terrain than serving as a plain instrument of official agendas. This film approaches the "slippery juncture" in which Steven Marsh rightly locates Luis García Berlanga's comedies, "inextricably linked to a discourse on Spanishness, whilst remaining its most vigorous critic" (99–100). In fact, a number of elements of *Fray Torero* are reminiscent of Berlanga's *¡Bienvenido, Mister Marshall!* (1952). The action takes places in a small town that remains nameless throughout the film to present it as a prototypical Castilian town, just like Villar del Río in Berlanga's classic. Critical approaches to *¡Bienvenido, Mister Marshall!* have pointed out the eternal, "timeless" quality afforded to the presentation of Villar del Río (Marsh 104; Rolph 13; Woods, "Rehearsing" 12) that goes along "with the town's glaring state of abandon" (Woods, "Rehearsing" 13), as attested, for example, by the clock tower in the main village square that does not work. Similarly, the convent in *Fray Torero* has a dilapidated appearance, which is highlighted in the description provided by the film's script: "Aunque su edificación es ostensiblemente antigua, el descuidado estado de su paredes y tejados hacen pensar más, observándolos, en la vejez que en la antigüedad" (although the building is ostensibly old, the rundown condition of its walls and roofs makes one think of old age rather than antiquity) (Sáenz de Heredia 1). Another similarity has to do with the self-conscious manufacturing of the town, and of national cultural difference, as a commodity for foreign tourists. And related to that, *Fray Torero* also presents an ensemble cast typical of the *sainete* tradition that acts as a chorus linking Spanish national traditions such as bullfighting and Catholic rituals to sometimes unorthodox practices.

What is absent, though, is Berlanga's famous use of the long take to produce a "cacophonic effect" in this chorus, which allowed a fluidity of relations among characters. This often triggered a spatial subversion of hierarchies through careful arrangement of the compositions, such as, for example, putting subaltern characters on top (Marsh 128). Sáenz de Heredia instead employs a more conventional shot/reverse shot structure that limits the potential for disruption of the social order in the choral scenes. Even more crucially, the happy ending that seals the concord of the community through the religious ritual situates *Fray Torero* well within the most conventional (and conservative) versions of the comedy genre. This is different from the ambiguous, often pessimistic resolutions of Berlanga's comedies, which put the finger directly on the fissures and gaps in the celebratory discourses of the nation. The conventional resolution of the conflict in *Fray Torero* neutralizes much of the dissident potential of the popular "invented traditions" and reactivates their role as the main pillars of official national discourses. But for a perceptive viewer, this does not fully erase that, along the way, they have served to expose through comic mimicry the invented quality – in the sense given by Hobsbawm – of those very discourses that hegemonic groups try to pass off as natural and eternal.

The same year that *Fray Torero* was released, Pedro Lazaga also mixed bullfighting and religion in *Nuevo en esta plaza* (1966), a biopic with hagiographic undertones about the heroic life of the matador Sebastián Palomo Linares, interpreted by Linares himself. Cashing in on the growing popularity of the bullfighter, the film attracted more than three million spectators (3,067,863) to the movie theatres. As in *Fray Torero,* the film glorifies the opportunities for social mobility within the developing Spanish society. Apart from the bullfighter, other poor rural characters make their way into the thriving urban environment. That is the case of Trini (Gracita Morales), the waitress in the village's bar who moves to the city to become a hotel housekeeper. Also as in *Fray Torero,* rural Spain appears as the repository of the spiritual values that nourish Spain's socioeconomic development. The religious hero (the bullfighter) is shot praying before each *corrida,* thus enhancing the religious undertones of the miracle of development (social mobility and the spread of wealth among the poor). Furthermore, the use of crosscutting editing during some of the sequences of the *corridas* alternates between shots of the religious saint in action and emphatic low-angle shots of his mother (played by Julia Gutiérrez Caba) praying in the Linares church before a statue of Christ. This recurrent portrayal of the "invented traditions" of bullfighting and Catholicism in tandem reminds viewers that the holy bullfighting hero, like Spain, thrives not only thanks to the divine intervention that rewards moral integrity but also because he does not lose sight of his cultural identity.

Emphatic low-angle shots also ennoble the moral figure of *El padre Manolo* (Ramón Torrado, 1966), in which Manolo Escobar stars as a "cura ye-yé" whose talents as a magician and a pop singer help him to support his parish and to carry out a number of social projects to benefit a working-class neighbourhood on the outskirts of Madrid. The customary "tradition versus modernity" schema appears through the contrast between this priest of a working-class district and his uncle, Father Pepe (Miguel Ligero), who on the surface despises his nephew's modern methods but deep down feels proud of Father Manolo's achievements. As usual, the by-product of this tension is the recognition of the need to bring together both forces. *El padre Manolo* adds a noir element to this typical framework of the comedy of development. By chance, Father Manolo becomes the witness to the death of a high-profile theatre entrepreneur. Father Manolo has a hunch that it was a homicide and investigates the case on his own. Each time he meets one of the suspects – three cousins who had financial motives to harm the victim – the scene appears with a recurrent pattern of camera angles: high-angle shots for the suspects followed by heroic low-angle shots of the priest that evince his moral elevation over the potential culprits. As in *Fray Torero*, camera angles take on an upfront function of classifying the moral profile of characters in opposing camps, thereby establishing a clear dividing line between moral forces that dislodges the film from the noir tradition. The noir touch thus remains on the surface and adorned with explicit references to Arthur Conan Doyle's Sherlock Holmes (worshipped by Father Manolo) and implicit ones to G.K. Chesterton's Father Brown. In appreciation for solving the crime, Father Manolo is allowed to perform in the theatre to raise funds. Predictably, it is a huge success, just like Torrado's film itself with 3,031,369 tickets sold.

Also as in *Fray Torero*, the clerical protagonist heals social conflicts and unites an optimistic community that accepts and reveres the spiritual leadership of the updated Church to guide them along the right path to modernization. The post-conciliar priest's talents – as a magician, singer, and detective – increase the scope and effectiveness of his apostolic mission, as he is able to appeal to secular sceptics and greedy capitalists. In *El padre Coplillas* (1969), Ramón Comas reactivates this "celebrity priest" formula with the story of Father Fernando (Juanito Valderrama), a rural Andalusian priest who finances his social projects to build a neighbourhood for poor people in an Andalusian village by singing *coplas* on television. Like his counterpart in Torrado's blockbuster, Father Fernando appropriates the conduits of consumer culture to modernize his rural community and, simultaneously, help a famous singer, Consuelo Montes (Dolores Abril), to find a proper husband in the rural community, the agricultural engineer Carlos (José Bastida). The subplot of Consuelo's story adds a small noir touch – when Consuelo is persecuted by her agent and almost dies in a car accident – and a melodramatic element: the moral clash between good and evil. The religious and decent Consuelo, whose honour is tested throughout the film, triumphs over her oppressors.

In the quintessential happy ending of the comedy genre – marriage – the triumphant figure of the priest unites the secular sceptics and the devout townspeople. This ending is only possible once the blending of tradition and modernity is worked out under the spiritual guidance of the priest. The inexorability of this merging for the welfare of the community is a recurrent motif throughout the film, but it is especially highlighted early in the narrative in a fundraising concert organized by the priest that frames the main thematic conflict of the film. Father Fernando recruits for the show two young ladies representing diverse social groups and the future of the town – and allegorically of Spain: Rocío (Silvia Tortosa), a young girl of modest origins who sings a *fandango*, and María José (Leonor Varela), the heiress of one of the rich landowners, who performs a pop song. Their attire identifies them with the young, modern generation: both wear very short dresses that recall the mini-skirt fever of the late 1960s. Particularly relevant is Rocío's performance, as she fuses her modern sartorial taste with her traditional musical choice. During her performance, mostly shot in aggrandizing low angle, the camera shows the street sign with the name of the plaza, the village square, "Plaza Menéndez Pelayo," which pays homage to the Spanish Catholic traditionalist thinker par excellence. Although it is not a cinematic trick but the actual location in the village of Cantillana where the film was shot – the village square still has the same name today – it is another element of the mise-en-scène that further focalizes the tradition-modernity conflict. The plaza is the spatial core of the village, the scenario of traditional folkloric celebrations that reaffirm its cultural identity, but it is also the point of entry of new influences that renew the community. The Spanish *fandango* and the non-Spanish "ye-yé" musical and clothing choices meet at the crossroads of this public square to signify that the blending of traditional Spanishness and European modernity is feasible. This blending is, of course, supervised by the town's spiritual leader and enabled by holy intervention. The film inscribes the ubiquitous providential presence through the recurrent use of what I term a "celestial shot": each time Father Fernando achieves something important or semi-miraculous, or simply overcomes a difficult situation, he looks up to the sky to express his gratitude for the celestial intercession on his behalf. These "celestial shots" are always accompanied by religious musical chords seasoned with a flamenco guitar touch, in a stereotypical rendition of Spanish cultural difference as closely tied to Andalusian folklore.

Conspicuously, what unites all the films discussed in this section is the leading role of clerical characters with artistic talents – singers, bullfighters, a magician – who achieve a high media profile that saves their poor communities, whether they are rural or working-class suburban. Bullfighting and popular music function as ideological banners that sustain and epitomize a form of Spanish national identity that is traditional and religious, but which can be combined with a moderate form of modernization. Another symbolic function of these celluloid religious figures with artistic talents has to do with the internal development of the Church in relation to the broader social context. These films are symptomatic of the Church's increasing awareness about its own historical condition in the midst of the first signs of the secularization process. Until the Vatican II Council, the Church had a triumphalist attitude that derived from the privileged position afforded to the ecclesiastical institutions by the regime. This boastful pride ensued from the perception of being the bearer of eternal truths. But with the mounting secularization process, Catholic doctrine had to compete with other interpretative frameworks to affirm its significance and scope of influence on Spanish society. Since the secularization process in Spain in the mid-1960s coincided, as in other Western countries, with economic modernization and the emergence of consumer society, this also entailed that the Church had to enter the marketplace of values to assert its status. And it had to do it with appealing strategies of apostolate so that it could grab the attention of the new affluent consumers.

My point is that these comedies of development presented religious leaders who mobilized masses by mastering talents highly valued in the consumer society as much as by their spiritual leadership and moral righteousness. As celebrity figures in Spain's emerging consumer society, the ecclesiastical characters of these films embodied a more up-to-date clergy that, influenced by Vatican II recommendations, accepted that the Church needed to become part of the modern world and to compete for a relevant spot in it. In this sense, the primary symbolic function of the religious figures of these films was more to imbue the Catholic Church with a liberal, and marketable, cultural identity and public image than to instil a deep sense of religiosity in Spanish society. Post–Vatican II comedies highlighted how the clergy could themselves become a commodity for consumption as well as active agents fuelling the development process in their roles as entrepreneurs, venerated artists, and advocates for urbanizing and real estate projects in their respective communities.

"¡Hay que motorizarse!": Mobility in Post–Vatican II Comedies

Post–Vatican II comedies also called attention to how economic modernization and the rise of massive consumer industries were tied not only to social mobility but also to physical, spatial mobility. Father Manolo rides a Vespa motorcycle that allows him to travel in the city and to make an impromptu trip to Segovia to interrogate one of the suspects of the crime; Father Fernando drives a *biscúter* to meet the bishop in Seville. In both cases clerical figures still use pre-conciliar modes of transportation. The full technological *aggiornamento* of cinematic clergy comes with Lazaga's *Sor Citröen* (1967), another popular post–Vatican II comedy (1,992,032 spectators) in which motorized mobility takes centre stage and clerical characters enjoy the comfort of riding in a modern automobile.

Mobility constituted a menace to the concept of rural society imagined by Franco in the early years of his regime. State propaganda privileged an agrarian nation based on myths of rural Castile and initially tried to prevent the migration of the peasantry to urban areas. However, the accelerated transformation of the economy in the 1960s and the boom of consumer culture demanded the rise of the urban labour force, resulting in numerous waves of rural migration to large metropolitan centres. Mobility was then promoted from above by the government, which was well aware of the need to move peasants to the cities to participate in the process of industrialization. This permutation in the official discourse about mobility and its practical materialization did not happen in an effortless manner. As Tatjana Pavlović states: "the move toward modernity/modernization was inexorable but never smooth. It entailed a continuous process of struggle and negotiation" ("España cambia" 219). The technocrats had the arduous task of appropriating a discourse tinged with transgressive undertones to support a gigantic technological and economic expansion that was still at the service of a non-democratic political structure. The official narrative about mobility had to subsume its dissident connotations of rebelliousness to the status quo within the generalized rhetoric of a stabilizing progress that generates social consent.

This use of mobility by technocrats operated as a strategy of calculated anti-essentialism – promotion of change and innovation – in order to reconcile modernization with compliance to the foundational values of the regime. It is at the core of this historical junction that I propose to assay the duplicitous significance of mobility in *Sor Citröen*. The film features Tomasa Carrasco (Gracita Morales), a young woman in her mid-twenties who moves to the bustling city of Madrid from the small village of La Robla (León) to become a nun. She serves in an orphanage and, driven by an altruistic impulse to raise funds to support the orphan children, she manages to convince the mother superior to buy a vehicle that will allow the nuns more mobility to carry out their mission. Accompanied by Sor Rafaela (Rafaela Aparicio), Sor Tomasa will be able to reach faraway neighbourhoods, thus increasing the fundraising profile of the convent. Her temerarious driving of the brand new Citröen 2CV across Madrid will gain her fame among traffic officers and city drivers, who baptize her "Sor Citröen."[6]

The choice of La Robla as her hometown is not fortuitous. At first, it just seems to be a prototype, a representation of rural Spain from which the unpolished protagonist migrates to the big city. Yet, there is more to the story. The village of La Robla is inextricably tied to the process of modernization in Spain. At the end of the nineteenth century, the Basque iron and steel industry needed to adjust its production costs by establishing a cheaper source of coal than the British Isles. With this goal in mind, the Basque bourgeoisie began an initiative to investigate how they could build a communication system to utilize the less exploited coalfields of León and Palencia. The result was the largest narrow-gauge railway constructed in Western Europe, beginning in La Robla and ending in Bilbao. For a century, the popular train called

"El Hullero" transported coal to support the blast furnace of Vizcaya. The train traversed five provinces for a total distance of 340 kilometres. By the end of the 1960s, though, the commissioned local company in charge of this railway, the Compañía de los Ferrocarriles de La Robla, went bankrupt, and by 1972 the national company FEVE had to take it over (Delgado García). This historical occurrence is retrieved by Pedro Masó, the scriptwriter and producer of the film. Interestingly, Sor Tomasa's father is the station master of La Robla, and his daughter, despite having "alma de ferroviario" (railwayman's spirit), decides to migrate to Madrid.

The story is thus situated in the context of the transition from a rural agrarian society to an urban and industrialized economy. Although Tomasa moves to Madrid for spiritual reasons rather than for material prosperity, she is still one of the six million people who migrated to cities in Spain between 1955 and 1975.[7] The film opens with a train that departs from La Robla but does not travel northbound towards Bilbao carrying coal; rather, it transports people, and its destination is Madrid. *Sor Citröen* begins by pinpointing the urban mobility of the *desarrollismo*. The moving train offers travelling shots of the countryside that it is leaving behind on its way to the urban centre. Farmers, cows, and vegetation appear as wayside elements for the moving voyeur – both Tomasa and the spectator – who traverses the rural topography at a fast pace. The camera does not tarry over the vision of the landscape, nor does it suggest a reflection on the implications of the abandoned rural scenery; it quickly passes through it while offering the title credits of the film. The train / camera soon arrives in Madrid, and the premises of the film are revealed unequivocally through both the opening sequence and the names of the crew members announced in the credits, which promise another instalment of what Nathan Richardson calls the "*paleto* film" from the Masó / Lazaga factory. With that label Richardson refers to "comedies of backward rural immigrants in the city" (*Postmodern* 21) that exploited the comical side of the conflict of values between the sophisticated – yet often corrupt – urban environment and the traditional morals of the *paleto* immigrant, usually taking sides with the latter. The team of producer and scriptwriter Pedro Masó, director Pedro Lazaga, composer Antón García Abril, and director of photography Juan Mariné had recently worked together to make *La ciudad no es para mí*, the quintessential *paleto* film and the biggest box-office success of the 1960s in Spanish cinema (4,296,281 tickets sold).

The similarity to *La ciudad no es para mí* is enhanced by the film's first scenes, which take place in Madrid. A series of long takes show the river Manzanares as part of the urban landscape of the city, rapidly followed by a zoom in to the frantic movement of automobiles in transit. With this sequence, cinematographer Juan Mariné underscores the transition from a rural background to the dynamism of a busy metropolis. Moreover, it immediately calls attention to the specific aspect of urban mobility that *Sor Citröen* will explore: the transformation of the cityscape as a consequence of the boom of the mass automobile industry in Spain.[8] Then, a matching zoom widens the frame until it reaches the other side of the river with the scene in which Sor Tomasa is about to take her driving test for the second time, thus individualizing the mobile crowd to the specific driver who will be the protagonist of the story. In *La ciudad no es para mí,* Juan Mariné also chooses to begin with a long shot of the familiar Madrid cityscape, which is recorded through a slow pan and a long take from the large park on the city's western edge, the Casa de Campo. While the cityscape is visible in the skyline, the trees and vegetation of the park dominate the foreground (Faulkner, *A Cinema* 60). This initial long take targeting a rural-like environment is followed by snapshots of the city and its frenetic rhythm, portrayed through rapid editing cuts that produce a "fast-paced montage of life in modern day Madrid" (Richardson, *Postmodern* 73). The sense of velocity and acceleration of urban life achieved through camera work and editing is accompanied by the effect of the rock music in the soundtrack, by the Uruguayan band Los Shakers, which adds a sense of ebullience and vibrancy. Clearly, the analogy between the two films in their presentation of Madrid is the result of a common technical crew, which could be recognized by the audience.

Although these first elements may suggest that *Sor Citröen* is another example of *paleto* cinema, the film will soon break the audience's expectations. The presentation of the urban landscape is not further contrasted with country life as in other *paleto* films. The spectator never gets a glimpse of the essence or the activity in the rural space of La Robla. Only the train station and the interior of Tomasa's father's house are shown. Country life is not portrayed as an idyllic place as opposed to the morally corrupt city. On the contrary, it seems that the film intends to celebrate the development of the urban metropolis at the cost of rural exodus. Tomasa's provincial origin is not even highlighted in her characterization, and her tribulations within the urban space do not come as a result of her lack of sophistication or rural naiveté, but rather as a result of her impulsive actions to help the orphan children. Furthermore, *Sor Citröen* ends with Sor Tomasa departing from Madrid to La Robla, yet not as a return of the *paleta* to her natural rural habitat, but as a stopover on her way to Bilbao, where she has been transferred by her superiors as a punishment for her irresponsible behaviour.

This resolution does not linger on the city/country opposition or on any other detail that could indicate a message eulogizing the rural space. Sor Tomasa's obsession with acquiring a motorized vehicle comically reflects the new consumer fever of Spanish society and also spotlights the star of the industrialization process: the automobile. Along with the SEAT 600, the Citröen 2CV became the crown jewel of the industry and also a symbol of the improved living conditions of Spain's middle class. The year before this film was made constituted a turning point for the Spanish automobile industry. As Santiago García Ochoa documents, in that year, 1966, production surpassed the demand for cars for the first time. The 57 per cent production increase generated a surplus of cars that led to more affordable prices and better financing conditions that stimulated mass consumption (93). In her main argument to persuade her superior to buy an automobile, Sor Tomasa appropriates the economic rhetoric of the technocrats, which by that time had been internalized and celebrated by a society that enjoyed the affluence accompanying *desarrollismo*: "Todo el día pedimos en veinte casas, con el coche pediremos en cien. Así aumentaremos la productividad, ¡hay que motorizarse!" (All day we can visit twenty houses; with the car we could visit one hundred. This way we will increase productivity. We have to motorize!). Later in the movie, when the mother superior asks about the hefty car payments, Sor Tomasa reiterates her faith in the profitable results of the investment.

Sor Tomasa's hypothesis proves right, and the purchase of the vehicle will bring positive effects. Although she gets in trouble because of her faulty driving and illegal parking manoeuvres, she manages to raise money even in those unorthodox circumstances. Particularly relevant is a scene in which she is about to be issued a parking ticket and to have her car towed, but she is able to turn the tables and convince the traffic officer, and all the surrounding pedestrians, to waive her penalty and, furthermore, to donate money to the orphanage. While underscoring the generosity of Spanish society, and therefore the preservation of moral values, this scene also illustrates its economic empowerment by displaying a crowd of people who can afford to contribute their spare money and subscribe to the charitable cause. We are certainly far from the years of hunger and the *racionamiento* (supplementary portions) of early Francoism; the comedy of *desarrollismo* proclaims that Spaniards are no longer an indigent population.

The purchase of the automobile augments the nuns' options for charity in multiple ways beyond pecuniary compensation. Thanks to the car, Sor Tomasa is able to save the life of Luisa, an orphan girl who accidentally injured her cervical spine. The car enables Sor Tomasa to get Luisa to the hospital La Paz (the icon of scientific modernization) in time for an emergency operation. This scene, once again, publicizes Spain's Catholic modernity. The use of the "synergical crosscutting" editing juxtaposes the surgery in the operating room and the entire orphanage praying for Luisa's salvation. The choice of this type of editing works to produce an association of ideas in the spectator: the synergy between technological and scientific progress and the merciful auspices of the Virgin Mary. A medium close-up of the image of the Virgin suggests that the positive outcome for Luisa is as much a consequence of efficacious medical assistance as a miraculous sacred intervention. The critical condition of the emergency – and thus the providential role of both the doctors and the Virgin – is accentuated by the accelerating editing tempo employed to connect the shots in the operating room. Rapid cuts show consecutive close-ups of the machinery, medical devices, X-rays of the girl's cervical spine, and the perspiring faces of doctors working hard to save her life. This analogy is further expressed in the subsequent scene in the hospital room where Luisa is convalescing. A medium shot shows the mother superior, Sor Tomasa, and another nun sitting with Luisa, while a celestial white light illuminates Luisa's angelic face, which is shown in a close-up that elicits the spectator's empathy. Non-diegetic religious music punctuates the benevolent mediation of divinity in the miraculous episode. Consequently, the dexterous camera work, editing, music, and lighting contribute to emphasize how the skilful efforts of the doctors and of Sor Tomasa, resorting to the latest developments in medicine and mechanical engineering, combine with holy protection.

Post-Conciliar Transgressions

Sor Tomasa, as an unconventional nun who is aware that spiritual values must stay in harmony with market demands and progress, and as a non-threatening clerical subject who has assimilated the changes brought by Vatican II, seems the perfect embodiment of a sanitized version of *desarrollismo*. Nevertheless, as with the secondary comic voices in *Fray Torero*, the overt and inflated defence of the official rhetoric that lies behind the comic façade may lead, precisely because of the abuse of the formula, to ambiguity. The playful and farcical tone that permeates the film might restrain spectators from taking the ideological precepts into serious consideration. Sor Tomasa is played by Gracita Morales, an actress who by 1967 was already one of the most prolific figures of Spanish comedy, creating a filmic type based on her unique voice. As Juan Ríos Carratalá explains, "su peculiar voz se impuso a cualquier otro aspecto, se rompió el equilibrio y se convirtió en un estereotipo" (her peculiar voice prevailed over any other trait of her character, upsetting the balance and becoming a type) easily recognized by the audience (54). Her partnership with José Luis López Vázquez and Rafaela Aparicio echoes popular products such as *Atraco a las tres* (1962), another film that exploits the corporeal features of these actors to produce comic effects. *Sor Citröen* profits from using López Vázquez's histrionic body movement to portray a *descuidero* (pickpocket), and from the comic contrast between Morales's petite body and her acute, imposing voice. Her size also contrasts with Aparicio's large and rotund figure, which is ridiculed in the scenes where she falls down in the playground and later when she is forced by Sor Tomasa to push the car all the way to a gas station.

With Sor Tomasa, Lazaga plays on Gracita Morales's physical features and chemistry with the audience to fabricate an affable post-conciliar figure who would presumably be appreciated by all spectators. Her personification of post-conciliar values is so hyperbolic that it acts as a distorted rendition of the impact of Vatican II on Spanish life. This over-the-top presentation, especially by comparison with the religious figures analysed in the previous section, had the effect of making all the more evident the divisions within the Church as well as its patent tensions with the state. The Vatican Council generated a polarization of views within the Spanish Church. Some factions exposed enthusiasm for innovation, while others held on to nostalgia for the past (Cárcel Ortí, *Historia de la Iglesia* 230). This created a significant gap, which only widened in the last few years of the regime, between what came to be known as the "two Churches." Certain sectors of the Church hierarchy held a reactionary position and tried to adapt conciliar measures to the specific context of Spain, and not the other way around. Feliciano Montero (100) and Vicente Cárcel Ortí (*La Iglesia y la transición* 262)

2.1 Slapstick elements in *Sor Citröen* (1967).
Permission to reproduce the still from EGEDA.

document how the Spanish bishops who participated in Vatican II were opposed until the very end to the issue of religious liberty that *Dignitatis Humanae*, the Declaration of Religious Freedom (1965), demanded. As the cartoonist Antón cleverly put it in the magazine *Signo*, "¡Hasta en lo conciliar ha de ser España diferente!" (Spain had to be different even in relation to Vatican II!) (quoted in Martín Descalzo 37). The regime also would have preferred to keep the Spanish "difference," but it had to accept the new principles implemented by the Vatican.

The last scene of *Sor Citröen* provides a clue that uncovers this controversy. In that scene, Sor Tomasa is about to take the train to Bilbao. Before getting on the train, she asks her father to give the signal for the train to depart. After much fussing with the bell, the camera zooms in to offer a view of an older priest on the train, who crosses himself and laments: "¡Lo que nos ha traído el Concilio!" (Whatever has the Vatican Council brought us!). The older priest, who deplores Sor Tomasa's informality, represents the traditionalist faction of the Spanish Church, while Sor Tomasa personifies the profile of the young clergy, who are more concerned with charity and social activism than with theological mysteries. Even though the tone of this closing scene recalls the overall humorous – and seemingly banal – air that pervades the film, I contend that we should reconsider Sor Tomasa's character with this line of inquiry in mind. Akin to the social concerns of the clergy inspired by Vatican II, Sor Tomasa prioritizes good will over observance of rules. She believes that her assigned role in the orphanage is not enough, and pursues the acquisition of the automobile to further in her social mission. In order to achieve what she believes is just, she faces down her superior's scepticism and social stereotypes about women drivers. Further, she constantly violates traffic norms and social codes. Sor Tomasa repeatedly challenges authority, again coinciding with the trend among post-conciliar clergy who campaigned for a rupture from the authoritarian Francoist regime. Although the film makes no single reference to concrete historical figures, it is significant that all the characters representing authority and power appear deflated. The police captain, the traffic agent, and the engineer examining Sor Tomasa all fail to execute their roles and yield to Sor Tomasa's pleas. They are supposed to punish Sor Tomasa for her reckless behaviour, but they end up overlooking her conduct and also supporting the orphanage.

One may argue that this is indeed mere propaganda aimed at projecting a renewed image of the status quo of the regime, less authoritarian and closer to the people and their needs, but it is also a mockery of bureaucratic inefficiency, in a very different fashion from the usual portrayal of Francoist officers in the Spanish cinema of that time. For example, in Fernando Palacios's *La gran familia* (1962), another comedy of development, the state bureaucracy proves to be efficient in quickly finding the lost child, Nando, and returning him to his family. As noted by Sally Faulkner, in this film "four different sets of state officials are shown to combine their efforts in what constitutes no less than a paean to bureaucratic efficiency" (*A Cinema* 32). Interestingly, the formula of the lost child in the modern city is repeated in *Sor Citröen*, even using the same name, Fernando, for the child who disappeared, yet this time he is tracked down by Sor Tomasa's persistence, not by competent public resources.

Even the mother superior acquiesces in Sor Tomasa's wishes. She is persuaded to buy the automobile and to keep it in spite of the first disastrous events. At the end of the film, she will again be convinced to keep Luisa and Fernando under the supervision and care of Sor Tomasa's father. This scene highlights Sor Tomasa's behaviour in the context of a challenge to authority. When she reminds her superior that she believed that charity was their mission, her superior replies: "Sí, pero con orden" (Yes, but as ordered). Duty and respect for authority are valued over humanity and generosity, hierarchical disposition and order over Christian virtues. The conspicuous presence of images of Christ in this scene strengthens the conflict. During this tense conversation, the mise-en-scène is carefully thought out, as a crucifix appears centred behind the two nuns, implying that the result of the negotiations will be affected by the divine judge. While the superior speaks on the phone with the Madre Provincial, Sor Tomasa turns to the image of the crucified Christ and asks for help. Reminiscent of the sacrifice of Christ for his people, Sor Tomasa jeopardizes her clerical position to assist the poor. She will have to be punished to ensure obedience to the established order. However, the need for this disciplinary action proves that her conduct constitutes a transgression of that very order, consequently showing its potential vulnerability.

Sor Tomasa's transgression should be weighed within the spatial terms that accompany her mobility, as "crossing boundaries." This entails her movement altering the precedence of a spatial ordering. She looks for the highway to heaven, but in so doing, she is taking detours that challenge normative geographies. The film explores the double and contradictory discourse on mobility during the years of development; while the official rhetoric praises the access of citizens to the mobility that comes with modernization, it simultaneously tries to regulate such movement through the proper channels. In this aspect of the film, Paul Virilio's thoughts on the ambivalent function of speed and movement in modernity cogently resonate. In his essay *Speed and Politics*, Virilio explains that public order in modern states is based on a regulation of transit, on the need to control the highway, to demarcate motion through the appropriate conduits (27). Virilio further notes that this is especially relevant in the context of undemocratic systems, since "the rise of totalitarianism goes hand-in-hand with the development of the state's hold over the circulation of the masses" (16). Francoism definitely matched Virilio's profile of "moving-power" inasmuch as it first prevented the migration of peasants to urban areas and later promoted movement of the labour force to help in the process of urban industrialization. Thereupon, mobility was used as a strategy at the mercy of the ruling classes, as a controlling mechanism ironically bringing stability for the social structure. Sor Tomasa's free motion and uncontrolled speed break traffic norms and disregard ecclesiastical hierarchy. This does not mean that *Sor Citröen* should be read as a cultural product expressing overt resistance to hegemonic norms. Resistance, as Tim

Cresswell notes, implies an intentional act directed against a rejected power system with the purpose of mitigating its jurisdiction and, ultimately, replacing it. Transgression, on the contrary, does not depend on the intention, but on the results, on the negative reaction by dominant agents who respond to it, who regard it as being "out of place" (22–3). Sor Tomasa is not driven by a subversive will, nor does she intend to undermine her superior's authority, but her mobility breaks – transgresses – normalcy. Although exclusively urged by altruistic motives, she does not pay heed to rules and customary practices and, above all, she manages to create an unconventional model of family at the end of the film, which differs from the official nuclear family supported by government policy.

Similarly, the characters of Trini and the pickpocket played by José Luis López Vázquez are mobile figures who unveil the fissures of the development narratives. At first, they seem to function merely as elements of comic relief. Also, they contribute to the characterization of Sor Tomasa's talent to reform sinners. Though she apparently guides them to decency, their reformation does not seem very convincing. One has the feeling that once Sor Tomasa leaves town, the *descuidero* will go back to his old ways. Their very presence in the film as outcasts, wandering characters who do not possess a permanent home or employment, further suggests that the developmental euphoria carries a dark underside. Not all have the same opportunities to enjoy the affluent society of the 1960s; some still occupy marginal spaces. Their condition as outsiders might not appear threatening because they are characterized as comic figures, easily digested by the overall celebratory discourse of social improvement, but they evince the cracks of that linear narrative. Considered, like Sor Tomasa, in light of the ambivalent connotations of mobility within this film, both figures bring disorder by means of their unrestrained mobility. Their movement is underground, unassimilated to the structures and norms of institutionalized power, beyond the grasp of the tentacles of the production system.

Unlike *Fray Torero*, the assimilation of these dissident elements does not take place through a happy ending that reunites the community. In fact, there is no such happy ending, since the film closes with Sor Tomasa being penalized and transferred to Bilbao. Instead, generic mixing does the healing magic through the symbolic deployment of slapstick comedy elements. Slapstick humour "is generally understood as physical humour of a robust and hyperbolized nature where stunts, acrobatics, pain, and violence are standard features" (Stott 87).

Although usually associated with the early American cinema and, concretely, with the works of Charlie Chaplin, Buster Keaton, and Harold Lloyd, examples of slapstick humour can be traced back to the classical Greek comedy. Slapstick comedy pivots around the excessiveness of the comic character's gestures and body movements. A central motif is the malleability of the comic body, indestructible even though it is constantly exposed to attack or physical danger (88). In *Sor Citröen,* Sor Tomasa and Sor Rafaela are frequently involved in comic situations involving physical pain that threatens their lives due to their lack of self-control. Both of them drive recklessly and run over a series of street vendors of melons, balloons, and ice-cream in different moments of the film. Sor Tomasa drives through red lights in downtown Madrid and creates traffic jams. Surprisingly, though, no signs of harm or wounds are ever present after their accidents and hazardous infractions. The only physical effect is Sor Rafaela's temporary lightheadedness, but there is no blood, no broken body parts, not even a bruise. This lack of injury to the slapstick body, which seems resistant to fragmentation or trauma, is indeed a convention of the genre. As Muriel Andrin points out, in slapstick comedy there is always "a great big noise but very little damage," which makes the slapstick universe "a perfect place for instant healing" (231). In the absence of a restorative happy ending, I believe that Lazaga deploys the slapstick bodies of Sor Tomasa and Sor Rafaela as the symbolic carriers of that healing of the social fabric. They lose self-control and their actions have transgressive effects, just as post–Vatican II shook the ground of the Catholic Church and even became a threat to Spain's confessional status. But in the end, the spectator never fears for the slapstick body, nor does he or she contemplate a fatal physical disaster. *Mutatis mutandis,* this film may well be inviting viewers to laugh at the slapstick national body of post–Vatican II Spain undergoing extreme velocity of change, some crashes, and disruption of the established order, yet no ultimate serious catastrophe.

Cinematic Counter-*Aggiornamento*

Similar to *Sor Citröen,* José Luis Sáenz de Heredia displayed in *¡Se armó el belén!* (1969) a comical depiction of the contradictions caused by what Josep Piñol calls the "aggiornamento a dos velocidades" of the Spanish clergy (*aggiornamento* at two velocities) (318). The meaning of this expression is twofold. On the one hand, it refers to the nebulous line, full of ambiguity, between official declarations of the Spanish Church's position in the aftermath of Vatican II and the concrete actions taken; on the other, this metaphor of mobility draws attention to the diverse degrees to which clergy from different generations and educational backgrounds assimilated the conciliar recommendations. The dramatic conflict, as in Lazaga's film, pivots on the diverging interpretations of what it means for the Spanish Catholic Church to become modern. The younger clergy represents the reformist faction willing to try new methods of apostolate in the modern world. The older clergy, embodied by Don Mariano (Paco Martínez Soria), represents traditional ecclesiastical sectors resistant to radical change. The difference from *Sor Citröen,* and from other post–Vatican II comedies for that matter, is that Sáenz de Heredia invites the spectator to identify with the traditional side by mocking the reformist initiatives.

Early in the film, Don Mariano is visited by Don Emilio (Javier Loyola), who, on behalf of the archbishop, instructs Don Mariano to modernize his parish to improve its ecclesiastical index ("índice eclesiástico"). This index quantifies apostolic accomplishments in terms of the number of weddings, baptisms, and communions officiated. Post-conciliar innovation is presented as aseptic statistics and macro-economic rhetoric devoid of any humane or spiritual component. Catholic *aggiornamento* seems to be a section of a *Plan de Desarrollo* whose success depends on the effective management of rationalized economic activity. Interestingly, the dialogue between the two clerical characters is filmed with a shot/reverse-shot structure alternating high-angle shots of Don Emilio and low-angle shots of Don Mariano that aggrandize his physical and moral figure. As in previous post–Vatican II comedies, camera angles serve to identify the moral quality of the characters. With this arrangement, Sáenz de Heredia takes sides with non-reformist views. The rest of the film narrates Don Mariano's failed attempts to modernize his parish. Don Mariano admits that he is old, incapable of adapting to the new times, and reconciles with the fact that he will be demoted to convent chaplain. A surprising narrative twist saves him. While he is convalescing in the hospital from an accident, a group of neighbours visits to let him know that the whole community wants him back in the parish. The film ends with the implied message that humane values prove more effective than modern methods to carry out the apostolate.

¡Se armó el belén! acts as a form of cinematic counter-*aggiornamento,* since it fits within a broader current in the Spanish cultural sphere that combated conciliar changes. That was the case with a wave of publications in the form of magazines such as *Montejurra, SP, El Español, El*

Cruzado Español, and *¿Qué Pasa?*, and a plethora of books that defended the confessional nature of Spain and warned, often with apocalyptic rhetoric, against the devastating effects of the *aggiornamento*, which is seen as the outcome of communist infiltration in the Church (Piñol 212–22). Although substituting mockery for the apocalyptic tone, Saénz de Heredia's film still equates the Church's modern outlook, and anything associated with modernity, with a mistake that could bring more harm than benefit to the community. In a revealing conversation between Don Mariano and Don José (Germán Cobos), the neighbourhood's doctor, the latter asserts that there is no room in the modern world for religion and the Church. Don José stands for the mainline secularization thesis of Western modernity that posits that religious institutions cannot compete with secular, scientific understanding of reality. For Don José, religion is an outdated issue, since in the modern world people are only interested in knowing about atomic bombs, television, and computers. By including the atomic bomb, a lethal weapon of mass destruction, among modernity's technological advances, Sáenz de Heredia insinuates, through Don José's words, that modern innovations, including the Church's *aggiornamento*, can have devastating effects for civilization. Moreover, he slips a concrete example into the narrative. Don Mariano tries to appeal to his parishioners with a television broadcast of their live nativity. The effort causes division and conflict in the community and leads to a major fight that almost kills Don Mariano. The film seems to suggest that modernity triggers social uncertainty and destabilizes the community.

In this dialectic between tradition and modernity, the emphasis on Don Mariano's aging process and health issues points to another ideological tenet of this film: the defence of the figure of the aging *caudillo*. Don Mariano stumbles while trying to walk up some stairs, falls off a rocking chair at home, and has to be taken to the hospital twice. Conciliar characters – Don Emilio and Don Melchor – constantly remind him of his old age and precarious health to imply that he should be replaced by a younger and more prepared priest. It is hard not to read his character in dialogue with the historical context of Francisco Franco's aging process and the advance of his Parkinson's disease. After all, José Luis Sáenz de Heredia was a profound admirer of Franco and had previously made two high-profile films devoted to praising his persona, *Raza* and *Franco, ese hombre*. As I examined in chapter 1, Sáenz de Heredia had already tried to counteract the anxiety over Franco's declining physical condition by venerating, even if fruitlessly, Franco's firm walk at the end of *Franco, ese hombre*. In *¡Se armó el belén!*, the filmmaker indicates that Franco is, like Don Mariano, still a valid leader for the national community.

Other details within the film further encourage this reading. A younger priest calls Don Mariano "inmovilista," which was a popular term used in political and ecclesiastical circles to describe the conservative factions of both the Church and the regime that resisted modernizing changes. Also, Don Emilio tells Don Mariano that his failure in the ecclesiastical index is due to his excessive focus on charisma to attract people to his parish. Again, the reference to the leader's charisma evokes the political sphere, as it alludes to the regime's changing strategy to assure political legitimacy. As I explained in the introduction, given Franco's aging and health issues, the technocratic cadres of the regime worried that charismatic and traditional legitimacy would not suffice to secure consent among new generations of Spaniards. They sought to emphasize political legitimacy on rational-legal grounds, so that obedience to authority would not rest on the figure of an individual sovereign but on satisfaction with the effective management of resources and the proper functioning of a legal-bureaucratic system that enabled citizens to improve their living conditions.

While his ideas to modernize the parish fail, Don Mariano finally succeeds in appealing to all his neighbours, regardless of their religious beliefs and ideological affiliations, through his charisma and humanity. In the final scene of the film, Don José, the left-wing doctor, assures the priest about his role by recognizing him as a mediator in reaching communal consent and declares: "Los hombres por encima de las ideas se pueden entender por el corazón" (Men can understand each other with their heart more than with their ideas). This statement, again shot in a low angle that magnifies the doctor's moral figure, certifies the appeasement of the political and religious divide that caused tensions in the community. It also represents the reconciliation of the "two Spains" that had fought against each other in the Civil War. Sáenz de Heredia indeed prepares spectators for this final scene of political reconciliation from the very first scene of the film. While Don Mariano is playing pool with Sebastián (Rafael López), an openly Republican supporter, they jokingly discuss their participation on opposing sides in the Battle of Brunete in the Spanish Civil War. The spectator is thereby invited to interpret all subsequent ideological discussions and conflicts in the film narrative as harking back to the fratricidal Civil War. The point that Sáenz de Heredia makes is that the leader's charisma – Don Mariano's in this neighbourhood and Franco's at the national level – suffices to eventually heal social division and overcome old political resentment.

Data and figures, such as the ones on the cards containing the low numbers in the ecclesiastical index of Don Mariano's parish, end up torn into pieces by Don Emilio. The final shot of the film is a symbolic close-up of the cards in the garbage can. The ending implies that just as post-conciliar modern techniques are inadequate in bringing people back into churches, so rational arguments, macroeconomic figures, and technological modernization are insufficient in attaining national consensus and seem only to elicit social conflict. What I am suggesting here is that in *¡Se armó el belén!* Sáenz de Heredia does not merely reveal his preference for pre-conciliar clergy and his suspicion about the effects of Vatican II on Spanish society. He also uses religious debates within the Spanish Church to put forward a political allegory about the way power was exercised in the late Franco period. More specifically, with this film he intervenes by sending a critical message to the regime administration about the danger of focusing excessively on rational-legal arguments for legitimacy and forgetting about the exceptional figure of the main architect of the system, the charismatic leader.

Also, different from the typical comedy of *desarrollismo*, *¡Se armó el belén!* presents a blatant picture of the shortcomings of the process of economic development, thus putting a question mark next to the performance-based rational legitimacy of the regime. As Manuel Palacio and Carmen Ciller notice in their brief analysis of this film, in the neighbourhood that this film presents, "the streets are not paved and the houses are closer to shacks than solid constructions" (59). In addition, class issues and injustices are explicitly mentioned. Ramón (Antonio Alfonso), a working-class neighbour, loses an arm because of the unsafe conditions of his workplace, and other young members of the community have trouble finding employment. A group of left-wing neighbours holds meetings to organize oppositional political activities in defence of workers. This is not the first time that a post–Vatican II comedy presents anti-Franco oppositional groups. Enrique Carreras's *Este cura*, which features a small-town post-conciliar priest who bravely faces the local political and economic powers to advocate for the poor and marginalized, also includes a comical scene of political dissidence. A group of college students influenced by Marxist ideology organize, with no degree of success, subversive anti-capitalist and anti-clerical activities. But left-wing dissidence in Carreras's film is depicted nonchalantly, as a harmless joke, while in *¡Se armó el belén!* the anti-Franco group is a well-organized association that includes some of the most important characters in the film, such as the doctor. Sáenz de Heredia presents the urban landscape of the late Franco period as an underdeveloped space full of poverty and political conflict. Only the charismatic holy leader, Don Mariano – and Franco by extension – can suture those tensions and ensure social consensus.

With *¡Se armó el belén!*, Sáenz de Heredia diverged from the most common configuration of the comedy of *desarrollismo*, including his previous film *Fray Torero*, to take a bold stand to warn against the development rhetoric and show his alliance with the old guard of the regime. This film specifically proves Paloma Aguilar's point when she fittingly suggests that, in analysing the case of late Francoism, it is interesting "to establish certain distinctions between the legitimacy of the régime and that of the leader himself" (40). With *¡Se armó el belén!*, Sáenz de Heredia sought to remind Spaniards that the social consensus and stability they enjoyed depended on staying as a nation under the sovereign leader divinely invested with power. While post–Vatican II comedies typically praised the modern and impersonal economic-theological paradigm of power that was becoming more prevalent in the late Franco period, this film insinuated that the right path was returning to political theology and relying on the figure of the sovereign. The other comedies analysed in this chapter drew attention to the prosperity of a country striving for modernity and led by the efficient economic planning of the administration, though some of them, and most notably *Sor Citröen*, left some room for interrogating this prevailing narrative.

These differing messages reveal the difficulty of pinning down whether a particular genre formula, and subgeneric forms of comedy in particular, serve conservative or progressive functions (Bishop 9). Certainly, one should no longer regard post–Vatican II comedies as an ideological vehicle that was merely imposed upon subordinate groups. Although they helped to shape public discourse by praising the new paradigm of power exercised in the last phase of the regime, they did so by commending the post–Vatican II Church, which was increasingly at odds with platforms of political power. The Spanish Church started to make structural demands of the regime that pointed towards a change in the political system. By the early 1970s, the majority in the Church wished to dislodge themselves from the regime and opted for democracy. Thus, the more these post–Vatican II comedies praised this renewed face of the Church, the more they embedded messages that lent themselves to dissident reception. Granted, the fictional solution to these tensions that most of the post–Vatican II comedies delivered was the adjustment of political powers to the changing times led by the Catholic Church, thus symbolically refurbishing the alliance between throne and altar. The reality was significantly different, since the Church was, *de jure*, still tied to the regime, yet had become a *de facto* opponent of the regime's political legitimacy and a force of political change.

As a subgeneric cycle, post–Vatican II comedies introduced a number of recurring and predictable visual features that viewers could recognize and use to make sense of these films that tackled pressing social issues with unique and not always coincidental perspectives. This is why the meaning of these post–Vatican II comedies is more effectively grasped by considering the aggregate impact of many films rather than just the distinctive statement of any given example of the cycle. Seen together, these films were symbolic representations that enabled Spanish audiences to reflect upon their shared values as well as upon the possibility of change and transformation of those collective values. This could partly explain why this subgenre attracted a massive audience, with numbers – more than three million spectators in some of the examined cases – that are out of reach for contemporary Spanish films. Most post–Vatican II comedies enabled Spaniards to envision a society that, while keeping its Catholic backbone, redefined many of its socioeconomic structures in tune with other Western European countries. Of course, insisting on the Catholic "difference" entailed keeping a patriarchal view of society. Gender roles became the one area in which the society imagined by these films seemed to be stuck in a tradition that was incompatible with modernity. Post–Vatican II comedies envisioned the implementation of European models of modern rationalized capitalism and certain social reforms associated with it (sometimes with disruptive effects), but still advocated for eluding some crucial values of the European liberal tradition. The purpose of next chapter is precisely to zoom in on the problematic gender roles of post–Vatican II comedies by analysing in depth the hitherto neglected nun films.

Chapter Three

Gender and Modernization in Nun Films

Women religious were prominent figures in Spanish cinema throughout the development years. Apart from the hagiographic films I analysed in chapter 1, popular celluloid nuns appeared in films such as *Melocotón en almíbar* (Antonio del Amo, 1960), *Canción de cuna,* and *La becerrada* (José María Forqué, 1963) in the early 1960s; and *Sor Citröen, Sor Ye-Yé, Encrucijada para una monja, Las cuatro bodas de Marisol* (Luis Lucia, 1967), *La novicia rebelde,* and *Una monja y un don Juan* (Mariano Ozores, 1973) in the post–Vatican II years.[1] Given how little we know about the actual situation of women religious in Spain during these years, nun films are a precious cultural document about how women religious experienced Vatican II and the post-conciliar crisis within Spain. Very much like their male counterparts in the post–Vatican II comedies that I analysed in the previous chapter, celluloid nuns embodied a marketable image of modern Catholicism. Most of all, as I set out to examine, nun films served as channels to reflect upon broader social issues. The hypothesis I want to propose here is that Spanish audiences did not massively consume nun films looking for answers to religious debates, but were enticed instead by the images of female subjectivity that these films fashioned against the backdrop of the shifting condition of women in the modernizing Spanish society.

The technocratic government approved some measures that improved women's legal status, especially pertaining to employment. The incorporation of women into public life was a sudden necessity, since "[i]ndustrialization created the need for women to enter the work force, from which laws and custom had previously excluded them; the laws were now abruptly changed" (Sieburth 160). This new legal framework was therefore far from a feminist initiative; rather, it was a convenient change to support economic development.[2] Although those advances had a limited scope, they still generated social anxiety over adjustments in gender relations. With this gender anxiety in mind, my argument is that the mass appeal of nun films in the late 1960s was indicative of a conservative reaction to threatening models of female independence that came as a result of women's entry into the job market. Celluloid nuns were used as instruments to disseminate backward-looking models of femininity. Nun films often featured young women who entered the convent because they did not fit into the schemes of normative heterosexuality. In some of the cases, as I will point out in my analyses of *Sor Ye-Yé* and *La novicia rebelde*, convent life was for rebellious women merely a step to becoming domesticated through marriage. The majority of the chapter will be devoted to showing how these films cinematically constructed those gender roles. I will pay close attention to the ideological effects created by the mix of the post–Vatican II comedy formula with generic conventions of the romantic comedy and the musical. Also, nun films shared the stylistic functionality of the broader subgenre of post–Vatican II comedies. I will illustrate how they effectively arranged certain aspects of the mise-en-scène such as lighting patterns, costume and make-up choices, and framing devices to shape gender-normative images of women deployed as counter-models to fluctuating models of womanhood on the rise in Spanish society.

Cinema's mode of addressing the condition of post–Vatican II nuns was important because of the massive appeal of popular cinema among Spanish audiences, especially among women. Since some of the celluloid nuns were played by stars who drew a huge number of followers, such as Marisol and Rocío Dúrcal, this entailed that cinematic nuns could influence patterns of behaviour among young Spanish women who identified with those filmic roles and the values they stood for. Also, women religious were particularly suitable models to be appropriated by cinema to stimulate social debates on gender issues because they were bridge figures situated someplace between the private and the public sphere, and between traditional and emancipated models of female subjectivity. In this sense, there was room for representations beyond the aforementioned reactionary models of womanhood. As Rebecca Sullivan notes in relation to the increasing popularity of nuns in Hollywood films in the 1960s, they "had the potential to disrupt the discourses of femininity since they operated outside the confines of heterosexual domesticity" (62). Nuns functioned fairly autonomously from men – though not from patriarchy – and homosocial relations wove throughout their everyday lives. Nuns were independent yet easily manageable female figures who served to cover and contain the growing image of working women with escalating access to financial independence – and thereby to sexual independence. My point is not to deem the context of Spain during the development years equal to that of the American culture in the 1960s that Sullivan examines, one in which the flourishing feminist consciousness was far more substantial and tangible.[3] Nor is it to suggest that nuns were influential feminist activists in late Francoism. However, celluloid nuns opened the door for multilayered spectatorial identifications. As I will highlight throughout the chapter, this included some daring depictions of independent-spirited nuns in *Encrucijada para una monja* and, to some extent, in *Sor Citröen*. This is why I believe that we should take more seriously the cinematic renderings of nuns in confessional films. In the next section, I briefly discuss the limitations of existing views on Spanish nun films and I delineate the critical path I intend to follow in the remainder of the chapter.

Critical Oversights

Nuns have occupied a negligible position in the broader scheme of religious cinema in Spain and elsewhere. Film historians have consistently derided nun films as tear-jerkers that portray idealized characters lacking any complexity. Referring to Hollywood nuns, Les and Barbara Keyser assert that they are "so holy and so unworldly and so impractical and so pious and so virginal and so innocent and so bubbly and so cheerful that they cannot be taken seriously" (141). Kathryn Schleich relates these undesirable representations of the celluloid nuns to "a long history of oppressing and alienating women" within the Catholic Church that ensues from "a deeply ingrained fear of women within the Church hierarchy" (9). While concurring with Schleich, I believe there is more to the story. The denigration of nuns in films also echoes a larger gender bias that begins with film criticism. Rebecca Sullivan observes that in the context of Hollywood, nun films "were almost always labelled as part of so-called women's culture, produced to appeal to female audiences by promoting lead female characters" (11). And that feminine pedigree was always a passport for a second-class rating. For instance, Ivan Butler described nun films as "pink-lampshade coziness" (qtd. in Keyser and Keyser 143), while Mary Ann Janosik claimed that nun roles in films were a sort of "cultural afterthought, needing kitschy talents or quirky gimmicks to explore trite social problems" (76). Before them, French critic Amédée Ayfre claimed that nun films offered fairy-tale nuns fabricated for twelve-year-old girls with no religious background (92). This quick sampling of the literature about nuns in Hollywood films reveals that we are in familiar territory: the association of aesthetic value with a masculine, rational realm, while cultural production that integrates "feminine" features is lambasted as kitschy and sentimental.[4]

Spanish film critics have not been any more benevolent in their assessment of nun films. Pro-regime film journals promoted films made for Catholic proselytizing, but they usually included a note clarifying, as José Torrella did in the pages of *Otro Cine*, that a true religious film should not be a "ñoño pasatiempo monjil" (an insipid nun's hobby) (5). In *SIPE*, a semi-official platform of the Church, the editors argued, in an article titled "Cinema y espíritu" written to encourage the production of religious films, that making films about and for nuns was a preposterous mistake: "'Cine para monjas' ¡Qué error! Ni para monjas, ni para beatas. Cine para hombres en el más firme, recio y viril de los sentidos" ("Films for nuns." What a mistake! We should not make films for nuns or for pious women. We should make films for men in the firmest, strongest and most virile sense) ("Cinema y espíritu"). Nun films were only endorsed as repositories of the essentialist virtues of the Spanish woman. For example, the poster announcing the release of *Sor Intrépida* (Rafael Gil, 1952) in *Primer Plano* (issue 629, 1952) made this point clear, as it announced a film that offered "[t]oda la gracia, todo el amor y todo el sacrificio de la mujer española" (all the grace, all the love, and all the sacrifice of the Spanish woman). The representation of Spanish nuns thus insists more on the adjective (their Spanish virtues) than on the noun (their status as nuns).[5] The poster mentions nothing about Sor Intrépida's role in a leper colony in India, only her sacrifice in the name of morally righteous Spanish women.

Critical views detached from regime orthodoxies worked with similar gender preconceptions. The editorial of the third issue of *Cinema Universitario*, a short-lived but influential oppositional film journal, called for "un cine bronco, áspero, que nos hable de las incidencias de la vida – del misionero, del sacerdote, del hombre – que derribe el museo de las ideas versallescas y nos lleve a esa vida real que siempre, hasta la fecha, nos ha escamoteado el cine religioso español" (a rough cinema that would tell us about the life incidences – of the missionary, the priest, the man – that would debunk the museum of decadent ideas and would show us the real life thus far absent in Spanish religious cinema) ("Sacerdocio y Curascope" 3). The messages from all sides of the ideological spectrum agreed in gender terms: religious films were valuable tools either for National-Catholic propaganda or as a form of social realism with a critical edge, but in either case we would be talking about an exclusively masculine universe. "Real life" issues and spiritual dilemmas seemed to be a male thing. Women, clerical or not, should not be protagonists or agents of religious cinema.

In a more wide-ranging look into religious cinema during Francoism, Diego Galán explored the roles of both priests and nuns. His account did not suffer from the gender bigotry of earlier assessments, as he evaluated all clergy roles in film in equal terms, rendering them as cardboard characters ("El cine 'político'" 99). Yet, he still relied heavily on a binary approach opposing the heroic roles of tough priests to the "sonrisas y canciones" (smiles and songs) and "caridad infinita" (endless charity) of the nuns (99). Once again, the celluloid clergy is distributed in contrasting camps of masculine heroism versus feminine feeling. Priests and monks at least show traits (toughness, heroism) as if they were made of flesh and blood. Women religious appear in two-dimensional depictions with no psychological development and are only equipped with "alegría cotidiana" (everyday joy) (99). It would be futile to dispute that many filmic representations of nuns during the Franco regime remained confined to fairly predictable roles. But Galán's view operates largely detached from the broader sociohistorical context of the films and, thereby, overlooks the possibility of any shift or evolution in the roles he describes. For him, Luis Lucia's *La orilla* simply confirms "la permanencia del género al cabo de los años" (the longevity of the genre) and *La novicia rebelde* is just a new version of *La hermana San Sulpicio* "en la que las canciones andaluzas se han 'actualizado', sin perder por ello su genuina esencia" (in which Andalusian songs have been "updated" without losing their genuine essence) ("El cine 'político'" 100). We are left to assume that all post–Vatican II nun films replicate the same formulaic pattern. María Jesús Ruiz Muñoz offers a less monolithic account and acknowledges that nun films of the development years introduced a noticeable evolution in external character depictions; however, she still pinpoints "un rotundo estancamiento" (a flat stagnation) with regard to the psychological complexity of the nuns as protagonists (95). For example, she maintains that Tomasa Carrasco in *Sor Citröen* is defined only by her stereotypical maternal role while Sor Sacrificio in *La novicia rebelde* tallies with the type of "enfermera-monja" (nurse-nun) that abounds in Spanish cinema (96).[6] For Ruiz, we would have to wait until the transition to democracy in the late 1970s for a shift to a humanization of the celluloid nuns, which for her resides in the representation of their human flaws, mainly sexual desires, such as the depiction of the "pecadora carnal" (carnal sinner) in *Cartas de amor de una monja* (Jordi Grau, 1978).

What is missing in these accounts is a more specific analysis of the formal and thematic features of nun films in relation to the concrete extra-filmic context from which these films emerge. There are more than four decades between the first film version of *La hermana San Sulpicio* (Florián Rey, 1927) and Luis Lucia's *La novicia rebelde* – with a 1952 version in between – yet both are discussed as providing identical nun roles. We need an assessment of nun films of the 1960s and early 1970s not as cosmetic variations of a familiar type, as imitative reproductions belonging to a static generic mould, but rather in their historical specificity. This means that to elucidate the relevance of nun films, one must also engage with the historical development of the institutional aspects of religion, in this case the situation of women religious in the aftermath of Vatican II in Spain, and, even more crucially, with the evolution of gender issues in the late Franco years. Nun films need to be examined as popular culture mediations between institutionalized religion, gender relations, and sociopolitical changes taking place in Spain. So before turning to the analysis of specific film texts, a brief account of the situation of women religious in the overall edifice of the Catholic Church is in order.

Post–Vatican II Nuns: An Unknown Collective

For all the sweeping changes the Second Vatican Council implemented in the Catholic Church's outlook, it did not modify its patriarchal structures in the least. Women religious were not present in the first two sessions of the council. When Pope John XXIII died, his successor, Paul VI, tried to amend that inexcusable situation, and a limited number of nuns (seventeen) were invited to participate in the 1964 and 1965 sessions. They were, however, confined to being mere auditors. Women religious were allowed to express their views in subcommittee meetings (Raguer Suñer 271), but not in the plenary sessions, not "even in matters that directly and exclusively affected their lives" (Kuhns 143). Pope John XXIII's universal call to *aggiornamento* intended to convert the Church into a community of "the People of God," but the Church still preserved its masculinist hierarchy. Even though that community "is called 'mother' and referred to with the pronoun 'she,' it is personified and governed by fathers and brothers only" (Schüssler Fiorenza 4). Women, a majority in the Catholic Church in terms of churchgoers and membership in religious orders, remained fairly invisible, as the "silenced majority" in the male-controlled organization (Schüssler Fiorenza 3). Conciliar documents as well as post–Vatican II papal declarations put a fair amount of emphasis on promoting the parity of women in the job market and in the broader society. However, as Francisco López Hernández-Herrera admitted in *Ecclesia,* Vatican II did not pay much attention to the situation of women within the Church. There is not a single conciliar document, not even a section of a document, devoted to the gender asymmetries in the Church (25). The asymmetries ensued from a male-defined theology and an "anti-feminist tradition" of canon law that has yet to be probed (Suenens 47). The Church was ready to see women as equal to men in the world, but not in its own world.

And yet, women religious underwent a renewal and had to renegotiate their role on the shifting ground of the Church. They read, debated, and struggled with the council's documents. Convents became sites of heated discussions between traditionalist and progressive nuns over the terms of their apostolate within the new framework of action delineated by the council. As just one example, Elizabeth Kuhns documents in her history of the habit that deliberations over the mandate to change the habit were far from simple and unanimous among religious orders (142–8). Three specific documents of Vatican II were especially relevant to the situation of women religious, even if they did not specifically address the gender question. The first one, *Lumen gentium,* the Dogmatic Constitution on the Church (1964), redefined the configuration of the Church as "the People of God" (chapter 2). This change had a profound impact on the way women perceived themselves in relation to the Church, no longer as "'daughters of the church' or even members, as if the Church were extraneous to themselves" (Riley 244). The renewed sense of belonging also led to a renewed shared responsibility to partake in the pastoral, liturgical, and dogmatic dimensions of the Church. In short, nuns felt for the first time in history that their voice and action mattered.

Gaudium et spes, the Pastoral Constitution on the Church in the Modern World (1965), introduced a radical turn in relation to the Church's previous opposition to modernity, since it called for a deep engagement in modern affairs. Chapter 4 of the Constitution spelled out that the role of the Church in the modern world was to assure "the dignity of the human person," and clergy had full responsibility to mobilize their resources, including political advocacy, to promote world justice and peace. This meant that nuns were summoned to come out of the cloister and engage in real issues. In this way, the council relaxed some of the strict rules that restrained nuns' activities and allowed them "greater freedom to experiment with new configurations of mission, community, and lifestyle" (Koehlinger 9–10). Despite the limited scope of Vatican II reforms regarding their leadership in the Church, nuns' mission took on extra significance in the 1960s. *Perfectae Caritatis*, the Decree on the Adaptation and Renewal of Religious Life (1965), expressed the terms and direction of that shift by requesting a "return to the sources of all Christian life and to the original spirit of the institutes" and an adaptation "to the changed conditions of our time" (2). This adaptation had to be ensured by the proper education of women religious to acquire "an adequate knowledge of the social conditions of the times they live in" (2d). Superiors in convents were charged with the duty of providing that suitable training. Thus, *Perfectae Caritatis* opened doors for nuns, who were expected to become better prepared to face the modern world and to play a crucial role in it. This decree mandated that convents and congregations should revisit their apostolic mission with an outward orientation to promote direct engagement with pressing issues of modern life.

Even though Vatican II had a profound impact on the situation and responsibilities of female congregations, the process of *aggiornamento* within convents has flown under the critical radar of studies on the impact of Vatican II in Spain. In the literature on this topic, it is hard to find any mention, even in passing, of the perspective of women religious at that crucial historical juncture. In an incisive article in *Cuadernos para el diálogo* cleverly titled "La monja, ese extraño personaje," a group of outspoken, yet anonymous, nuns – they signed the article as "un equipo de religiosas" – stated that women religious were a largely unknown group that was simplistically homogenized as a uniform collective without any diversity (69). As a case in point, in their sociological study *La Iglesia española contemporánea*, scholars Jesús Vázquez, Félix Medín, and Luis Méndez offered concrete data on the state of female religious orders in the late 1960s and early 1970s and pinpointed their decrease in membership. However, they left unexplored the reasons for and consequences of such a decline:

> Como puede observarse, en este apartado dedicado a las religiosas, únicamente se han señalado datos cuantitativos. Los cualitativos, es decir, la problemática y perspectivas de las comunidades religiosas femeninas

> creemos que representan aspectos, si no iguales, muy semejantes a los de los religiosos. Por cuanto todo lo dicho anteriormente de ellos es aplicable a las religiosas. (182)
>
> As one can observe, we have only mentioned quantitative data in this section dedicated to women religious. We believe that qualitative data, that is, the issues and standpoints of female religious communities, entail aspects that, if not equal, are similar to those of male religious orders. All that was said in relation to male clergy is therefore applicable to women religious.

In denying any specificity to the standpoint and agency of female religious orders and of women religious in the aftermath of Vatican II, this study did not constitute an anomaly. Rather, it represented a constant in the vast corpus of scholarship on the changes in the Church in the late Franco regime. An invariable factor in the equation is that the viewpoint and intervention of women religious in this crucial period remains, at best, an afterthought; at worst, utterly overlooked. This is why the perspective of film production, in which women religious had a prominent role, becomes especially relevant.

Female (Auto)Mobility

Women's increasing numbers in the labour force meant that they could gain access to motor vehicles. This is dramatized in *Sor Citröen,* as Sor Tomasa wanders freely around Madrid, although it is her position as a nun that truly allows her freedom of movement. Furthermore, Sor Tomasa's driving adventures do not promote radical female emancipation but a reinforcement of the role of women as mothers. In using the car mostly to drive the two orphaned children she nurtures, Sor Tomasa becomes, according to Ryan Prout, "a mother-by-proxy" (123). Rather than threatening existing gender asymmetries in Spanish society, this film might be suggesting that the growing numbers of women drivers would serve to maintain those asymmetries in the context of an increasingly modernized society. Women would be merely relocating their maternal roles to the automobile, which becomes a mobile family space.

Secular women in this film remain confined to domestic spaces. Such is the case with Rosalía, a woman who married following Sor Tomasa's advice and who has to endure her husband's physical abuse. When asked about his violent impulses, her husband claims that his behaviour is a reaction to her failure to comply with the role of a traditional wife, as she is unable to handle the money for the household, cannot sew or iron properly, and arouses other men's desires. Rosalía falls short in performing her expected role of *ángel del hogar* (angel of the hearth), the old-fashioned model of female conduct based on abnegation and subordination to patriarchal domination. This model was officially restored when the government updated implementation of the 1889 Civil Code in 1938, which "made married women legally subordinate to their husbands" (Shubert 214). Rosalía's revelation of domestic violence to Sor Tomasa is shot in a nonchalant and comical tone. Sor Tomasa blames Rosalía for most likely provoking her husband to beat her up, and concludes that "las mujeres son débiles y necesitan la confianza y el cuidado de sus maridos" (women are weak and need the trust and support of their husbands).[7] The only secular woman in the film in a public space is La Trini, a thief dressed like a nun who is arrested by the police. Sor Tomasa commits to reforming this lost sheep and to guiding her in the proper direction: marriage and motherhood. This comedy of *desarrollismo,* despite showing snapshots of a changing society, still cages women in the private sphere and serves to affirm a reactionary set of traditional female values.

Sor Tomasa enjoys freedom of movement, but all her trips are humanitarian gestures, either to raise money for the orphanage or to take Luisa to see her brother Fernando, who lives in an orphanage for boys. Her mobility, therefore, is not for the sake of leisure or personal fulfilment, but a means to carry out community service. She is not the embodiment of a 1960s version of the *flâneuse,* the mobile female urban figure emerging in the late nineteenth century whose gaze, according to Anne Friedberg, was mobilized in the new public spaces of modernity, such as the department store and the movie theatre (36). The need to encourage the development of the emergent consumer society could provide a good excuse to empower unsupervised female mobility. *Sor Citröen,* in its contradictory message, celebrates modernization, yet shows that unrestricted female mobility can lead to a sexual freedom that is deleterious to society. La Trini, freely roaming the streets, becomes a contaminating influence on society; only a nun, trustworthy in her moral behaviour, is granted the privilege of socially sanctioned mobility.

That privilege, though, does not liberate her from mockery. The film repeatedly ridicules Sor Tomasa's driving endeavours. In her first appearance, Sor Tomasa fails the driving test by making a basic mistake: she changes gears without even starting the car. Later in the film she will be able to pass the exam, but only because she brings with her an array of images of saints. The implication is that sacred intervention enables the achievement, not Sor Tomasa's skills. In fact, in her first ride after getting her licence and purchasing the car, she hits just about every pedestrian who gets in her way and ends up in the police station. Thanks to her ability to drive, Sor Tomasa will be able to save both Luisa and Fernando – when he gets lost in the city; yet she never has a proper command of driving. On her very last ride, she does not stop at a red traffic light and almost causes another accident. When she leaves town, Sor Rafaela takes over the role of the driver for the community of nuns, and soon proves her ineptitude in manoeuvring the car by hitting another street salesman.

A similar scenario appears in *La novicia rebelde*, where Sor Sacrificio (Rocío Dúrcal) arrives at the convent to become a novice recklessly driving her convertible. She almost runs over a group of nuns at the door of the convent and then damages a sculpture while trying to park the car. The car that Sor Sacrificio is given to drive to Granada is a Citröen 2CV AK250, which is an almost identical model to the 2CV that Sor Tomasa drives in *Sor Citröen*. Another similarity between Sor Sacrificio and Sor Tomasa is that both cause car wrecks and other physical disasters. In my view, with the choice of the car and the insistence on the novice's wild driving, Luis Lucia seeks to imitate Pedro Lazaga's film for commercial purposes. And it worked, as *La novicia rebelde* attracted 1,346,691 spectators to the movie theatres.

In this mockery of women's driving skills, both *Sor Citröen* and *La novicia rebelde* echo stereotypes of female ineptitude at operating a vehicle and, by extension, any machine requiring technological expertise. Those stereotypes were grounded in the very nature of the automobile, a powerful and complex machine apparently more suitable for male hands. In his insightful study on folklore concerning the behaviour of women drivers, Michael Berger explains that the negative clichés emerged because "[e]verything about the car seemed masculine, from the coordination and strength required to operate it, to the dirt and grease connected with its maintenance" (257). Automobiles, or any other motorized means of transportation, are associated with masculinity, even though "women have been driving cars since they were invented" and have contributed to shaping automobile culture (Clarke 9). This is what Dick Hebdige calls "mechanical sexism": the motorized machine is a material sign that produces gender differences (186). Although these authors refer specifically to the contexts of British and US culture, their observations also apply to the context of Spain under Franco.

As an illustration, the examiner in charge of Sor Tomasa's driving test bemoans the escalating number of female drivers when he is informed that the next examinee is a woman: "¡Otra! ¡Qué epidemia!" (Another woman! What an epidemic!). In spite of their usual presentation in a jocose and seemingly harmless manner, these commonplaces reveal concerns deeply rooted in the social psyche. I am referring to the aforementioned precept of the 1938 Civil Code that kept women in a domestic sphere, distant from the dangers of the public domain. The automobile could grant women flexibility to pursue their dreams beyond the self-sacrificing model of femininity tied to motherhood and domesticity. The examiner's choice of the word "epidemia" conveys the sense of a diseased society threatened by the virus of female access to mobility, which compromises the core values of the community. By and large, *Sor Citröen* celebrates mobility as a metaphor for Spain's modernization and progress during the years of development, but it is a socially stratified and controlled movement, operating within a web of power relations. *Sor Citröen* illustrates the predicament of the comedy of *desarrollismo,* which originates in the need to reconcile an image of modernity and a rejuvenated version of a mobile nation with the commitment to perpetuate the pillars of its social hierarchy.

The Nun-in-Love Film

The extraordinary success of the Hollywood production *The Sound of Music* (Robert Wise, 1965) inspired Spanish producers to reactivate the tried-and-tested formula of the "nun-in-love film" in the late 1960s. The Spanish film industry had already manufactured huge hits with this formula, such as *La hermana San Sulpicio* (Florián Rey, 1927, 1934; Luis Lucia, 1952) and *Sor Angélica* (Francisco Gargallo, 1934; Joaquín Romero Marchent, 1954). Veteran director Luis Lucia was already familiar with the formula, since in 1952 he directed Carmen Sevilla, at that time one of the biggest stars of Spanish cinema, in the leading role of the third adaptation of *La hermana San Sulpicio*. In the early 1970s, and prior to making one more adaptation of that nineteenth-century novel in *La novicia rebelde,* Lucia deployed the formula with different intentions in *La orilla* (1970). This was a more ambitious, and far less commercial (558,226 spectators), project that constituted the final instalment of what Román Gubern called "el ciclo de reconciliación nacional" (cycle of national conciliation): films that revisited the Civil War by downplaying the ideological division that threw Spain into a fratricidal war and by portraying a false appeasement between the two factions (*La guerra* 148).[8] Luis Lucia cast a wounded anarchist lieutenant, Juan (Julián Mateos), who has to find refuge in a convent towards the end of the war and develops romantic feelings for one of the novices, Sister Leticia (Dianik Zurakowska), who has previously donated her blood for Juan. The blood transfusion symbolically unites two individuals on opposing sides of the war – and on different sides of the symbolic river to which the movie title refers. To deliver the message of "national reconciliation," Luis Lucia imprinted his script with unrealistic dialogue between the anarchist, the nuns, and a Nationalist official who becomes fond of Juan and does not turn him in. Far from the religious interpretation of the Civil War as a "crusade war" in which the Nationalist side led by the holy Franco saved Spain from the danger of communism, *La orilla* portrays the war as a fratricidal mistake. No one is blamed for it; there are no villains in this story, only victims. Apart from downplaying the ideological components of the war, Lucia also exempted Spanish nuns (and actresses) from any anti-nationalist and immoral behaviour by casting a Polish actress in the role of the novice who escapes with her anarchist lover. Clearly, Lucia was careful not to overstep any boundaries of the still vigorous censorship. The *Premio Especial del Sindicato Nacional del Espectáculo*, which was ultimately awarded to this film, was on the line for him.

Luis Lucia tried the "nun-in-love film" again a year later with *La novicia rebelde*, with better results (1,346,691 spectators). These box-office figures probably owed less to his mastering of the formula than to the appeal of Rocío Dúrcal, who by then had equalled Marisol as the biggest young female star of Spanish cinema. *La novicia* is loosely based on Armando Palacio Valdés's novel *La hermana San Sulpicio* (1888). The chosen title, which matches the title of the Spanish-dubbed version of *The Sound of Music* released in Latin America (not the Spanish one, which was *Sonrisas y lágrimas*), highlights the profit-oriented motivation to make another version of Palacio Valdés's novel. *La novicia* features Rocío Dúrcal as Gloria Alvar González, a wealthy cattle rancher who receives God's calling to become a nun. Given her prior education as a nurse, she is sent to serve in a hospital in Granada during her novitiate. While working at the hospital, Sor Sacrificio falls in love with the hospital director, the Mexican-born doctor Ceferino Sanjurjo (Guillermo Murray). At the end of the film, instead of taking the veil for life, she leaves the congregation to marry Ceferino. Although this plot bears some resemblance to the novel, the differences are significant. First of all, the film is narrated from Gloria's point of view instead of the doctor's. This point-of-view displacement also extends to other aspects: Ceferino is originally from Mexico instead of Galicia, and Gloria becomes Sister Sacrificio instead of San Sulpicio. Also, the Galician origin of the doctor generates a "fish-out-of-water" situation in the novel, for he filters his feeling of estrangement from the Andalusian customs with irony. That alienation of the outsider becomes mere touristic fascination in *La novicia rebelde*. Before starting his job in Granada, Ceferino Sanjurjo indulges himself in a tour of Andalusia. Spectacular long takes of monuments such as the Giralda tower present a postcard image of Seville. Then, while in Granada, Ceferino takes Sor Sacrificio, Sor Estefanía (Isabel Garcés), and Father Sabino (Ángel Garasa) on a touristic excursion to visit the Alhambra and to see a flamenco show at the Sacromonte. The richly textured and sometimes acid view of the Andalusian folklore of Palacio Valdés's novel dissolves here into an uncritical sightseeing brochure.

A documentary-style montage of the Alhambra and the Generalife that is shot with a handheld camera offers the pinnacle of this touristic pamphlet. At the same time, we overhear a conversation between Ceferino Sanjurjo and Sor Sacrificio regarding the state of their patients: tourism and scientific innovation filtered through the voice of a Church representative; it smells like *desarrollismo* spirit. The emphasis on clichéd elements of Spanish "difference" (bullfighting, flamenco, sun, and Moorish architecture) resonates with the "Spain Is Different" slogan that Manuel Fraga orchestrated in the offices of the Ministry of Information and Tourism. As a co-production with Mexico (hence the Mexican *galán*) with potential to make a splash in Latin American markets, *La novicia rebelde* was a model comedy of development. It is no wonder that Lucia still enjoyed official support in the 1970s.

The other "nun-in-love" commercial hit of these years was *Sor Ye-Yé*, a co-production of Aspa Films with Mexico directed by Ramón Fernández and with a script written by confessional film connoisseurs Vicente Escrivá and José María Sánchez Silva. The casting of Mexican stars Hilda Aguirre and Enrique Guzmán – at that time at the peak of his popularity as a singer in Latin America – made the film an international blockbuster and also generated excellent box-office results in Spain. The signature of Aspa Films and Vicente Escrivá is noticeable throughout the film in a number of narrative elements that the seasoned scriptwriter had already employed in *Sor Intrépida*. In the latter, Soledad (Dominique Blanchar) is a famous singer who surprisingly decides to give up her fame and fortune to join a religious congregation. In *Sor Ye-Yé,* María is a young orphan woman who sings in a night club with the pop music band "Los Yaqui voladores" before entering the convent. Both characters live under the tutelage of rich and eccentric aunts. Both novices enter a convent that is going through serious financial difficulties, and both try to remedy that situation with an impromptu visit to a bank to get a loan for their respective convents. When the banking tactic fails, the novices temporarily relieve the convents' woes by contributing donations from their wealthy aunts. Further affinities between the two films include a harsh nun who initially criticizes the novices, and a turning-point episode in which the older nun intercepts a letter written by the novice and becomes aware of the novice's good intentions. Drawing on a familiar formula, Vicente Escrivá nonetheless adapts it to the post–Vatican II times. While *Sor Intrépida,* as part of the political-religious cycle of the team Rafael Gil–Vicente Escrivá, was made to praise the values of National-Catholicism, and hence the female lead dies as a religious martyr in the Spanish colonies in Asia, *Sor Ye-Yé* pays tribute to Vatican II reforms, even if in a comic fashion.

What unites *La novicia rebelde* and *Sor Ye-Yé,* and what prompts me to discuss them in tandem, is that they deploy a similar blend of popular genre formulas to secure commercial success. In fact, one could say that these two films took to the extreme what the editors of *Cinema Universitario* sarcastically termed the tradition of the "plato combinado" (combo plate) ("Editorial" 5). With this culinary metaphor, these editors referred to the opportunistic pick'n'mix of popular film formulas to elaborate new commercial recipes for Spanish cinema.[9] Both films included in their generic recipe the post–Vatican II comedy + romantic comedy + musical. *La novicia rebelde* also added a touch of the bullfighting film. Genre analysis proves crucial here to understand the messages these films deliver and, related to that, the reasons behind their commercial appeal to audiences. The analysis of the blended generic elements at play in these films will help us elucidate what the love plot and the musical numbers contribute to the conflict between tradition and modernity underlying post–Vatican II comedies and, conversely, if and how the pro–Vatican II religious discourses shape the historically and culturally specific representations of gender roles, love, and sexuality that these two comedies deliver.

As I explained in the previous chapter, the generic distinction of post–Vatican II comedies depends on the centrality of the iconography of modernity. The core of the story line of both films takes place in the interior of a modern hospital that is indicative of scientific development. *La novicia rebelde* highlights this by recurrently showing long shots of the Hospital San Onofre, whose name already symbolizes that science and religion are perfectly compatible. Shots of medical instruments and sophisticated machinery flaunt the technological modernization of Spain in the development era, although they are interspersed with cautionary messages that indicate there is still a long way to go to complete this modernization. National resources are still insufficient, given that Ceferino Sanjurjo has to be recruited from Mexico to manage the San Onofre medical centre. This lack of medical talent is made even more patent in *Sor Ye-Yé*, since the ophthalmologist who performs eye surgery on one of the children in the nuns' orphanage has to be flown in from Germany. The clear message is that Spain, like the orphan child in the film, is not completely out of the tunnel and needs Europe to see the light. Yet, by recruiting foreign talent, the country also shows its willingness to change and overcome its scientific backwardness.

La novicia highlights this point by loading its narrative and visual style with other icons of technological modernity such as the long shots of the airplane that brings Ceferino to Spain, the automobiles that the doctor and Gloria drive, and even a helicopter that delivers an injured person in time for surgery. But the crucial aspect is that this modernity comes with the aid of divine intervention, as announced in the prologue of the film. Gloria explains, while speaking to the camera and, thus, breaking the fourth wall, that "allá arriba, los que se ocupan por velar por el destino amoroso de la gente acababan de dar un toque maestro al botón de las recomendaciones. Y como precisamente es un invento español, miren ustedes lo bien que funcionó la cosa" (up there, the ones who take care of people's destinies made a recommendation. And given that it is a Spanish invention, you shall see how well it works). This prologue epitomizes the notion of Catholic-infused modernity that this book examines. Gloria looks elegantly dressed and accessorized in a studio decorated in minimalist fashion with expensive-looking furniture. She plays music on a record player and draws attention to the telephone. Again, the point is to saturate the narrative with clues that introduce the spectator into a world of luxury goods, material possessions, and technological sophistication. This presentation sets the film in a Spain that is on the cutting edge of technological innovation and modern consumer culture. However, as stated in that prologue, Catholic morality is still an essential component of this nation chosen by God, since Gloria refers to providential destiny as a Spanish invention.

La novicia rebelde paints a colourful picture of the seemingly untroubled coexistence of modernization and Spanish "difference," and Sor Sacrificio embodies that dynamic tension. Her religious faith and purity (she never had a boyfriend) contrast sharply with many "modern" traits of her character: she recklessly drives her convertible car; she has deep knowledge of "masculine" activities such as automotive mechanics and bullfighting; humility is not her strength; last but not least, she has an impulsive personality and a tendency to break rules. On the stage of the comedy of development, modernization and tradition are not mutually exclusive. And neither are competing models of the apostolate of the Catholic Church. Just as in *Sor Citröen*, the divisions within the Church appear in a tongue-and-cheek fashion in both *Sor Ye-Yé* and *La novicia rebelde*. In the former, Sor María and Sor Emilia (Ofelia Guilmáin) stand for the "for" and "against" camps of the ecclesiastical debates over conciliar reforms. In the latter, Father Sabino and Sor Estefanía represent the old guard of these debates that disagreed with many of the sweeping changes Vatican II brought. In their conversations they introduce their atavistic positions on ceremonial issues such as the unfortunate relaxation of the clergy's sartorial codes and the relinquishing of Latin in the Mass. On a deeper level, Father Sabino expresses his disagreement with the Church's new mission to intervene in temporal matters. On the other side of the spectrum, Sor Sacrificio and the Madre Provincial stand for the pro-renewal sectors of the Church, open-minded clergy eager to embrace the beneficial aspects of modernity.

The core of the ideological suture of this film lies in the non-mutually exclusive status of the divergences between the two sides of the tradition-versus-modernity debate and in the synergy between disparate characters. Sor Sacrificio's insubordinate profile is tamed by her purity, which makes her "not too modern," while Sor Estefanía, who on the surface stands for the reactionary faction of the Church, is the one who mimics the language of the technocrats' "economic miracle." In a high-angle shot that comically emphasizes the visual effect of her words, Sor Estefanía asks Sor Sacrificio which professional route she wants to take to contribute monetarily to the convent. To the latter's surprise, she adds: "Usted no se puede imaginar el entusiasmo con el que vivimos en este convento lo de la sociedad de consumo" (You have no idea how enthusiastically we embrace consumer society in this convent). Towards the end of the film, it is Father Sabino who demonstrates his consumerist taste when he buys Gloria a modern-fitted dress – hemmed above the knees – to expedite her express transformation on the road to becoming a modern secular woman. Sor Estafanía supports the priest's adept choice by claiming that the dress showcases "el estampado que se lleva esta temporada" (the pattern in fashion this year). Once again, she proves her up-to-date knowledge of commercial trends.

Closing the gap between tradition and modernity even more, Father Sabino at some point offers to engage in a debate about "la encíclica Humanae Vitae y, si me apuras, sobre el celibato" (the Humanae Vitae encyclical and even about celibacy). Despite the jocose tone of the scene, this is not just a passing mention. The *Humanae Vitae* was a controversial encyclical letter written by Pope Paul VI in 1968 that sanctioned acceptable and non-acceptable forms of sexual practices and affection. Most polemically, this document prohibited all forms of artificial contraception (section 14) and certified the innate link of sexual acts to procreation within the framework of heterosexual, God-blessed marriages. "Conjugal love," the encyclical states, is "ordained toward the procreation and education of children" (section 9). The encyclical was well received by the conservative sectors of the Church, but criticized by reformist factions that felt that the so-called "encíclica de la contradicción" did not live up to the expectations of renewal that the Constitution *Gaudium et Spes* had created (Guerrero 29). The *Humanae Vitae* encapsulated – and still does today, almost half a century after its release – the Church's traditional view on marriage and marital relations, and it had crucial implications in the aftermath of Vatican II. The Church was committed to fight for democracy and human rights, but not quite ready to overcome its conservative views on gender and sexuality.

In presenting old-fashioned clergy in the avant-garde of consumerist trends and willing to argue about the legitimacy of the Vatican's reactionary views on human sexuality, Luis Lucia is not merely seeking to humorously reflect Vatican II's updating of the Church's old guard. Nor is he trying to present a straightforward subversive scenario of reverse ideological roles: a parody of the atavistic position of the Church hierarchy, comically presented in an absurd suspension of its authority. Similarly, the insistence on Sor Sacrificio's traditional core values underneath her modern façade, and especially on her virginity, is more than a strategy to circumvent the tentacles of censorship for a commercial romantic comedy. What I am trying to emphasize here is that characters in this film are defined by a "not too" ontological status. Despite all her "modern" qualifications, Gloria's purity attests that she is "not too" modern. Despite functioning throughout the film as factors of containment of modernity, Father Sabino and Sor Estefanía are "not too" atavistic. This "not too" ontology is not merely political wishy-washiness seeking to please spectators on all sides of the ideological spectrum. Rather, it is a more intricate manoeuvre of ideological suture that might be better conceptualized along the lines of what Slavoj Žižek has called the "ideological antioxidants" of modern societies (1). For Žižek, modern political systems – whether democratic or totalitarian – operate by a process of internal cleansing of "free radicals." Like Celestial Seasonings green tea, political systems contain antioxidant properties to help "the body maintain its natural good health" (1). I propose to interpret Lucia's film as a cinematic version of these ideological antioxidants. In this case, free radicals symbolically correspond not only to extremist versions of either Catholic traditionalism or the post–Vatican II "Church of contestation," both equally undesirable in the society free of ideological conflicts envisioned by the technocrats, but also to threatening forms of female mobility and emancipation. Just as antioxidants are used as dietary supplements to protect our cells against the effects of free radicals, Lucia's film crafts a fantasy of a healthy social body devoid of any political free radical.

Corporeal metaphors such as the one I have just suggested were indeed crucial in the regime's rhetorical framework and, as Aurora Morcillo argues, "women's bodies played a central role in the political imagination" of Francoist Spain to symbolically connect the "Spanish body politic" with "the allegorical female body of the nation" (*The Seduction* 13). Bearing in mind this importance of corporeally gendered metaphors in public discourse, *La novicia rebelde* illustrates one of these threatening free radicals to be tamed: the emancipated and mobile female. For example, the "chica ye-yé," which emerged in the Spanish social fabric in the 1960s, was triggered in equal terms by the sexual revolution – however diluted this process was in Francoist Spain – and by the opening of Spain to international consumer trends. A model of femininity that came to Spain from abroad, *la chica ye-yé* rapidly spread in *aperturista* Spain as an icon of the sociocultural renovation taking place worldwide in the 1960s. The *chica ye-yé* was a figure that ensued from the orbit of pop culture, especially pop music, as the sexy performer who dared to challenge, among other things, the sartorial codes in vogue for young women. The use of the miniskirt popularized by the British designer Mary Quant, one of the main emblems of the

"Swinging Sixties" in London, epitomized this rebellion articulated through clothing options.

Ramón Fernández's *Sor Ye-Yé* had already cloistered the *chica ye-yé* in a convent on her way to becoming a submissive wife. But before changing her habit for bridal wear, Sor María shows her congregation the path to renewal and, thereby, survival within the modern world. She finds the solution to the convent's problems by competing and winning the grand prize in the San Remo Festival of popular music. As mandated by Vatican II, Sor María responds creatively to the challenges of modern times. Also, she undertakes a crucial element of the spirit of the conciliar document *Perfectae Caritatis*. This decree had recommended that the focal point of religious life should shift from the religious order as a whole to the individual person within the order. As long as the superior had provided the appropriate training and the nuns had achieved spiritual maturity, nuns were allowed to exercise more agency and independence in choosing the missions of their apostolate. The eighth section of the decree stated that "apostolic activity must spring from intimate union with Him [Christ]," which meant that a nun could take on her own apostolic missions without the superior's approval. As Amy Koehlinger notes, this was a huge innovation, since a nun "who believed that she was being divinely led toward a particular ministry could claim the newly legitimized basis of individual conscience for apostolic preferences beyond the scope of her congregation" (48). In essence, both Sor María in this film and Sor Tomasa in *Sor Citröen* are post-conciliar nuns who respond to the calls of the council's mandates. But the problem, and the source of most of the comical situations in both films, is that neither of them has the spiritual maturity or training required to make apostolic decisions. This is why Sor Tomasa is punished and relocated to a different convent and city, and Sor María is advised to leave the convent to become a married woman. Still, their enthusiasm and initiative reactivate their convents' mission. Sor María sheds light on the route the Church should take to maintain its status as a relevant institution within an increasingly modernized society: an open-minded and flexible mindset, like the one shown by the mother superior of this convent to adapt the apostolate to the spirit of the times.

Singing for Marriage

María and Gloria, with their impulsive personality and, in Gloria's case, with her financial independence, were free birds flying in a society not quite ready for gender equality. This is why enclosing them in a convent, a sanctuary of purity and sexual inviolability, constituted an efficient path to contain a latent challenge to traditional feminine roles. The convent offered a decent and controllable alternative for young women like them who did not fit into the strict schemes of heterosexual domesticity. Their modern yet "not too modern" status acts as a filmic attempt to counteract the burgeoning images of femininity in the *aperturista* society. In case dressing the female stars in a nun's habit was not enough to cleanse the free radical of threatening forms of femininity, *Sor Ye-Yé* and *La novicia rebelde* encompass one more strategy to strengthen their function as ideological antioxidant. I am referring to the tactical integration of generic elements of the romantic comedy and the musical into both films. Seminal studies on romantic comedies and musicals have conceptualized them as conservative forms of entertainment with a recurrent structure consisting of a heterosexual romance with a happy ending that brings together opposing social groups (Altman, *The American*; Neale and Krutnik; Schatz). The main conflict at stake in these two films is competing models of femininity that need to be reconciled. As in romantic comedies and musicals, Fernández and Lucia present energetic protagonists while simultaneously creating "censorial narrative structures to surround them" (Sutton 196). Gloria is potentially a threat to those gender hierarchies, since she is a highly successful entrepreneur in the masculine realm of bullfighting and cattle ranching. On top of that, she is a single woman thus far not interested in dating men.

In both cases, the attempt to be a religious woman appears as a stepping stone to learning to be a "real woman," as an intermediate stage of the transformations María and Gloria experience under the direction of male figures. That learning process culminates when the rebellious female protagonist expresses her pleasure in being domesticated and in becoming a woman-object for the male. As Gloria tells Father Sabino: "Si usted supiese lo bien que se pasa cuando a una la domestican" (If you only knew how great it feels to be domesticated). At the end of the film, when she reunites with Ceferino on the road, she tells him she has transformed her attire and her identity (from religious habits to her feminine dress) to please him. The reconciliation scene on the road cuts to a predictable marriage scene. The tension between competing gender roles is therefore resolved through marriage. The dreams of the energetic protagonist may come true, but only as long as they remain within the purview of patriarchal values.

Visually, the prevalence of this gender hierarchy is represented by two recurring technical conventions that by now can be considered hallmarks of confessional cinema. The first one is the tactical use of framing devices. When the sexual tension between Sor Sacrificio and Doctor Sanjurjo in *La novicia rebelde* begins to be evident, the camera angulation chosen to frame the interactions between the two characters shifts to a noticeable gendered pattern: low angles to aggrandize the figure of the male doctor and high angles to curtail the domesticated female. A second but equally fundamental stylistic convention to inscribe the gender ideology of the films is the lighting pattern. In both films, the romantic scenes between the novices and their soon-to-be husbands are lit by permeating the female characters with abundant light through the balanced use of the key, fill, and back lights to avoid any shine or unflattering shadows in their faces. The purpose of this lighting technique, as we have seen in other religious films of this era, is to present an idealized angelic image of the female lead that visually suggests her flawless moral profile. The meticulous use of the lighting techniques also constructs the relationship between male and female characters in both films according to conventional representations of heterosexual couples in romantic comedies. In *Sor Ye-Yé*, the flame of love between Sor María and the doctor, Juan (Manuel Gil), ignites in a late night encounter. Sor María is working the night shift at the orphanage, and the doctor conveniently goes to check on the sick children. A medium shot of their unexpected encounter shows the angelic Sor María radiating chastity. The overhead light catches her hair prominently and slightly brightens his figure. This prevalent convention suggesting that the man is being illuminated by the woman is therefore a visual marker hinting at the territory of a romantic comedy, suggesting that the man feels a desire for the light she exudes. Love is in the air. Interestingly, *La novicia rebelde* also contains a night scene between the lovers in a hospital room with the same lighting conventions.

Beneath the veil, these nuns incarnate a model of femininity mastered by Rocío Dúrcal in the first part of her acting career. As I have argued elsewhere, Rocío Dúrcal embodied a specific type of Cinderella of the development years, modern yet decent, usually of low class origins, and who can move up in society through marriage if she proves her qualities (purity being the most important one) (82). Although the novice in *Sor Ye-Yé* is played by Hilda Aguirre, reviews upon its release pointed out that Aguirre "está muy en la línea física y expresiva de Rocío Dúrcal" (has similar physical features and acting style to Rocío

Dúrcal) ("*Sor Ye-Yé*"). In both films, women's purity and willingness to be domesticated are rewarded with marriage. By the end of the 1960s, the Cinderella recipe seemed exhausted, as Rocío Dúrcal began to star in films such as *Cristina Guzmán* (1968) and *Las Leandras* (1969), in which her characters were not as decent or fully clad. *La novicia rebelde* appeared not only as a final attempt to stretch the commercial formula one more time, but also as an opportunity to sanitize the image of the star.[10] Granted, María's and, above all, Gloria's wealthy origins make access to a higher class unnecessary, but the Cinderella motif is still operative in these films. Although they both end up marrying doctors and, as a result, returning to the upper middle classes, they have previously renounced their class status and luxuries to enter the convent. In Gloria's case, she has donated all her money. The point is that they are not "gold-diggers" aspiring to climb the social ladder; rather, what they ultimately desire is to fit into the heteronormative social system and become middle-class, "normal" women through marriage. But to achieve that, they need to renounce their economic independence and accept male authority and guidance.

Sor Ye-Yé and *La novicia rebelde* thus integrate the most reactionary undertones of the Cinderella motif of classic romantic comedies. They dramatize that women's escalating incorporation into the Spanish public sphere as workforce and their subsequent attainment of financial independence could pose a threat to the male supremacy in the social structure. Spanish women could suddenly channel their desires toward their own improvement and not toward being rewarded with marriage. Both films squeeze in generic elements of the romantic comedy to mitigate any possible social transgression and restore the positions of the sexual-economic order. Therefore, at stake in these post–Vatican II comedies is not so much the impact of the renewal of convent life, and the changing role of women religious within the Church in particular, but reaffirming patriarchal authority as the norm in the economic and sexual spheres.

What is unique about *Sor Ye-Yé* and *La novicia rebelde* in relation to the classic Hollywood romantic comedy is that the gender ideology underlying the love plots is framed within a religious discourse. Catholic morality is still an essential component of the acceptable models of womanhood they endorse. National-Catholicism promoted a traditional notion of womanhood that rested upon Catholic virtues such as self-sacrifice, obedience, and chastity. As Aurora Morcillo has shown, this model, which she calls "true Catholic womanhood" (*True* 3), draws heavily on sixteenth-century treatises on the education of Christian women, especially Juan Luis Vives's *Instrucción de la mujer cristiana* (1523) and Fray Luis de León's *La perfecta casada* (1583). With the modernization process, women's incorporation into the job market, and the new popular models of femininity that emerged from the thriving consumer society, the official model of womanhood had to be adjusted to the changing times. The emergence of "the consumer-housewife model" brought the image of Spanish women closer to the model of "consumer female ideal" that was prevailing in Western capitalist countries (Morcillo, *True* 4). But it is important to keep in mind that this adjusted model was still shaped to the service of a Catholic morality. Spanish women were necessary as labour force and consumers, but "their presence in the public sphere had to maintain the Christian values prescribed by the regime" (Morcillo, *True* 55). *Sor Ye-Yé* and *La novicia rebelde* present mass culture representatives of this new official model of womanhood. Gloria "wins" Ceferino for the Catholic cause by convincing him to attend Mass; María takes care of Juan's struggles with domestic activities. Every time Juan appears on the screen, he is a walking fashion disaster, whether because of an unbuttoned white coat, a wrongly tied tie, or socks that do not match the clothes. Apart from creating some of the most rib-tickling moments of the film, there are also ideological implications for Juan's tribulations with clothing. The masculine character is constructed as a professionally successful bachelor who needs a woman for domestic things. The message is that both men and women are better off in a traditional marriage with the proper gendered division of labour.

Humour is crucial in the generic mix that these post–Vatican II comedies present. Genre scholars have traditionally differentiated the romantic comedy from the comedian comedy, and have regarded the presence of comic gags in romantic comedies as a distraction to narrative (Karnick 126–30; Karnick and Jenkins 80–1; Neale and Krutnik 17). Celestino Deleyto has shown, writing about the Hollywood context, that such a differentiation is tied to the notion of genre as belonging that I questioned in the previous chapter. It emerges from the understanding of a genre as a group of films with a rigid set of features that need to be present or absent in order to claim genre belonging. By posing a theoretical barrier that establishes romantic happy endings and laughter as generically incompatible, this prevailing view neglects that in practice humour is a central ingredient in many romantic comedies and, consequently, should be included in any theory of this genre (23).

This is certainly the case with the two post–Vatican II comedies I am analysing here. The romantic bonds between the nuns and their respective doctors grow from the initial laughable situations of misunderstanding and quarrels often caused by the reckless behaviour of the impulsive nuns. In *La novicia rebelde,* these comic gags include uproarious slapstick moments when Gloria almost runs over Ceferino in Seville's city centre, then hits his car when reversing hers at a gas station, and provokes an explosion in Ceferino's car by pretending to possess mechanical expertise. Instead of an interruption to the narrative logic of these two films, the comic situations in *Sor Ye-Yé* and *La novicia rebelde* form what Deleyto calls a "comic, protective, erotically-charged space" in the sense that it protects the future lovers "from the strictures of social conventions and psychological inhibitions" (23). This is a space in which reality can be transformed by creating an "erotic utopia" projected "as an antidote against the sexual and affective frustrations of everyday life" (35). It is a space that triggers the otherwise impossible flirtation between the lovers. Nuns are not supposed to flirt with doctors in real life. But this comic space enables the films to get away with presenting novices engaging in courtship without crossing the line of the scandalous and the nonsensical.

Musical numbers embedded in both films also contribute to the creation of this utopian space of transformation where romance is possible. They lift viewers from the *hic et nunc* into the territory of romantic love. The numbers in musicals project, according to Richard Dyer, a sense of utopia not by constructing "models of utopian worlds, as in the classic utopias of Sir Thomas More, William Morris, et al"; rather, they present "what utopia would feel like rather than how it would be organized" ("Entertainment" 177). And that feeling could not be more clear-cut in these two films: happiness, happiness, and more happiness. The very titles of some of the songs performed, such as "Alegría del Señor" and "Vivir, vivir, vivir" in *La novicia rebelde,* indicate that they are musical sermons on happiness. However, the two films differ in the way they integrate those numbers. In *Sor Ye-Yé,* most of the musical numbers are part of the diegetic space of the film and serve to advance the narrative – for example, Sor María's rehearsals and actual performances in the San Remo Festival – or serve as devices for characterization – to depict the *chica ye-yé* at the beginning of the film. In *La novicia rebelde,* most of the numbers appear as dream sequences.

On the surface, the dream device may seem to diminish the narrative relevance of the songs and, in this way, support negative assessments of the musical that deem it an escapist genre made only for entertainment. The narrative/musical number split is indeed, according to Rick Altman, what defines the musical as a genre, and the interpretation of this relationship has divided evaluative approaches to this genre into opposing camps. As Altman points out, some critics of the musical argue that "the numbers appear unreal by comparison with the narrative" and these discrepancies "in content, tone, and treatment" make the genre a particularly frivolous one (*Genre* 190). For others, the textual mechanisms of the musical numbers and the way they make spectators active participants in the fantasy they convey are much more complex than is often assumed, at times even having a self-reflective avant-garde function (Feuer 12–13; Collins 135–40). In *La novicia rebelde*, the productive tension between the narrative and the musical numbers presented through dream devices is instrumental in creating the utopian space that compels spectators to suspend their disbelief and participate in this fantasy world leading to a happy ending. As in the classical Hollywood musical, Sor Sacrificio sees her dream "as if it were projected onto a screen," thus sharing the same limited reality with the spectator, "while the dream and the film both enjoy a freedom from the normal physical laws of time, space, and causality" (Altman, *The American* 61). Let us remember that the spectator was already directly addressed in the preface by Gloria/Sor Sacrificio and therefore invited to participate in the world of the film and in the joyful musical numbers.

But apart from compelling the diegetic audience into sharing the enjoyment, the musical numbers are also instrumental in performing and, thereby, upholding the main ideological tenets of this post–Vatican II comedy, which have to do mainly with conservative gender roles. Take, for example, the first musical number in the convent. This is the first of a series of dream-like numbers that project the protagonist's feelings and her inner transformations. Sor Sacrificio ecstatically contemplates herself in a mirror in her new nun attire and this leads her to an oneiric meditation. The sound of the convent bells acts as what Altman calls the "audio dissolve" of musicals. If video dissolves are used as an editing device to connect one shot to another by visual superimposition, "the audio dissolve superimposes sounds in order to pass from one sound track to another" (*The American* 63). In this case, the audio dissolve involves the transition from the diegetic track (the sound of the bells) to the music track (the bells as part of the orchestral accompaniment of the musical number). Through this audio dissolve, the spectator is magically transported along with Sor Sacrificio to an abstract scenographic stage outside of the spatial and temporal coordinates of the empirical world. Dúrcal and an entourage of female backup dancers appear dressed in lavish pink habits and perform their number with a perfectly synchronized choreography that exaggerates the feeling of joy conveyed by the lyrics of the song "Alegría del Señor." The nuns situate themselves in three groups placed in a circular arrangement around three large church bells. The groups break out in dance, and the main performer, an oneiric version of Sor Sacrificio dressed in a slightly darker pink habit, appears from the back. Backup dancers start to dance in circular patterns around the bells and then around Sor Sacrificio, who is herself spinning around. An editing cut takes us to a long shot in high angle of the backup dancers sitting in a semicircle and knitting. The insistence on the circular presentation brings to mind traditional symbols of femininity and female sexuality. The joyful music and lyrics suggest female ecstasy about life in the convent. Since professing the vows of a woman religious entails becoming, figuratively speaking, a spouse of Christ, the circular arrangements in this performance could evoke the circular symbol of the wedding ring that suggests a pledge of eternal love and fidelity.

Later in the film, another dream sequence further emphasizes Sor Sacrificio's fantasies of becoming a traditional housewife who accepts her submissive role within the patriarchal order. The sacred space of the church witnesses the first strong hint of the development of romantic bonds between her and Ceferino. Sor Sacrificio invites Ceferino to Sunday morning Mass. A close-up of the figure of the Virgin Mary hanging in the chapel announces the divine intervention in the upcoming scene. While Sor Sacrificio is singing Charles Gounod's version of "Ave María," Ceferino walks into the chapel, and in a series of shot/reverse shots the two characters stare at each other, revealing their joy. In the last shot, in which Ceferino turns back to look up at Sor Sacrificio as she is singing, the methodically planned framing shows the figure of the Virgin Mary next to Ceferino, thus highlighting the divine blessing of the romance between the protagonists and, just as importantly, that one more soul is recruited for the Catholic cause. An audio dissolve takes us, through the use of the diegetic music, from the concrete world of the religious service into a dream sequence in which Sor Sacrificio imagines herself in bridal wear. The musical numbers thus perform the transformation of the rebellious dreamer into a conformist. The tension between narrative and musical numbers is finally resolved and the narrative overtakes the numbers in the happy ending. Sor Sacrificio's dreams come true and she gets her husband, yet she also has to accept reactionary gender norms, including heteronormative society's definition of women as passive and domesticated.

The most cunning aspect of the cinematic rendering of the nuns in these dream sequences is that they all appear associated with stereotypical depictions of female beauty. Close-ups of Sor Sacrificio in the first dream sequence highlight her pink eye shadow and lipstick – matching her habit – and her perfectly plucked eyebrows. The mise-en-scène of both sequences constructs – as seen in the costumes, make-up, set design, and performance – an image of women religious as beautiful models to be contemplated, as projection of desire – of the director and the audience alike – and as a source of identification for female viewers who are interpellated into sharing this image of women as passive recipients. A similar construction of the image of Sor María in relation to mainstream conventions of female beauty appears in *Sor Ye-Yé*. Once the novice settles down in the convent, a scene shows her happily lying in bed. The lighting treatment illuminates her face, highlighting the make-up on her lips and eyes as well as her impeccably plucked eyebrows. Given that at the beginning of both films these two novices were struggling to fit into the niche of compulsory heterosexuality, the purpose of the copious use of cosmetics to groom them is, undoubtedly, to make them appear perfectly heterosexual. As some feminist scholars have pointed out, the use of make-up is a conventional marker of female heterosexuality (Dellinger and Williams 159) and a ubiquitous aspect of the construction of femininity in contemporary societies (Jeffreys 114). What I am suggesting is that these two "nun-in-love films" do not merely present traditional gender roles through thematic patterns but also construct, through cinematic techniques and tactical choices in the mise-en-scène, celluloid images of women (religious) tied to gender structures pervasive in society.

Another song certifies the ideological manoeuvring behind the musical numbers. "La marcha de la paz," with music and lyrics by none other than Junior, Rocío Dúrcal's husband in real life, is an anti-war appeal to endorse a conservative ideological agenda. Dúrcal sings that she desires peace in the world, but that peace is not to be achieved through activism but rather by conforming to the system: "Quien se queja de vicio, ya me saca de quicio" (Those who complain for the sake of complaining get on my nerves). The song conveys a conformist agenda advocating for compliance with the current political order – the peace and prosperity under Franco – and against any form of protest.

3.1 The construction of female heterosexuality through make-up in *La novicia rebelde* (1971). Permission to reproduce the still from EGEDA.

The message of obedient optimism is again reinforced by the mise-en-scène of the number, especially by the gaudy yellow dress embroidered with musical notes that Sor Sacrificio wears. This musical number should be framed within the context of the post–May 1968 youth protests against hegemonic political systems and their military interventions (i.e., the Vietnam War), but also, at the national level, within the turmoil caused by the cultural and political opposition to the Franco regime, including the actions instigated by the progressive factions of the Church. The message of the musical number is clear: stop whining, smile and enjoy the prosperity of Spain's *desarrollismo*. The Arcadian sensibility of the musical defuses social forces of protest and threatening forms of femininity. Through a poetics of happiness, the audience is interpellated into a communal celebration of conformist social values and sutured into a world of prosperity and false peace. *La novicia rebelde* assembles a fabricated utopia of Spain during the development years, where women only have to learn to be "real women" – becoming submissive wives who knit instead of being entrepreneurs – to enter a world of wealth and luxury, and where divine powers will reward those who adapt to the patriarchal system.

As we have seen, the mise-en-scène, camera work, and editing, along with the mix of generic elements of the romantic comedy and the musical, deployed in both "nun-in-love" films are efficient cinematic mechanisms to deliver conservative messages regarding gender roles and love relationships. Interestingly, they simultaneously contain the seed for a different kind of reading. Similar to *Sor Citröen*, in which I identified a stream of transgression, articulated through the trope of dissident mobility, some of the romantic scenes between the novices and the doctors border the morally unacceptable. By way of illustration, let us return to the church scene in *La novicia rebelde*. Ceferino and Sor Sacrificio's exchanged looks in the church imprint that sacred space with a sexual undercurrent that surpasses the rules of decorum for a divinely sanctioned romance. There is something lascivious not only in the smiles they exchange but also, especially, in Ceferino's compulsion, triggered by Sor Sacrificio's voice, to turn his head back to look up at her. My point is not to assert that Luis Lucia pioneered the *destape* fever that was to spread in the Spanish film industry. Oddly enough, and eager as Spanish audiences of the 1970s were to perceive any type of sexual undertone on the big screen, the erotic subtext of *La novicia rebelde* may seem more obvious to a twenty-first-century viewer than to one of the early 1970s.[11]

Seen today, *La novicia rebelde* appears to have an air of sacrilegious sexuality that probably surpasses Lucia's intentions. A similar perverse effect is created by the strong emphasis on the physical appearance – make-up, plucked eyebrows, and fake eyelashes – and the clothing choices of the female lead. Sor Sacrificio wears fitted and stylish habits that were made by couture designer Manuel Pertegaz. Vatican II had mandated, through the Decree *Perfectae Caritatis*, a refashioning of nuns' habits. The idea was that as "signs of a consecrated life, religious habits should be simple and modest, at once poor and becoming. They should meet the requirements of health and be suited to the circumstances of time and place as well as to the services required of those who wear them" (quoted in Valentine 141). Needless to say, Sor Sacrificio's couture habits are far from looking poor. Instead of being crafted for practicality and hygiene, they are designed to be displayed on the runway. Although the sartorial codes of *La novicia* reinforce the conservative ideological lustre of the film, as part of Gloria's training in traditional femininity, the over-the-top presentation of her physique deviates a tad from the chaste "Rocío Dúrcal look" of her Cinderella cycle of the 1960s. Even though the lighting treatment of Gloria/Sor

Sacrificio that I analysed before matches the idealized angelic image of celluloid religious figures, her "grooming" is too overstated to pass as a "natural" everyday practice for women, let alone women religious. Instead, this eroticized image of Rocío Dúrcal's face and body appears closer to the soft-core nun porn genre in vogue in Europe in the 1970s, which reached Spanish screens during the *destape* fever of the transition in films such as *Venus de fuego* (Germán Llorente, 1979) and *Inés de Villalonga, 1870* (Jaime J. Balcázar, 1979). In hindsight, Dúrcal was closer in *La novicia rebelde* to her last film role as a wealthy wife who has a lesbian affair – with *destape* star Bárbara Rey – in the highly erotic *Me siento extraña* (Enrique Martí Maqueda, 1977) than to her debut, also directed by Lucia, in *Canción de juventud* (1962).

In both *Sor Ye-Yé* and *La novicia rebelde,* the need to captivate a wide spectrum of moviegoers paradoxically had perverse effects. Selling heterosexual desire through the physical appeal of the stars, Hilda Aguirre and Rocío Dúrcal, became a priority. The over-the-top exhibition of the stars' appeal through costume, make-up, lighting, and camera work certainly succeeded in enticing the desired audience, but it also imprinted the films with erotic undertones that conflicted with their otherwise tight conservative messages. While cultural critics have long considered ideological orthodoxy and commercial success as organic partners in pro-regime cultural production, these two films show that these two logics (the commercial and the ideological) were not always inherently well matched. In my view, this means we should give far more credit to the massive audiences that consumed these commercial comedies and could detect and engage with their protean shape and the incongruities of their representational mechanisms. This also means that trying to grasp an all-encompassing picture of popular confessional cinema in late Francoism may be a tremendously frustrating venture. Instead of pulling our hair out trying to reach a perfectly aligned outlook, we should accept Sally Faulkner's invitation and continue to explore the fascinating cracks in this "cinema of contradiction."

Testing the Feminist Waters

The most courageous nun film the Spanish film industry dared to make during these years was Julio Buchs's *Encrucijada para una monja*. This film was a co-production with Italy that tells the story of a nun, Sister María (Rosanna Schiaffino), who gets pregnant after being raped by insurgent soldiers in the Belgian Congo. Once the nun returns to Belgium, she is pressured to choose between keeping the baby and giving it away. While she is making her decision, a doctor, Pierre Lemmon (John Richardson), tries to make her transition into a secular lifestyle easier by offering to marry her. When the story line seemed bound to have a conventional happy ending that would bring closure to the nun's internal conflict and seal her social integration via the ideological trappings of heterosexual marriage, the film closes with a surprising twist. Sister María renounces her vows and rejects the marriage proposal to become an independent single mother. Corny as this plot line may seem for a contemporary viewer, the resolution was nothing short of bold in the context of the 1960s in Spain. The controversial topic paid dividends (2,673,726 tickets sold), and the commercial formula of the "missionary nun-raped-by-primitive-African-natives" was revisited by Mario Camus in *Esa mujer* (1969), a film commissioned by Cesáreo González for Suevia Films. Unlike *Encrucijada,* however, *Esa mujer* was made with no intention to contribute to ecclesiastical or ethical debates, since the only devotion it fostered was Sara Montiel's popular appeal. Instead of spiritual or moral quandaries, the film dwelt on Montiel's distinctive repertoire: her melodramatic songs, her lavish outfits, and her affected performance. Although her cinematographic cachet was visibly waning, Cesáreo González decided to take a second shot at dressing Sarita in a nun's habit, after the commercial flop of *Pecado de amor* (1962). And this time it paid off. *Esa mujer* was not as lucrative as *Encrucijada* but it still generated satisfactory box-office figures (1,374,096 spectators).

The cases of *Encrucijada* and *Esa mujer* once again illustrate how the commercial potential of celluloid nuns had less to do with embodying the post–Vatican II renewal of convent life than with personifying other issues of social interest. First of all, the nun stories in both films seemed to be instruments to express colonial anxieties over the decolonization process in Africa. While the beginning of *Esa mujer* takes place in an indeterminate African country facing a local rebellion and *Encrucijada* is set in the former Belgian colony, Spanish audiences could easily draw parallels with the independence process affecting Spain's own colonial possessions in Africa. Let us not forget that in 1968, only one year after *Encrucijada* was released and one year before *Esa mujer,* the regime gave in to the escalating pressures coming from both the United Nations and Equatoguinean nationalists and granted independence to the new Republic of Equatorial Guinea. The "decolonization anxiety" emerges in both films through the deployment of hackneyed formulas of the missionary film genre; namely, the clichéd portrayal of "primitive"

Africa as a pre-modern and uncivilized territory with indomitable individuals naturally inclined to violence and whose bloody actions against the European colonial order destroy the modernizing impulses in their own countries. Especially insidious is the portrayal of colonial conflicts in *Encrucijada*. The film credits appear over a montage of newspaper clippings about the violent massacres carried out by African natives against the European civilizing presence in the Belgian Congo, juxtaposed with images of a group of black Africans playing music with sinister tones. By straightforward association, the film links African culture and people to genocide. The cinematic presentation of the arrival of nationalist African soldiers at the missionary convent further reinforces this association through a long shot of a contingent of dark figures walking mechanically towards the convent as if they were mindless zombies on the hunt for human flesh.

Once the story line settles on European soil, the dramatic centre of gravity veers to the individual struggles of Sister María. Although in principle those struggles are of a spiritual nature, about what is acceptable and what is not for a woman religious under sacred vows, they are visually represented as issues of shifting gender roles and women's independence. The first shocking clue is the thick make-up on her face, which includes mascara, eyeliner, mauve eye shadow, and red lipstick. The numerous close-ups of her face objectify the nun's image and compel viewers to regard her character in relation to gender stereotypes and assumptions about external beauty. Sister María is beautified for the desiring gaze of Pierre and the spectators. The woman religious is visually presented and subsequently judged by characters and viewers alike by dropping the second noun, as a woman of flesh and blood. This is especially highlighted by the red lipstick, which historically has elicited a wide spectrum of connotations ranging from sin and defiance to feminine self-confidence and strength. It works as a visual cue that Sister María is no longer a virgin, but simultaneously foreshadows her assertive behaviour in the closing scenes of the film.

Other aspects of the mise-en-scène, along with choices in the cinematography, underline that what is at issue here is gender roles. Most of the interior scenes are photographed with dark filters to evoke Sister María's gloomy state of mind. But the shadows in which she has to navigate are not just metaphorical but quite literal. The lighting treatment of this nun significantly differs from what viewers are accustomed to with other celluloid nuns. Instead of the balanced three-point lighting system that gave nuns an ethereal, angelic aspect in *Sor Ye-Yé* and

La novicia rebelde, Sister María in *Encrucijada* usually appears with shadows under her nose and mouth. Particularly conspicuous in this regard is a scene in which she is having a nightmare and her sister Lisa (Mara Cruz) comes to her aid. The nun is lying in bed, and the unflattering lighting chosen to illuminate her figure shows that she is profusely sweating, which gives her face a shiny appearance. As I pointed out in chapter 1, cinematic representations of idealized forms of white femininity have traditionally avoided, through the meticulous technical deployment of lighting and make-up, shine and sweat, because they connote physicality, be that related to labour or sexual activity. Sister María has the finger pointed at her not only by her hypocritical family members and by her superiors, who worry about the Congregation's dirtied reputation, but also by the technical lighting conventions, as she cannot enjoy the glow that permeates idealized female characters.

The closing scene, in which the lighting pattern is conspicuously broken, makes a noteworthy exception. As Sister María talks to her male confessor (played by Ángel Picazo) about the brave decision she has made, hard key and fill lights illuminate her figure significantly more than thus far in the film, especially by comparison with the poorly lit figure of the priest. The scene is also punctuated by melodramatic non-diegetic music that is radically different from the sinister sounds of African drums that appeared in the initial credits and then reappear each time the nun remembers or talks about her traumatic experience in the mission. Lighting and music thus work in tandem here to imply that Sister María has been cinematically redeemed – for the first time she appears with an angelic look – by means of her conscious assumption of a maternal role. However, Sister María's visual redemption is still limited. She is no longer pure or virginal, even if it was not her fault, and she assumes a non-traditional maternal choice outside of the sphere of the nuclear family. So she is not afforded all the visual privileges of other nuns. For example, the backlight that provides an exalting halo to idealized female characters is absent. In the hierarchical visual economy of confessional cinema, Sister María is still placed below other female models, but at least she is allowed to come out of the shadows. This is no small accomplishment. Celluloid nuns who transgress boundaries are subsequently punished – as we have seen in *Sor Citröen* – and the ones tempted by carnal desires immediately domesticated through marriage – *Sor Ye-Yé* and *La novicia rebelde*. In contrast, *Encrucijada* allows its female lead the independence to choose a lifestyle that does not conform to the rigid gender roles of patriarchal society.

María might not glow like other nuns, but she has agency instead. This is quite daring, indeed, for a religious film.

Like other post–Vatican II nun films, *Encrucijada para una monja* drew massive audiences into the movie theatres less because it explored in depth how women religious experienced the changes of the council than because it addressed female models of subjectivity in the changing Spanish society of the late 1960s. *Encrucijada* presents a celluloid nun who is given the choice to break with prescribed gender roles. She opts for emancipation from the patriarchal supervision of both the Church hierarchy and a future husband, even if one gets the feeling that her secular life will be full of obstacles and social prejudices. This pro-feminist message sets this film apart from the previously analysed nun films that upheld traditional models of gender identity and the dichotomy of a masculinized rational public sphere versus the feminized private sphere. The blockbusters *Sor Ye-yé* and *La novicia rebelde* were effective in reinforcing that capitalist development and modernization could occur at a fast pace without compromising traditional Catholic morality, especially in relation to women's rights. These films appropriated religion mostly as a factor of containment rather than as an agent of social change in the late 1960s and early 1970s. With the exception of *Encrucijada*, the Spanish film industry thus seemed to evolve at a similar pace to the Catholic Church: it embraced modern values but it stayed very traditional when it came to gender and sexuality. In this way, it fed the vast audiences that went to see these films with reactionary models of womanhood that counteracted the incipient feminist movement in Spain.

Chapter Four

Narratives of Suspicion: Religion in the *Nuevo Cine Español*

The return of Luis Buñuel to Spain in 1960 to make *Viridiana* after more than two decades in exile was a landmark event in the history of Spanish cinema. It was crucial, first of all, because of the significance of that film in terms of quality and international resonance – it was awarded the Palme D'Or at the 1961 Cannes Film Festival. Second, *Viridiana* was relevant because of the scandal it generated. The review of the film published in *L'Osservatore romano* the day after its triumph in Cannes, which condemned *Viridiana* for being blasphemous, prompted a political crisis. José Muñoz Fontán, the government director of cinematography, was forced to resign and was immediately replaced by the Falangist Jesús Suevos. The film was banned from commercial release in Spain and no mention of it was allowed in the press or on the radio (Sánchez Biosca, *Luis Buñuel* 22). While acclaimed around the world, *Viridiana* did not even exist in Spain until it could finally be screened there in 1977. The scandal exposed the limitations of the *apertura* of the development years and of the new image of modernity that the regime intended to project by co-opting the work of progressive filmmakers.

Although religious issues had always been central throughout his filmography, with *Viridiana* Buñuel continued the deeper theological exploration that he began with *Nazarín*, as he later would in *El ángel exterminador*, *Simón del desierto*, and *La Voie Lactée*. Attacks on organized religion were main ingredients in his early films, but the difference was that with *Nazarín*, where he crafted his own vision of the passion of Christ via the novelistic world of Benito Pérez Galdós, Buñuel began to address religion as something related to inner beliefs, not just as external practice (Sánchez Biosca, "Scenes" 173). In *Viridiana*, Buñuel engaged a number of religious themes and theological notions – related to the meaning of charity, chastity, devotion, and liturgy – in a narrative simultaneously "replete with the most varied perversions (fetishism, necrophilia, transvestism)" (173). Most scholarly approaches to the film have explored this irreverent play with religious and erotic references to point out the humorous effects it causes (Sánchez Biosca, "Scenes") or to showcase it as representative of Buñuel's distinctive "anti-religious films" (Ivan Butler 190–7). Along with Víctor Fuentes (*Los mundos* 159) and Elizabeth Scarlett (62), I believe that the union of mysticism and eroticism in *Viridiana* goes beyond producing humorous effects and displaying anti-clerical belligerence (though both are certainly present) and should be addressed as part of a radical reworking of a Christian vision of the sacred. Different from the hagiographic films in vogue in Spain at that time, in which charity and saccharine piety always triumph over evil, the main character (played by Silvia Pinal) fails to create a Christian community in the age of secularization. But Viridiana's failed pursuit of charity and compassion, her becoming a Christian "broken idol" (Scarlett 37), purifies her as a saintly figure. Despite her flawed conduct – or perhaps because of it – Viridiana appears closer to the original spirit of Christianity, to the Church of the poor and the marginalized.

Viridiana and Nazario (Francisco Rabal), the protagonist in *Nazarín*, are what Ernest Ferlita calls "frustrated practitioners of 'pure' Christianity" (154). It is not by chance that Buñuel explored theological issues more deeply in his films from 1958 on. This shift to the sacred coincides with the election of Pope John XXIII and the subsequent renovation of the Church with Vatican II. This is why Fuentes argues that films like *Nazarín* and *Viridiana* not only dialogue with but also prefigure the spirit of *aggiornamento*, driven by the urge to reconcile faith with the modern world through a return to the essence of Christianity that will imbue the Church in the 1960s (*Buñuel* 171–3). In *Viridiana*, Buñuel demolishes in ludic fashion some of the pre-modern religious forces lingering in Spanish Catholicism. But he also shows, through the character of Jorge (Francisco Rabal), who for Nathan Richardson embodies "amoral and destructive modernity," that modernity understood as rampant capitalist expansion is not his "choice to fill the void left by discredited religion" (*Constructing* 164). Spiritual quest still mattered for Buñuel in trying to make sense of the modern world.

The return of Buñuel to Spain, even if short-lived, was also important because he got in touch with a new generation of filmmakers who were to follow his path. Scholars of Spanish cinema have pointed out the impact of this occurrence on the young directors coming out of the Instituto de Investigaciones y Experiencias Cinematográficas who attempted to innovate filmmaking trends in Spain in the 1960s (Fuentes, *Los mundos* 139). As is well known, these young directors benefited from the state subsidies and the new code of censorship that José María García Escudero, director of cinematography between 1962 and 1967, put in place to support the quality filmmaking of what became labelled as *Nuevo Cine Español* (NCE). The encounter of these young directors with Buñuel could be read as a symbolic "passing of the torch" of an auteurist type of cinema that tangled with censorship officials over its explicit or implied messages that demythologized some of the ideological tenets of the regime. Notably, many NCE directors inherited what John Hopewell deems an "obsession" of Spanish art film directors with religion that derived from "the mental legacy of Buñuel," as seen in the recurrent representation of the inexorable links of sexuality to sin and religion, and in the condemnation of the marriage between ecclesiastical and political powers (32).

My aim in this chapter is to examine more in depth how NCE filmmakers engaged religion in their films. A common thread uniting an otherwise diverse group of filmmakers, producers, and crew members who became associated with the NCE was that religion was oppression writ large and always perceived with suspicion. As Marvin D'Lugo and Paul Julian Smith have contended, many NCE directors incorporated the strategies of cinematic auteurism at the height of fashion in other European cinemas as "an effort to embrace an international model through which to counter the stifling containment of Francoist culture" (113). But this adoption of European filmmaking trends "could never fully obviate the national context" and, above all, the dire reality of an authoritarian regime that impeded civil and artistic freedoms. The Spanish auteurist tradition developed as an anti-Francoist endeavour, thus somewhat singling out Spanish auteurs in relation to European auteurs (115). This is why the young directors of the NCE drew on Buñuel's attacks on the authoritarian structures of the Church, and on the ominous effects of religious intolerance so deeply ingrained in Spanish traditionalism, to condemn the confessional status of Spain. But they overlooked what made Buñuel's films universally appealing for scholars examining the intersections between religion and film: the exploration of the creative, and even revolutionary, potential of religion, once it is stripped of its ties to power hierarchies and repressive structures. Unlike Buñuel following the release of *Nazarín*, they chose not to look at theological notions as potentially empowering responses to the contradictions of modernization processes in Spain. As I will show in my analyses of key films by Basilio Martín Patino, Carlos Saura, Francisco Regueiro, and Pedro Olea, the young directors of the NCE exposed what I identified in the introduction as normative secularism, for religion was inescapably (and somewhat reductively) depicted in their films as a repressive force and, thereby, incompatible with modernity.

Remembering the Crusade Church: Basilio Martín Patino

Basilio Martín Patino's feature-length debut, *Nueve cartas a Berta* (1966), is considered one of the most emblematic works of the *Nuevo Cine Español*. Awarded with the Silver Shell at the San Sebastián Film Festival, the film also had a better commercial run than expected, as attested by the total number of tickets sold (417,965), but especially by the twelve weeks it was shown in Madrid theatres (Cines Pompeya and Cine Palace) after its release in February 1967 (Vaquerizo García 139). In comparison with other NCE debut films such as Julio Diamante's *Los que fuimos a la guerra* (1963), Jordi Grau's *Noche de verano* (1963), and Manuel Summers's *Del rosa … al amarillo* (1963), *Nueve cartas* was a blockbuster. Casimiro Torreiro goes so far as to argue that *Nueve cartas* should be regarded as a "manifiesto-compendio" (manifesto-synthesis) of the achievements and the shortcomings of the whole movement ("¿Una dictadura liberal?" 318). Among the achievements, critics have pointed out the formal innovations that Patino integrated in a coming-of-age story that, while told in linear terms, also included documentary-style techniques and formal conventions typically associated with art cinema such as freeze-frames, slow-motion shots, narrative ellipses, disruptive soundtrack, and rapid montage, among others (Faulkner, *A Cinema* 136; Keller 947; Nieto Ferrando, *Posibilismos* 50; Zunzunegui 71–8).

Nueve cartas a Berta comprises the rebellious mindset – both aesthetic and political – that Geoffrey Nowell-Smith attributes to the European "new cinemas" of the 1960s (3). The film narrates the existential failure of the protagonist, Lorenzo Carvajal (Emilio Gutiérrez Caba), a college student who after a study abroad program in England returns to his native Salamanca. Lorenzo initially expresses his estrangement from his conservative family, from his friends and girlfriend, and even from the city – metaphorically evoking the traditional Spanish society under Franco – in letters read in voice-over to Berta, the daughter of an exiled

Spanish author with whom Lorenzo has had a romance in England. Patino strengthens the protagonist's feelings of alienation and existential loss with a plethora of visual disruptions that provoke the spectator's emotional detachment from the character. Patino hoped that spectators would experience the same sense of disillusionment and anguish as Lorenzo does in the film. The ultimate goal was to portray a harsh picture of Spanish society in the 1960s that would contradict the developmental euphoria of the regime's rhetoric. These formal disruptions include unusual choices in camera work, editing, and even the soundtrack with its "intrusive, irritating musical score and conflicts in dubbing between Lorenzo's voice in dialogue and voice-over" (Faulkner, *A Cinema* 136).

I wish to complement existing studies of this film by briefly highlighting the key role that Lorenzo's religious crisis has in his existential anguish and in his life choices. The importance of religion in Lorenzo's dissatisfaction is present throughout the film, as his girlfriend (Elsa Baeza) and mother (Mary Carrillo) interpret his absenteeism from Sunday Mass as a sign of his malaise. In the segment corresponding to the seventh letter, "Pretérito imperfecto," Lorenzo attends a spiritual retreat outside of Madrid with other college students. He hopes that the retreat will help him resolve his doubts about his faith and bring him closer to God, but it only serves to exacerbate his feeling of oppression. This is visually expressed by images of confinement. We hear Lorenzo sharing with Berta his joy about the possibility of finding a good and understanding God "sin Inquisición, sin miedos, sin vulgaridad" (without Inquisition, without fears, without vulgarity), but simultaneously we see him descending a staircase behind iron bars that are reminiscent of imprisonment. An editing cut takes us to a medium shot of Lorenzo sitting in his room and meditating in front of a crucifix while he expresses his desire to communicate directly with God. As he is articulating these thoughts, the camera tilts upward to capture a barred window that again suggests confinement.

Lorenzo somatizes his feeling of oppression through a stomach ache and difficulty in sleeping during the spiritual retreat. A speech by Father Echarri (Fernando Sánchez Polack) buries Lorenzo's hopes for a more modern type of Church, as the priest lectures the young pupils about the inferiority of science, reason, and any kind of intellectual activity in relation to the power of blind faith. The camera zooms in on the priest, which gives him a centrality in the composition that signifies the Church's overbearing presence in Spanish society, but this technique simultaneously isolates him visually while he says that "un intelectual está al borde de perder su alma por exceso de saber baldío" (an intellectual is on the verge of losing his soul due to an excess of waste knowledge).[1] Subtly, Patino visually performs what will soon be a reality check for the Spanish Church: the realization that it was out of touch with the theological currents throughout the Catholic world and, therefore, not in a position of spiritual leadership. The economy was not the only area that had suffered from Franco's autarky; Spain was also theologically underdeveloped, as attested by Father Echarri's backward views, and could no longer congratulate itself as the spiritual reserve of the Western world. Although Lorenzo's spiritual doubts lead him to abandon the retreat, he eventually capitulates to the teachings of Father Echarri, or at least chooses passive compliance with them by renouncing intellectual reflection. Instead of engaging Berta's enthusiastic thoughts about John XXIII and Vatican II, he declines further discussion about the update of the Church in the modern world by saying that "tampoco quiero indagar más ni estoy preparado para ello" (I don't want to delve into it and I don't feel prepared for that). Guided by Berta, Lorenzo could have redirected his spiritual crisis towards a renewed post–Vatican II faith. Instead, he prefers to stop asking himself the big questions and to stop questioning the authority of the pre-conciliar Church.

To help Lorenzo recover from an illness that is symptomatic of his existential angst, his parents send him to spend some time during Holy Week with his uncle (Manuel Domínguez), a rural priest. This section of the film is symbolically entitled "Un mundo feliz," an ironic intertextual reference to the Spanish title of Aldous Huxley's novel *Brave New World* (1932). If Huxley's acclaimed novel was an ironic jab at the excesses of the technological advances of modernity, Patino here inverts the target to satirically refer to the false happiness of the "bendito atraso" (blessed backwardness) in National-Catholic Spain. The time spent with his reactionary uncle, the representative of an old-fashioned preconciliar Church that has not gone through the *aggiornamento,* marks the turning point in Lorenzo's switch from rebellion to conformity. As he sits though a religious ceremony conducted by his uncle, he wonders, "y ¿por qué tengo yo que arreglar el mundo?" (Why do I have to fix the problems of the world?). In case Lorenzo had any further doubts, during a walking tour in the mountains his uncle lectures him on the advantages of the rural lifestyle over the corrupt modern urban civilization and proceeds to list a dismal state of affairs at the international level. He ends his speech by claiming the Iberian superiority as the spiritual reserve of the world over communist countries and Western capitalist nations, which are involved in violent conflicts in contrast to the peace Spaniards enjoy under Franco. Long shots of the characters chatting in an idyllic landscape in the mountains symbolically suggest Lorenzo's spiritual (and political) cleansing during his visit with his uncle. The implied message the village priest transmits to Lorenzo is the sacredness of the regime's foundational principles and, accordingly, the legitimacy of those who rule under those principles.

Patino thus articulates the religious factor as a choice between the retrograde Church with political ties to the regime – epitomized by Lorenzo's uncle and by Father Echarri – and a post–Vatican II renewed spirituality that Berta – the representative of modernity in a broad sense – tries to instil in Lorenzo. He tacitly accepts the familiar option by refusing to inquire further into the implications of the conciliar reform. Ultimately, Lorenzo decides to follow Father Echarri's advice and refuses to know too much. In the context of this film, knowledge equals religious dissension; non-reflexive faith is compliant bliss. Similarly, Lorenzo takes to heart his uncle's words and cuts his ties to the equally damaging "foreign" intrusions by renouncing his relationship with Berta – and with his French friends, whom Lorenzo's family declines to host – and by staying with his traditional Spanish girlfriend. Lorenzo's gradual loss of his rebellious spirit and his adaptation to the existential platitudes of provincial life in Salamanca are formally signposted by a change in the sound devices. As Sally Faulkner aptly notes, Lorenzo's conformism towards the end of the film goes together with a soothing formal effect that materializes in "the harmonization of diegetic and non-diegetic sound" and their alignment with the image in the final sequences (*A Cinema* 137). Lorenzo goes back to his family house in Salamanca and adapts to conservative values. In return, his parents reward him with a brand new television, which signifies his interpellation into the deceptive happiness of Spain's sacred technocracy and consumer society in the 1960s.

After the commercial failure of his second feature-length film, *Del amor y otras soledades* (1969), Basilio Martín Patino turned his back on the mainstream circuits of the industry and made three documentary films that were not conceived as a unified series but resulted in a sort of "intuitive trilogy" (Sanz Ferreruela, "Reconstruyendo" 492). The three films – *Canciones para después de una guerra, Queridísimos verdugos,* and *Caudillo* – had problems with censorship and could not be released until the post-Franco period. *Canciones* was a censorship scandal similar to the "*Viridiana* affair." As Patino explained in an interview, the film was initially approved by the censorship board. Patino was promised reimbursement of 40 per cent of the film's total costs and the "special interest" classification, which assured permission for the film to be exported and, moreover, to represent Spain at international festivals (Castro 319). But the film was never released in 1971 and instead suffered what Juan Antonio Pérez Millán calls a "witch hunt" ("caza de brujas") (121), and what Ernesto Pastor Martín refers to as a "Gordian knot" ("nudo gordiano") (287), motivated by a private screening for government officials at which President Carrero Blanco demanded that approval for release be revoked.

Canciones was quarantined for five years but did not lose its controversial aura. Once released in 1976, it suffered more attacks, although this time from left-wing critics, who expressed their disappointment with the ambiguity of the film and even regarded Patino as a retrograde filmmaker complicit with the regime (Font, "Canciones"). At a time when Spanish cinema was highly politicized, critics expected from Patino a frontal, literal attack on the regime. The subsequent releases of *Queridísimo verdugos* and *Caudillo* in 1977 elicited similar reactions from critics who unreasonably judged these films, made during the dictatorship, with a post-Franco lens. Even more recently, critics such as Augusto M. Torres have maintained this unfair assessment by reproaching Martín Patino for making politically ambiguous films. Torres considers *Caudillo* a film that was made to satisfy all parties, and one that supposedly criticized and praised the dictator in equal terms (141). Ironically enough, Patino made *Canciones* because of his disillusionment with the commercial pressures of the industry and with an artistic and ethical-political goal in mind, yet the recognition he obtained for this film was exactly the opposite of the one he probably anticipated. It was disapproved by both the right and the left; however, it was a commercial success with 830,911 spectators.

Canciones is a documentary film about the early post–Civil War years (between 1939 and 1954) that corresponds to the type that Bill Nichols calls "interactive documentary," one in which the filmmaker's point of view about the material becomes evident (33). Patino retrieves abundant archival materials, both filmic (available footage from newsreels and films) and non-filmic (magazine covers, newspaper clippings, photographs, and propagandistic pamphlets), and combines them with the evocative power of popular songs of the period. He employs a collage technique that he perfected during his years as a pioneer of advertising in Spain (Bellido López 69; Hopewell 127) to compose a sentimental yet caustic chronicle of the postwar years. Patino intended to reclaim the historical memory of the defeated in the Civil War while simultaneously unveiling the oppressive mechanisms of control that platforms of power used to subdue any dissenting position.

The key stylistic element of *Canciones* is the ironic discourse that ensues from the juxtaposition of contrasting images and from the dialectical opposition between the images and the soundtrack. Especially adroit is Patino's use of popular songs that were thought to be escapist entertainment complicit with the ruling regime in such a way that they become re-semanticized with corrosive meanings. This is why José Colmeiro discusses Patino's film as comparable to Manuel Vázquez Montalbán's project of recuperation of historical memory through popular culture in his poetry and in influential essays such as *Crónica sentimental de España* (1971) and *Cancionero general* (1972) (91). Recognizing the power of collective memory to bring communities together and to create social identities (Halbwachs), Patino prompts viewers to revisit popular songs and other materials from perspectives that differ from the official memory orchestrated by the Francoist regime. Popular songs, along with photographs and commemorations such as the Victory Parade of the Civil War, appear in *Canciones* as what Pierre Nora calls *lieux de mémoire* (sites of memory), which he defines as "any significant entity, whether material or non-material in nature, which by dint of human will or the work of time has become a symbolic element of the memorial heritage of any community" (xvii). Sites of memory can be places (archives, cities, and memorials, among others), concepts (commemorations and rituals), and objects (monuments and emblems) that become invested with symbolic meanings that bind together a community. Although sites of memory are typically associated with official memory, what Patino proposes with *Canciones* is to revisit those institutionalized sites in order to re-historicize them also in symbolic terms but with dissenting meanings. Carrero Blanco understood the danger of such a proposition, and this is why he banned the film from commercial release.

Among the inadmissible elements of *Canciones,* the new censorship file spotlighted the irreverent representation of religion and the Catholic Church (Pastor Martín 300). The public dimension of religion in the postwar years features prominently, and almost always negatively, in *Canciones*. The second segment includes a brief image of two nuns who smile while giving the fascist salute. Immediately thereafter, people surround a priest and small children kiss his hand. At the end of this segment, we see footage of ecclesiastical representatives among the presiding authorities in the Victory Parade in the streets of Madrid that commemorates the Nationalists' victory in the war. Notwithstanding what critics like Domènec Font and Augusto Torres have said, there is no ambiguity in the message that Patino sends in these initial stages of the film: he wants to accentuate that the Church chose to become a political accomplice of the regime.

Midway through the film, two sections are devoted entirely to the social influence of the Church. In section 23 a religious canticle accompanies images of the celebrations related to the "Congreso Eucarístico Internacional" held in Barcelona in 1952. We see a parade led by ecclesiastical authorities in the presence of civil and military officials in which footage of devotees kneeling down in religious fervour serves as the testament of the heyday of National-Catholicism. In disruptive fashion, Patino accompanies the joyous scenes with a female voice-over that laments the "depurations" of the moral conduct of citizens in the early postwar period and, by visual association, calls attention to the role of the Church in those infamous processes of supposedly moral, but in reality political, cleansing. The segment ends with a shot of Pope Pius XII clapping, which hints at the Vatican endorsement of the Francoist regime.

The Church's control over education is the topic of the segment 26. The song "La chunga" serves as background to a highly elaborated collage, inspired by the Soviet montage by collision, which creates shocking analogies and contrasts. Images related to strict classroom instruction are crosscut with images of leisure activities such as a puppet show, amusement park rides, and comic books. The voice-overs – one male and one female – create a sharp contrast to those images of entertainment. Apart from mentioning the fear of sin and hell that ecclesiastical educators instilled in the young pupils, these voices outline a long list of pious exercises students had to perform in the classroom, such as praying the rosary, spiritual retreats, novenas, Easter Triduum, and so on. The footage of the "fun activities" shows a recurrent pattern: people (both children and adults) spin around in numerous rotating circular platforms that include carousels, Ferris wheels, and other rides in amusement parks. Meanwhile, the lyrics of the song speak of the misfortune of a woman inexorably subjected to patriarchal control. In my view, the editing insinuates a diagnosis of the reasons for the infantilization of the Spanish population under Franco. The coercive religious education inculcates in children fears that limit their capacity to make free choices and to develop their critical thinking skills. The repetitive images of puppets that move like automatons reiterating the same gestures metaphorically evoke people's subordination – like the female character of the song – to a circular fate predetermined by the emasculating ecclesiastical powers. Through the collision of images and sounds, Patino seems to suggest that people never unshackle themselves from that religious indoctrination, as they live perpetually spinning around in the carousel of a life controlled by the hooks of National-Catholicism – just like Lorenzo in *Nueve cartas a Berta*.

Several segments throughout the documentary also spotlight how deeply ingrained religion was in the structures of the Spanish film industry in the 1940s and 1950s. Segments 24 and 32 include footage of the glamorous premieres of *La fe* (1947) and *Reina Santa* (1947), both films directed by Rafael Gil. Segment 30 includes the announcement of the premiere of *Locura de amor* (1948), followed by some images of the film in segment 39, along with footage from *Alba de América* (1951), *Agustina de Aragón* (1950), and *¡A mí la legión!* (1942), all of them directed by Juan de Orduña. The choice of directors and films was not arbitrary. Rafael Gil and Juan de Orduña were two of the most acclaimed pro-regime filmmakers and made a number of confessional films that touted the spirit of National-Catholicism. As always, Patino's editing choices to insert these references in the overall narrative were meticulously planned. He juxtaposed the footage from the premiere of *Reina Santa* with images from *Ladri di biciclette* (Vittorio de Sica, 1948). Patino wanted the viewer to realize that, while Spanish cinema was flooded with cardboard and propagandistic historical melodramas, other national cinemas were producing groundbreaking cinematic ventures, such as Italian neo-realism. The montage from Juan de Orduña's films was cut together with images of activities of the Falange and its Sección Femenina, thus calling attention to the ties of Orduña and his confessional films to the institutional apparatuses of the regime.

Towards the end of the film, there are two more meaningful references to the impact of religion on the public sphere of Spain under Franco. Section 45 includes a newspaper clipping announcing the Vatican's approval of Opus Dei as a Secular Institute in the late 1940s. This shot appears amid contrasting images of, on the one hand, fancy bars and clubs with English-language names that evince the penetration of American influence in Spain and, on the other, poor farmers eating with their hands. Another newspaper clipping offers predictions about the positive impact of the tourism boom on the national balance of payments and the Madrid stock market. The segment highlights the notorious association of the Opus Dei organization with financial elites and their disdain for the poor classes. Also, it foreshadows the role of the Opus Dei technocrats in the modernization of the economy during the development years. Close-ups of ragged-looking farmers and of situations of extreme poverty ironically remind spectators of the gap between the rich and the poor and, consequently, allude to the dark side of the developmental triumphalism of the regime. In between these images, newspaper clippings announce the imminent death of Stalin and the communist disaster of the Korean War (1950–3). The song "A lo loco" (literally "wildly") adds yet another ironic meaning that emerges from the combination of visual and aural codes. In this case, it helps to insinuate that Spain's switch from the autarkic to the technocratic economic model was a reckless march towards rampant (pro-American) capitalism orchestrated by the Opus Dei technocrats that neglected the needs of the disenfranchised populations. The last meaningful religious reference of the documentary appears in section 47. Newspaper clippings announce the signing of the concordat with the Vatican in 1953 while we hear the hymn of Catholic Action, a lay Catholic organization created to foster Catholic influence in society. This segment ends with images of Pope Pius XII and Franco that typify the configuration of the Catholic state led by civil and ecclesiastical powers in equal terms.

Basilio Martín Patino also denounces the political entanglement between the regime and the Church in *Caudillo*. If *Canciones* documented the silenced memory of the vanquished in the early postwar years, *Caudillo* goes back to account for the period between the beginning of the military hostilities and the end of the war. Like *Canciones*, it is a documentary built as a collage of diverse archival materials such as footage of the war, interviews and testimonies of participants in the military operations, photographs, and newspaper clippings. Also like *Canciones*, its corrosive political message derives from the sense of irony created by the crafty editing of the materials. Although the use of a voice-over narrator could initially suggest a sense of "objectivity," thus bringing *Caudillo* closer to the "expository mode" following Bill Nichols's typology of documentaries (34–8), this impression is instantly undercut by the unexpected juxtapositions that upend the meanings of historical events and materials pertaining to the Francoist side of the war. The film also includes plenty of footage from the other side – including testimonies about communists and anarchists – but these materials are not subjected to Patino's ironic inversions and keep their original propagandistic illocutionary force. Despite the aforementioned accusations of ambiguity, Patino showed his political stripes quite explicitly with his editing choices.

As a matter of fact, Patino wastes no time in laying out the premises of his project. The film opens with an extreme long shot of a town with a prominent church tower and then cuts to footage in black and white of wounded soldiers entering a battleground, alternating with shots in colour of a town in ruins. A travelling shot gives us a tour of those ruins and identifies them: they are the famous ruins of Belchite, a small town in the province of Zaragoza that was the site of the Battle of Belchite of the Civil War between 24 August and 6 September 1937. A voice-over narrator comes into play by stating that "hubo una vez un hombre enviado por Dios para salvar a España" (once upon a time a man was sent by God to save Spain), and we immediately see what I identified in previous chapters as a "celestial shot": a low-angle shot shows skylight, apparently of heavenly origin, that comes through a hole in the ruined church roof and is evocative of the providential intervention in reality that the voice-over suggests. The combination of the soundtrack and contrasting images invites viewers to establish a causative relationship between past and present and ironically implies that the providential saviour, Francisco Franco, led Spain to its destruction.

To a certain extent, Patino is not exaggerating, since Franco was indeed responsible for the state of the ruins in Belchite. The Battle of Belchite became a symbolic episode of epic containment of the Nationalist soldiers who were besieged by the Republican army (Thomas 704–6). After the Civil War, Franco ordered that the ruins of Belchite should be kept in memory of the sacrifice and resilience of his soldiers, and he sent left-wing war prisoners to rebuild Belchite on an adjacent site (the town we see in the initial long shot). His line of thinking was that, since the Republicans destroyed the town with their siege, they should rebuild it with their own hands. Franco made Belchite a *lieu de mémoire* symbolically endowed with the siege mentality that was so important to revamp "Spanishness" from the Francoist angle. Sites of memory like Belchite were used not only to celebrate the crusade spirit of the war but also to dramatize in heroic terms the reality of the postwar years: Spain's self-imposed isolation from the rest of the world during the autarkic period. The polyvalent applications of the "siege" metaphor explain, as Núria

Triana-Toribio has noted, its recurrent presence in the high-profile historical films that are known as *cine de cruzada* in the 1940s and early 1950s (44–50).

Unlike the 1940s historical melodramas, Patino's film does not evoke the siege of Belchite to commemorate the purifying force of violence that was ideologically appropriated to activate a renewed sense of national consciousness. Instead, Patino undermines the traditional type of legitimacy of the Franco regime that was grounded on political theology. This first sequence sets the tone for Patino's intentions in relation to his subject matter. It highlights yet ironically twists – by associating it with ruins and destruction – the meaning of two of the main tenets sustaining the regime: the conceptualization of the Civil War as a religious crusade and the providential nature of Franco's leadership. These two elements of the ideological crust of the regime are redundantly evoked throughout the film. Shortly after the sequence of the Belchite ruins, the voice-over narrator states that the Nationalists' coup d'etat "era otra vez la España que desde hace mil años levanta la espada en defensa de los valores espirituales y de la ortodoxia religiosa. Siempre en nombre de Dios" (was again the Spain that for a thousand years has raised the sword to defend spiritual values and religious orthodoxy. Always in the name of God). A number of statements along these lines are backed by the testimony of ex-combatants who declare that the ideas of God and the Fatherland were the motivations that urged them to fight in defence of traditional values that seemed under attack.

Previous approaches to this film have criticized Patino's excessive insistence on supernatural notions of providence (Sanz Ferreruela, "Reconstruyendo" 504; Nahum García Martínez 198). More than a flaw in the planning of the film, I believe that the redundancy of the religiously infused propagandistic messages is an attempt to imitate the regime's own overuse of them. The repetitive images of the Church's political alliance with Franco elicit the same effect. Numerous sequences show footage of public commemorations in which we see military and ecclesiastical authorities together, including images of several open-air Masses celebrated during the Civil War to venerate the Nationalists' victories. The film closes with yet another instance of the religious justification of Franco's persona and his right to exercise power. While we see an image of Franco receiving the *Cruz Laureada de San Fernando*, the narrator reminds the viewer, one more time, that "era nada menos que Franco, caudillo de España por la gracia de Dios" (It was none other than Franco, *caudillo* by the grace of God). The point is to bombard – pun intended – the viewer with the same verbose rhetoric with which the regime brainwashed the Spanish population to justify overturning the democratically elected government of the Second Republic. Patino hoped that an active viewer would get the ironic trick of his co-optation of the regime's iterative discourse, in the sense that it brought to the fore how the regime's ideological varnish operated like a catchy song on a top-forty station: it was aired repeatedly until it became a familiar tune that everyone recognized, some worshipped, most people unconsciously sang along with, but few dared to question for its lack of substance.

Irony turns into caricature when Patino focuses on the figure of Franco. *Caudillo* was conceptualized as an anti-hagiographic documentary about Francisco Franco to demystify his profile as the heroic saint whom God sent to redeem Spain from the communist and the atheist threat. In so doing, Patino articulated *Caudillo* as the filmic nemesis of Sáenz de Heredia's *Franco, ese hombre*. As I mentioned before, he inundated the narrative with references and voice-over commentaries about Franco's messianic nature but juxtaposed them with footage that showed death and destruction as the outcome of Franco's actions – an aspect omitted by *Franco, ese hombre*. After reiterating, one more time, that the war was a religious crusade led by Franco, the narrator proceeds to outline the material and human devastation his leadership caused: five hundred thousand households and one hundred towns destroyed, two million prisoners, five hundred thousand exiles, and one million deaths. Like Sáenz de Heredia's hagiographic documentary, Patino traces Franco's military trajectory leading up to his commanding role in the Civil War and mentions his miraculous salvation from enemy attacks. Franco's recovery is attributed to his *baraka*, a term that Moors used to refer to the good luck that accompanied leaders who seemed to be chosen by God. But the almost comical fashion Patino uses to explain this supernatural intervention greatly differs from the reverential treatment of Franco's salvation in *Franco, ese hombre*.

Moreover, Patino ridicules Franco's personal life and even his physical figure. More so than its anti-model, *Franco, ese hombre*, Patino's documentary displays Franco in a number of intimate and family-related settings. Once again, sarcasm and caricature shape these episodes. As Alberto Nahum García Martínez contends, the scene that covers Franco's wedding demystifies his heroic military figure and mocks a key moment of his life by using "una música acelerada y de letra grotesca – *El barberillo de Lavapiés*" (quick-paced music with grotesque lyrics – *El barberillo de Lavapiés*) (184). Patino also reproduces some of Franco's public speeches to spotlight his affected and high-pitched voice as well as his unimpressive physical presence. In one of the multiple occasions in which the narrator underlines Franco's immaculate Catholic pedigree by stating that, according to Pius XII, he was the golden boy of the Church among all the heads of state, the narrator also diminishes Franco's eminence right away by referring to his short physical stature: "Era, pese a su estatura, un verdadero gigante" (Franco was, despite his short height, a true giant).

All in all, *Canciones para después de una guerra* and *Caudillo* were pioneering efforts of what Jorge Nieto Ferrando calls the "destape documental de los setenta" (the documentary explosion of the seventies), referring to a mini-boom of political documentaries, including high-profile ones like Jaime Chávarri's *El desencanto* (1976), made in the first years of the transition (*Posibilismos* 89). Many of these documentaries looked back at the Francoist period from a critical point of view to denounce the Church's endorsement of the regime. This was the case of *Raza, el espíritu de Franco* (Gonzalo Herralde, 1977), which also demystified Franco's saintly figure, and *La vieja memoria* (Jaime Camino, 1977), which mentions the Church's condemnation of the Second Republic and its sympathy for the regime. As with Patino's *Caudillo,* what these documentaries failed to offer was a less biased position that would have also accounted for all the reasons why the Catholic Church sided with Nationalists – for example, the anti-clerical campaigns during the Second Republic. During the politicized years of the transition, the priority was not to offer a comprehensive, nuanced view of the subject, but to restore the memory of the defeated. This is why these documentary efforts addressed religion to trace an ideological line that separated two seemingly irreconcilable sides, and they pointed the finger at the ecclesiastical hierarchy for having chosen the wrong side of the war.

The Anti-Clerical Legacy of Buñuel in Carlos Saura

Scholars of Spanish cinema unanimously consider Carlos Saura the closest heir of Luis Buñuel (Quintana, "A Poetics" 87; Sánchez Vidal 20). More than any of his fellow post-war directors, Saura productively integrated Buñuel's filmic vision and cultural sensibilities into his own auteurist universe. Apart from inheriting Buñuel's use of dream sequences and his anti-clerical critique, perversely mixed with eroticism, Saura also took on Buñuel's "role of the troublemaker whose films disturbed the uneasy calm of the 'peace of Franco'" (Higginbotham 77). These three traces of Buñuel's legacy in Saura's work are especially patent in the last two films he made under Franco, *La prima Angélica* (1974) and *Cría cuervos* (1975).[2]

La prima Angélica was the first film to openly talk about the Civil War from the point of view of the defeated (D'Lugo 166; Jurado Morales 365; Sánchez Vidal 63). The film narrates the trip that Luis (José Luis López Vázquez), a middle-aged bachelor who lives in Barcelona, makes to Segovia to transport his mother's remains to be buried in the family tomb. The physical journey also becomes a journey into his traumatic memories of the war, which compel him to analyse the reasons for his current state of immaturity. Luis is one of the paradigmatic examples that Marsha Kinder conceptualized as "the children of Franco," characters that were almost alter egos of a generation of filmmakers who saw themselves as "childlike adults who are obsessed with distorted visions of the past" ("The Children" 59). During his stay with Aunt Pilar (Josefina Díaz), Luis encounters objects, situations, places, and people that take him back to his memories of the war and early post-war days. Instead of employing the conventional flashback, Saura plays with both moments, the past and the present, as if they were part of the same temporal plane, often without making any technical transitions between them. López Vázquez plays both the adult Luis and the eight-year-old Luisito, as present and past memories intermingle. The splitting of the character, first of all, emphasizes the mental infantilization suffered by "the children of Franco" in their adulthood, and, moreover, it suggests the scenario of individual and collective stagnation after more than three decades under an authoritarian regime.

This innovative cinematic rendering of memory and history goes hand-in-hand with an equally distinct editing style. Apart from conflating the temporal planes of the film, Saura also violates continuity style by presenting more than once events that happen only once in the story (i.e., the scene of the bombing of the school, the road stop of Luis and his family on their way to Segovia). To make sure that narrative connections are clear for the spectator despite these disruptions to the temporal order of events, Saura tactically deploys graphic patterns of editing. A prominent example of this appears in the transition from a point-of-view shot of Miguel's wounded leg from the perspective of the child Luisito to a close-up of Anselmo's leg in the diegetic present of the story (both Miguel and Anselmo are played by the same actor, Fernando Delgado). Typically used in non-narrative films to make abstract associations between shots (Bordwell and Thompson 301), graphic editing here is put at the service of narrative. The approximate graphic continuity in camera distance, framing, and lighting of both shots of the legs informs the spectator about the subjective process taking place in Luis's psyche by which he associates his brutal uncle Miguel (who used to batter him as a kid) with his cousin-in-law Anselmo. More than visually connecting two characters, the graphic continuity also has ideological implications: it links the brutal fascist who won the war to the representative of the new cadres of the regime in the development years. Discontinuity editing is used, paradoxically, to depict ideological continuity in the regime.

Another narrative alternative to the continuity system deployed by Saura to make temporal connections between present and past is the salient use of the jump cut. As abrupt changes between two shots of the same subjects or objects that "are cut together but are not sufficiently different in camera distance and angle," jump cuts typically result in a perceptible jump on the screen (Bordwell and Thompson 303). For the sake of narrative continuity, the editing style of mainstream films tends to avoid jump cuts by including abundant shot/reverse shots and by following the thirty-degree rule (making sure that every camera position is changed by at least thirty degrees in relation to the preceding one). As with the graphic editing, jump cuts are mostly associated with non-narrative films, for they convey an impression of fragmentation of time and space. In addition, they tend to produce a disorienting effect in the spectator, who is "troubled by the noncausality of the images and the narrative" (Hayward 205). But in *La prima Angélica* Saura uses this technical device for narrative purposes. During Luis's first visit as an adult to his old school, he hears the sound of drums and a flute, which, along with the contemplation of a painting featuring the martyr Saint Sebastian riddled with arrows, leads him back to another episode of his childhood. The painting serves as a temporal bridge for the two moments. From Luis's subjective point of view, a zoom lens brings the painting into a close-up, followed by a jump cut to the same painting without changing the camera angle but with a change in lighting (a darkened setting with very soft fill light). The shift in lighting is the visual cue to signal the temporal transition and, therefore, to guide spectators to a previous moment in the narrative. After zooming out from the close-up of the painting, the camera tilts to show a group of boys and men dressed as Roman soldiers as part of a martial parade that accompanies a religious ceremony. As they are about to enter the chapel, Luisito is chosen by a priest to stand guard next to a sculpture of a *Cristo yacente* (dead Christ). The priest approaches him to remind him: "Recuerda, inmovilidad absoluta, como si fueras de mármol" (Remember, absolute immobility, as if you were made of marble). Like Saint Sebastian and Jesus Christ, Luisito appears as a martyr, embodying in this case the suffering of a generation of Spaniards who were petrified by the immobilizing ecclesiastical machinery in the post-war years.

The scene insinuates an identification of Luisito with both relics of religious martyrdom. It is important to note the air of eroticized violence that pervades the whole scene. Images of Saint Sebastian's arrow-pierced and semi-naked body have inspired many interpretations of his figure in (homo)erotic terms – most notably, Derek Jarman's film *Sebastianne* (1976). In fact, the combination of erotic nudity and tortured flesh – symbolizing the torture of closeted sexuality – has made Saint Sebastian "the patron saint of homosexual men" since at least the nineteenth century (Kaye 86). Similarly, the *Cristo yacente* belongs to an influential tradition of religious art that emerged in the baroque period in Spain. Commissioned by King Philip III, Gregorio Fernández sculpted the first *Cristo yacente* in 1614–15, leading to a school of followers and imitators. As Noël Valis suggests in her perceptive interpretation of this altarpiece, the sculpture exudes an air of "disturbing beauty derived from violent, protracted death" (57–8). The images of both the dead, yet desirable, Jesus and of the perforated Saint Sebastian incarnate the repressed sexuality inherent in the representations of violence that appear in a great deal of Christian art. Interestingly, Saura immediately accentuates the sexual subtext of the sequence. Angélica (María Clara Fernández) walks into the chapel with her mother. Once she sits down for Mass, Angélica and Luisito exchange flirtatious looks, imbuing the scene with a flux of desire that viewers already know that Father Florentino will censor and punish. Sexuality becomes attached for Luisito, and by extension for several generations of Spaniards, to sin, violence, and death. It is no wonder that the adult Luis is a forty-something bachelor whose sexual life seems permanently damaged by a backward religious indoctrination, condemned to recalling his position of inactive voyeur as a child who spied on his aunt (Lola Cardona) while she was bathing.

Images of martyrdom during Francoism were typically associated with the cult of sacrificial violence that the neo-Catholic revival used as a strategy to uphold the status quo. However, Saura divests martyrdom of pious connotations. The suffering of the martyrs Luis and Angélica, forced to separate for life and to renounce their feelings, leads to physical – Luisito battered by his uncle Miguel – and psychological torture resulting in trauma. Also pointless are the sufferings of Luisito's aunt, the nun played by Julieta Serrano who has self-inflicted sores on her hands that she offers to Jesus Christ in exchange for Christ's converting the political and anti-clerical stands of Luisito's father. Luis remembers her after he notices the absence of a painting of a crucified nun – another religious image featuring mortified flesh as a way of sublimating and, thus, repressing sexual desires – that used to be in his aunt's house. During a nightmare that functions as an explicit homage to the use of dream sequences in Buñuel's films, the vision of a tortured nun haunts Luis. The nun – a younger version of his own aunt – walks towards his bed with one hand holding a candle, the other hand showing an open wound, a metal lock sealing her lips, and a worm coming out of her habit. By illuminating the scene in low-key, with a hard light on the creepy spectre of the nun and almost no fill or back lights, Saura creates a chiaroscuro effect that underlines the sinister connotations on Luis's psyche. The image of the lock preventing the nun from speaking also suggests that both the vanquished and the victors of the war were doomed to muteness and lack of agency. While the former were obliged to be silent witnesses of the horror inflicted upon them, the latter could only utter trite ideological messages imposed from above.

La prima Angélica is indeed full of religious iconography mixed with references to eroticism and violence that by cumulative effect reiterate the overbearing and emasculating presence of religion in the education of post-war children, including their sentimental education, as remembered by the adult Luis. As Nathan Richardson has observed, this is spatially represented by depicting the church, the religious school, and the family home as the three disciplinary spaces in charge of producing subjectivity, even if sometimes with contradictory effects (*Postmodern* 119). The interrogation scene with Father Florentino indicates that the Church was the main guarantor of a retrograde morality that inhibited the nascent sexuality of children and instilled in them a paralysing fear of sin. The interrogation alternates low-angle shots that magnify the figure of the infuriated priest with high-angle shots that underline the fear of the terrified Luisito. The sombre air of the scene is further reinforced by the low-key lighting treatment, with a hard key light on the priest and on Luisito but tenuous fill and background illumination, creating a shadowy effect and a feeling of confinement. This lighting treatment is emphasized even more by the contrast with the preceding scene, in which Luisito and Angélica are flirting in an open field, with the resultant connotations of freedom and openness in opposition to the visual imprisonment of interior scenes. Also, as with the case of Miguel/Anselmo, the same actor, José Luis Heredia, plays the role of the authoritarian priest, Father Florentino, who interrogates Luisito for having kissed his cousin Angélica, and of Felipe Sagún, the priest who facilitates the interment of Luis's mother. By using the same actor, Saura implies is that there is continuity between the crusade Church and the Church of the late Franco period.

Two more scenes are crucial in conveying the coercive impact of the Catholic Church on children and the endurance of that coercion in the last phase of the regime. In a second visit back to his old school, a travelling shot shows Luis walking down some stairs on his way to the chapel. The camera is situated at a considerable distance so that four layers of iron bars of the staircases separate the spectator from the figure of Luis, which visually suggests the incarceration that Luisito must have felt while studying in the religious institution. Luis enters the chapel, sees the altar with images of the crucifixion and the Virgin Mary, and affirms that "más o menos esto está igual" (this remains more or less the same), which hints at a broader immobility of ecclesiastical institutions. Another important scene to suggest religious oppression is one towards the end of the film in which a priest lectures young pupils about the meaning of divine punishment in the afterlife for those who die in sin. The parable he uses is the story of a bombing of a school by the Republican air forces in a Nationalist zone, which causes the death of an eleven-year-old child in the playground. As the priest wonders if the dead boy was God-fearing and avoided sin, the camera shows the priest in an enlarging low-angle shot that, combined with the shadowy lighting (in low-key, with weak fill and background lights creating ominous shadows in the classroom), intensifies the fear he provokes in the young students, including Luisito, as Saura offers individual close-ups of their reactions. Again, to emphasize the gloomy air conveyed by the lighting and framing patterns, Saura chooses to edit this scene in stark contrast with the previous one, another outdoor scene in which Luis/Angélica and Luisito/Angélica kiss each other on the roof of the building. The recurrent association of open outdoor areas with freedom and healthy sexuality and interior spaces in the religious school and in the family house with imprisonment and coercion becomes a powerful motif that epitomizes the ideological message of the film.

An editing cut takes viewers from the sermon to another recollection of the scene of the bombing of the school refectory with which the film began – this time with diegetic sound and no slow motion – which suggests, as Marvin D'Lugo notes, that "Luis sees the sermon as a kind of framing device for the scene of the bombing" (124). The re-enactment of these repressed memories appears to help Luis grasp the sociopolitical implications of events that he has thus far internalized as shameful traumas. That is, Luis "is able to perceive a perceptual distance from his memories" (121), and this allows him to rationalize their causes and consequences. This recognition, however, does not seem to lead him anywhere other than to escape from that past. Saura renders Luis's catharsis in less than optimistic terms. There is no clue that Luis's traumatic memories will be healed, just as there is no prospect for a change at a national level. As Nathan Richardson has summarized, this film reveals "each and every space in late-Francoist Spain as completely locked into a stifling hierarchical system of power" (*Postmodern* 114). Through editing choices, composition, and lighting patterns, Saura exposes the coercive modus operandi of National-Catholicism and the emptiness surrounding the religious fervour attached to a traditional view of Spanish history. Furthermore, he leaves no room for hope, as he suggests that Spanish society continues to be subjugated to the same institutions of repressive power.

Many regard *La prima Angélica* as the most audacious of Saura's politically charged films of the late Franco period. Tom Whittaker goes even further, for he deems the film "the most incendiary of Querejeta's productions" (13), while José Jurado Morales argues that it "was instrumental in undermining the Franco regime" (367). Apart from the daring thematic elements and cinematic properties that I have shown, the seditious fame of the film was largely due to the unique context of its reception. The case of *La prima* was comparable to the other two biggest censorship scandals during the late Franco period, Luis Buñuel's *Viridiana* and Patino's *Canciones*. In fact, Diego Galán wrote an entire book telling the tortuous story of its approval by the censorship board and the attacks the film endured from right-wing extremist groups. The first two drafts of the script were rejected, and the third one was accepted pending a number of required modifications to be made during shooting (*Venturas* 42–3). Upon watching the final product, the censorship board approved it for release and selected it to represent Spain at Cannes, but without granting the film the "special interest" classification that provided state subsidies, because Saura neglected most of the requested amendments. Among those, Saura did not cut the most controversial scene, involving a wounded soldier dressed in Falangist uniform, whose plaster cast forces his arm into a permanent fascist salute.

Also, Saura did not follow the warning of the censorship file that stipulated that he would not treat characters as political, religious, or military symbols (Hernández Les 193). *La prima* was apparently not good enough for special interest classification, yet it was selected for Cannes, where the director won the Grand Jury Award.

The case of *La prima Angélica* proved the contradictions behind the *aperturismo* that Carlos Arias Navarro announced in his inaugural speech as Spain's newly appointed president on 12 February 1974. In that speech he promised a number of liberal reforms that immediately became known as "el espíritu del 12 de febrero." The reformist spirit of February, however, faded away in March, when a number of political crises led the Arias administration to revert back to repressive measures. Among those crises, three stood out. The first one was the "Añoveros affair," caused by a sermon of the bishop of Bilbao that contained a defence of Basque cultural identity. The political turmoil caused by this scandal threatened to fracture the already tense situation between Church and state, as Arias Navarro tried to expel the prelate from Spain, and the Church hierarchy responded by backing Monsignor Añoveros and by threatening to excommunicate Arias Navarro. Franco intervened and forced Arias to backpedal (Barrera, *Historia* 46; Payne 205; Tusell 416). The second political crisis emerged from the execution of the Catalan anarchist Salvador Puig Antich on 2 March 1974, which provoked an international uproar against the Franco regime (Preston 766). The third was the reaction of the conservative clique of the regime, the so-called bunker, against the decision of the minister of information, Pío Cabanillas, to allow the media to report on the "Carnation Revolution" that ended the pro-Catholic authoritarian regime of Salazar in Portugal (Barrera, *Historia* 47). In just a few months, the spirit of February had been buried.

This context of political turmoil explains the aggressive reaction of right-wing groups to the premiere of *La prima Angélica*. A group of young men tried to steal footage of the film while it was being screened at the Cine Amaya in Madrid. Because of this unfortunate event, a unit of police officers protected its opening at the Cine Balmes in Barcelona. However, that protection did not deter extremists, as a bomb exploded in the movie theatre two months after the film's premiere (Jurado Morales 359). In order to prevent further incidents, and possibly also because of political lobbying by the most conservative factions of the regime, *La prima Angélica* was withdrawn from exhibition and from distribution on 14 July 1974 (Galán, *Venturas* 145). Despite this deplorable attack on civil liberties, right-wing extremists ended up benefiting this film, at least in commercial terms. The news about the political scandal drove audiences to the theatres, and *La prima Angélica* became the first hit of the Querejeta factory with a total count of 1,410,361 spectators (Hernández Les 311).

La prima Angélica became a point of contention between the *aperturista* group of the minister Pío Cabanillas and the so-called *inmovilistas,* which ended with the political defeat of the former and the resignation of Cabanillas as minister. The political co-opting of this film called attention to the increasing fracture between reformist and conservative sides that would lead to the splintering of pro-regime factions and eventually to their political demise after the death of Franco. As I have been arguing throughout this book, an important factor in this tense political scenario was the escalating disaffection of the Church with the political platforms of the regime. Ironically enough, *La prima Angélica* was not attacked for bringing to the fore the schism between state and Church or for displaying the dissident sectors within the Church that collaborated with forces opposed to the regime. Rather, it triggered violent assaults for representing the memory of the "crusade Church" that allied with the winners of the Civil War and for suggesting that things had not changed much in forty years.

The publicity surrounding the release of *La prima Angélica* boosted the commercial run of Saura's next film, *Cría cuervos* (1,292,417 spectators). This film also deals with memory and trauma – individual and collective – in relation to repression under Franco, and also calls attention to the adverse role religion had in causing that trauma. In this case, the focus is on a family representing the "winners" of the war. The protagonist is a nine-year-old child, Ana (Ana Torrent), who exemplifies the hardship suffered by Spanish women during Francoism due to the conservative environment and the strict religious education in which they were brought up. For many critics, her story is one of capitulation to the authoritarian forces that have shaped her identity (Edwards, *Indecent* 98; Evans 22; Medina 136). Despite her rebellion against such an oppressive setting and against the expectations to become a traditional woman, critics brand her as a helpless victim who ultimately succumbs to those forces (Evans 17) and adheres to the lessons of her conservative religious education (Deveny 220; Hopewell 139). The portrayal of the negative effects of religious education on female subjectivity is especially explicit in the character of Ana's mother (Geraldine Chaplin). She is a submissive wife who gave up her professional career and her talent as a piano player. When she is about to die in a bed with a large crucifix mounted above the headboard, she tells Ana: "Todo es mentira. No hay nada" (It is all a lie. There is nothing). Ana (with the spectator) sees blood emanating from her groin area, and, as Elizabeth Scarlett notes, the mother conveys to her daughter a sense of existential emptiness and her feeling that she has been sacrificed "on the altar of motherhood, with her reproductive organs plagued by a metaphorical illness one assumes is ovarian or uterine cancer" (108). The death of Ana's father is also connected to Catholic iconography, since Ana finds his inert body on the bed in a position that Scarlett interprets as similar to the *Cristo yacente* (107).

Other critics would have us read Ana's story in positive terms as suggestive of a metaphorical emancipation from the repressive past for post-Franco Spain (D'Lugo 130; Hardcastle 399; Stone 101). Jo Labanyi regards the resolution of the film as a "happy end" that she links to a "modernization narrative" in the broader national context ("Memory" 98). In the final sequence, Ana and her sisters abandon the family house to go back to school after the summer break. By leaving the family house, Ana is also leaving the environment causing her trauma. A travelling shot in high angle shows the three sisters walking in a noisy street and passing several billboard signs announcing commercial products. This travelling shot emphasizes movement over the paralysis within the family house, and the noise, traffic, and billboards are cues of Spain's modernization. Saura seems to suggest that, like Ana, Spain is leaving behind repressive traditions and walking along the path of modernization. Yet, as the three sisters reach their destination, nuns are waiting for them in front of the religious school, thereby implying that the girls are entering another disciplinary space that will shape their subjectivity. This ambiguity of the film's ending makes it hard, as in the case of *La prima,* to draw a definitive hopeful conclusion for Ana's (and Spain's) future. The vagueness surrounding the scenes of adult Ana (also played by Geraldine Chaplin) reinforces this point. We do not know anything about her life as an adult, and she seems far from having resolved her trauma. If anything, the adult Ana looks and sounds just as confused as the nine-year-old Ana. For all we know, she is still trying to figure things out. And that is all we know, because Saura's indirect style leaves a convenient ellipsis here that furnishes no verdicts about Ana's development and about the successful completion of a coming-of-age allegory for post-Franco Spain. Elizabeth Scarlett reads this uncertainty as a dissident gesture against "the false security" of the pro-regime religious films and the conservative gender codes with which they enticed women to sacrifice themselves as repositories of society's moral values "in exchange for eternal reward" (110).

The only certain thing is that for Carlos Saura, just as for Basilio Martín Patino, religion was a coercive factor hampering subjectivity. As we have seen, both auteurs engaged the religious question filtered through the memory of the Civil War and early Francoist period to point out the ubiquitous and deleterious effect of religion on their education. For Saura and Patino, to talk about religion was to talk about the institutional power of the crusade Church and, moreover, to articulate a frontal attack against that power. The visual styles of their acclaimed films recurrently linked religion to oppression, confinement, and even death through editing choices, composition, framing, and lighting patterns. Unlike Buñuel, however, their critique of institutionalized religion was not accompanied by an exploration of the possibility that spirituality, once free from the constraints of rigid doctrine and authoritarian hierarchies, might have a creative function within the modern world. Also, it is surprising that, given their concern with criticizing the confessional status of the Spanish state, neither Saura nor Patino – except for a brief mention in *Canciones* – decided to delve into the role of the Opus Dei organization in connection to platforms of political power from the 1950s on. Other young directors associated with the NCE did, and this is where I turn in the next section.

Uncovering Opus Dei

The political domain was not the only site in the public sphere of late Francoism where one can notice the impact of the Opus Dei organization. The tentacles of what its critics call "Octopus Dei" also worked their way into the cultural field (Hutchinson 163; Orbaneja Aragón 12). Some of the platforms associated with Opus Dei included the publishing companies Rialp and Magisterio Español, the magazines *Mundo Cristiano* and *Telva,* and the business weekly *Actualidad Económica.* Within the film industry, important venues such as the production companies Procusa and Ariel, the distribution company Dipenfa-Filmayer, the Cine Club Monterols, and the film journal *Documentos Cinematográficos* were somewhat linked to Opus Dei.[3] Despite these and other connections to the field of cultural production, Opus Dei flew under the radar when it came to representations within cultural products. In this sense, it will not take us long to make an inventory of films that directly addressed the Opus Dei organization during the Francoist regime. Apart from the brief mention in Patino's *Canciones*, only three other films come to my mind: *El buen amor* (Francisco Regueiro, 1963), *La casa sin fronteras* (Pedro Olea, 1972), and *La trastienda* (Jordi Grau, made in 1975, though released in 1976). And the three of them, regrettably, have gone barely noticed in the history of Spanish cinema.

The main explanation for this representational scarcity is most likely Opus Dei's infamous secrecy. Opus Dei's founder, José María Escrivá de Balaguer, always claimed that it was easy to find out about the organization (*Conversaciones* 56). The reality was, however, that its constitution remained sealed until 1982 even to the majority of its members, and members were instructed not to reveal their status or the names of other members, as stipulated by articles 190 and 191 of that internal constitution (Michael Walsh 120). Opus Dei's justification for this secrecy, which they prefer to call "strategy of discretion" (Hutchinson 105), is the apostolate. Discretion ensures maximum efficiency in their aggressive recruiting practices, "fishing" in the Opus internal lingo (Michael Walsh 162), as Escrivá himself wrote in *Camino* (1934), the foundational spiritual text of Opus Dei: "If you hold your tongue, you'll gain greater effectiveness in your apostolic undertakings" (maxim 648, *The Way* 152). Opus Dei proved to be savvy in using media channels, including those of the film industry, to influence public opinion, while at the same time keeping its own public exposure to the minimum.

Censorship also helped Opus Dei to keep a low profile. For all the liberal promise of the new *Ley de Prensa* (1966) that Fraga crafted, its reactive rather than proactive course of action allowed platforms of power to exercise even more control over the field of cultural production. This was especially patent during the heyday of the political infiltration of Opus Dei technocrats into the monochromatic government (1969–73), when no critical perspective on Opus Dei was allowed to be published, and if any was, it was immediately wiped away. For example, Luis Carandell documents that Josep Dalmau's *Contrapunts al Camí de l'Opus Dei* (1969), a spiritual response to Escrivá's *Camino*, was sequestered immediately after its publication, and it took a while until it could be re-released. Other critical perspectives on Opus Dei had to wait until 1974, once the Opus Dei technocrats were no longer occupying influential political positions, to get the green light for publication, such as Evangelina Jardiel's *¿Por qué no es usted del Opus Dei?* and Alberto Moncada's *El Opus Dei. Una interpretación* (Carandell 32). The Opus Dei intelligentsia again proved their political dexterity by appropriating the legal framework implemented by their political rivals – Fraga's press law – to micromanage their own public image.

Of course, the success of the strategy of discretion/secrecy has not come without a price, for it has triggered a suspicious attitude about the true colours of Opus Dei and about its connections with platforms of power. Accordingly, this suspicion looms large in the cinematic representations of the religious organization in the few examples that I identified above. In the remaining pages of this chapter I will examine them to showcase how *El buen amor* briefly and timorously suggested those connections, while *La casa sin fronteras* vicariously attacked them through a visual aesthetic of disturbance (portraying an organization that resembles Opus Dei as a sinister one through technical devices such as low-key and high-contrast lighting patterns and a distressing musical score). It is in *La trastienda*, made under a far more relaxed censorship code in the last months of the regime, that we find a more thorough and frontal cinematic representation of Opus Dei. Disguised in erotic scandal and democratic promise, Jordi Grau's film actually encompassed a defence of the Opus Dei ethic and its role in the modernization of Spain during the late Franco period, as well as a jab at the dismissal of Opus Dei technocrats from the last administration of the Franco regime.

The Good Love and the Opus Dei Shadow

Francisco Regueiro's *El buen amor*, one of the first outcomes of the *Nuevo Cine Español*, experienced the same fate as its predecessors and of most of its successors: some critical splash abroad, divided reviews at home, and little commercial success. *El buen amor* entered into the official competition of the 1963 Cannes Festival, where it was enthusiastically received and was supposedly a contender for one of the main awards (Barbáchano 65).[4] Unlike comparable films such as *Nueve cartas a Berta*, which offers similar ingredients – youth dissatisfaction, realist aesthetics, and sociopolitical critique of the regime – *El buen amor* has received scant critical attention and has remained a hidden jewel of Spanish cinema. The film features the lovers Jose (Simón Andreu) and Mari Carmen (Marta del Val), who take a train to spend a day alone in Toledo in a (futile) attempt to escape the routines of their dull existence in Madrid. During that day, they visit many of Toledo's monumental sites but end up just as bored as in their daily lives. Like *Nueve cartas a Berta, El buen amor* lingers on the discontent, emptiness, and emasculation of a whole generation of young Spaniards during the post-war years. Unlike the former film, though, *El buen amor* offers no sense of rebellion against those adverse circumstances. Heavily influenced by Italian neorealism, Regueiro records, with a series of monotonous, yet meticulously planned, sequence shots, the characters' wanderings in the streets of Toledo. Jose and Mari Carmen stroll and eat lunch, smoke cigarettes and have a number of ludicrous fights, but none of these actions serves to build a climax in the plot. Rather, they create a sum of meaningless events that enmesh the couple in the tedious cadence of provincial life until it is time to return to their routine existence in Madrid. Long takes of these insignificant events are typically shot with frontal views and a considerable distance between the characters and the camera. It is as if the director wanted to prevent spectators from penetrating into Jose and Mari Carmen's inner personas, or to supply a visual cue that highlights their emptiness.

As pointless actions accumulate, the trail of one of the numerous characters they run into during the day expands. In the train station Jose comes across a college friend named José María (a noticeable reference to Opus Dei's "Father"), who joined Opus Dei the previous year. Even though they only have a quick chat and José María does not appear again in the film, this encounter seems to have a considerable effect on the protagonists, for they continue to talk about him in their later conversations. Mari Carmen mentions José María's physical allure and complains that all handsome boys join Opus Dei, while Jose refers to his great academic and professional potential, as he is simultaneously pursuing several college degrees. On the surface, José María is a minor character in the film, but he gains symbolic weight when contrasted with the two lovers. He embodies positive qualities such as discipline and success, while both Jose and Mari Carmen express their dissatisfaction with their lives and future prospects.

Initially, José María appears to be just another secondary character among the many that the two protagonists run into who belong to either the armed forces or religious groups. Along with some *guardias civiles* and a group of nuns, José María seems like another hurdle that limits the freedom the two lovers seek – Jose does not even dare to introduce him to Mari Carmen, as if feeling morally guilty for escaping with his girlfriend. Nevertheless, we cannot overlook that José María is the only one of those secondary characters that reappears, even if only in conversation, and in a favourable light. I would argue that he functions as a narrative counterpoint, as a contrasting shadow of determination, to the purposeless protagonists. When Jose and Mari Carmen sit in a cafeteria to kill some time, the shadow of José María returns, as if propelling them to re-enact some sort of mirror stage, as it were, in which the shadow they evoke, by exuding an image of wholeness and a sense of direction that they lack, appears to multiply their own feeling of disillusionment. Jose María stands for the strong will of a high-achieving cadre soon to be in control of directive positions in the Spanish public sphere. In this way, *El buen amor* offers, however unconsciously, a prophetic statement about Opus Dei infiltration in relevant public positions, one that will reach its climax by the end of the decade. This statement was brief, timidly articulated – after all, Regueiro was still working under the rigid pre-1964 censorship norms – and it echoed the partisan views public opinion had formed about this religious organization.

The House without Scruples and the Holy Mafia

Pedro Olea enlisted in *La casa sin fronteras* a sound international cast and technical crew to make a film that tried to follow in the footsteps of Carlos Saura (Gregori 815). Apart from recruiting some of Saura's usual suspects (Geraldine Chaplin, Luis Cuadrado), he got Viveca Lindfors on board, the Swedish-born Hollywood star turned into muse of the NCE – she also worked with Miguel Picazo on *Oscuros sueños de agosto* (1967) and with Claudio Guerín in *La campana del infierno* (1973). The film received warm reviews (Gortari; Santiago Miguel; Carreño), entered the official competition of the 1972 Berlin Film Festival, and was selected to represent Spain in the American Academy Awards (not nominated). Despite this critical support, it was a commercial flop with only 162,389 tickets sold. Based on the short story "La casa sin fronteras (Lluvia)" by Mexican author José Agustín, a horror tale with metaphysical and Kafkaesque undertones, *La casa sin fronteras* centres on a powerful international sect that operates with dubious ends and punishes insurgence through bloody means. The protagonist is Daniel (Tony Isbert), a provincial young man who is recruited to work for the secret organization. After some successful small tasks, Daniel gets a bigger assignment: finding Anabel Campos (Geraldine Chaplin), another young recruit who has disappeared from the organization's house in mysterious circumstances. Daniel tracks her down, but once Anabel tells him that she ran away when she found out about the organization's venal purposes, he decides to escape abroad with her instead of turning her in. The attempt is fruitless, as they are captured and eventually tortured to death. With its cyclical structure – it begins and ends with an execution and the arrival of a young man who will be recruited – the film aspires to be a universal parable on the constrictions imposed on human freedom by powerful organizations of any sort.

Although Olea was careful not to make any direct reference to Opus Dei and has always been elusive about this issue in press interviews to avoid problems (Casas and Torreiro 93; Castro 18), he still had some hiccups with the censorship board, which believed the ominous organization depicted was Opus Dei (Castro 18).[5] But the film's parabolic aura undoubtedly helped it to receive the censors' approval. As it happened with many Spanish art-house films of the 1960s and 1970s, censors finally gave *La casa sin fronteras* a pass because they expected it to have a reduced distribution among film elites and no success with a broader audience. And they could not have been more accurate in their predictions. In part to get through this censorship hurdle, but also to try to capture the essence of Saura's oblique style and labyrinthine narrative paths, Olea overloads the story with enigmatic characters and vague references. These include a creepy session involving the occult, Daniel's terrifying nightmares, and a scary jigsaw puzzle that Daniel completes, which contains a reproduction of an execution scene taken from an Albrecht Dürer etching that announces his own fate in the near future. Carlos Losilla regards this overuse of shadowy elements as "un trascendentalismo metafórico a lo Querejeta" (a metaphorical transcendentalism à la Querejeta) (68). The allusion to Opus Dei, or to anything else for that matter, remains in an abstract domain that is hard to pinpoint in concrete space-time coordinates. Unlike Saura's historically rooted political allegories, Olea's *La casa sin fronteras* lacks any sense of historical texture.

To be fair, *La casa sin fronteras* is more than the truncated project of a would-be Saura. First of all, it is consistent with some of Olea's thematic and stylistic trademarks. As in most of his films based on literary texts – *El bosque del lobo* (1970), *Tormento* (1974), *Un hombre llamado Flor de Otoño* (1978), and *El maestro de esgrima* (1992) – the main characters are marginal with respect to the sociohistorical conditions in which they live and are not able to survive within those hostile conditions (Losilla 63). Also as in many of his films, there is a tragic resolution involving the execution of the main characters – *El bosque del lobo, Pim, pam, pum ... ¡Fuego!* (1975), *Un hombre llamado Flor de Otoño*, and *Akelarre* (1984). Overall, the film has a number of tangible technical and aesthetic merits. The superb use of locations in Bilbao, adeptly photographed by Luis Cuadrado, provides a distressing effect on familiar urban scenarios such as the Abando train station and the Palacio de Ibaigane as the headquarters of the sect. Olea also methodically planned the interior scenes by using a low-key lighting approach that creates shadows and evokes a climate of mystery and secrecy. The execution scenes (including the one of the main leads, Daniel and Anabel) are particularly salient within this visual aesthetic of disturbance, as they create some vivid chiaroscuros that intensify the sinister air surrounding the secret organization that operates in the house without boundaries.

There are a number of details in the depiction of this organization that resonate with the functioning of Opus Dei. When Daniel visits the house for the first time, he is able to glimpse a meeting of members discussing their recruitment progress, which they hope will satisfy "el gran canciller" (the great chancellor). One could note the resemblance to the vertical inner structure of Opus Dei, whose "gran canciller" is "el Padre" (Escrivá de Balaguer), the only free member of the organization, placed at the top of the hierarchy and holding his authority over the rest of the members (Guillén 107). Opus Dei is vertically organized and promotes absolute and uncontestable obedience to the figure of the Father, which Michael Walsh calls "the ideology of submission" within the Opus Dei structures (118). Another scene containing a hint happens when Daniel returns to the house to clarify the terms of his assignment and only finds two construction workers, who confirm his task while threatening him with the consequences of failure. This enigmatic scene points to the very etymological meaning of the name Opus Dei, "the work of God" in Latin, here suggested through the "construction" metaphor.

The main activities of the organization portrayed in the film seem to be, first, recruitment, with the "prefecto externo" (José Orjas) as the main "hook" for "fishing" for new recruits who arrive at the train station, and, second, making sure there are no dissenting views. Those who dare to challenge commands are cruelly penalized with the "castigo final" (final punishment): torture and death. Again, these activities appear to echo the hard-line proselytizing that Opus Dei members are compelled to carry out and the harsh treatment of dissenters and dropouts (Michael Walsh 171), respectively. The biographical accounts and memories of former Opus Dei members recurrently expose that any member daring to separate from Opus Dei immediately becomes a "non-person," excluded from all of the organization's networks that could facilitate that person's adaptation into a new life and subjected to a number of reprisals (Tapia 286–300). A fictional enactment of that process of retaliation appears, albeit in exaggerated fashion, in the gory executions we see in *La casa sin fronteras,* in which the organization converts dissidents into non-persons by taking their lives.

Rather than seeking to carve out a realistic profile, *La casa sin fronteras* builds on popular suspicions about Opus Dei's shadowy practices to create a horror tale. But it also builds, again in an overstated style, on Escrivá de Balaguer's *Camino.* Elvira's long and pompous speech to Anabel about the nature of the secret organization echoes some of the most controversial maxims from *Camino.* Elvira (Viveca Lindfors) welcomes Anabel to their group of "esclarecidos," composed of a select minority, thus echoing Opus Dei's ill-reputed elitism and its "apostolado de la inteligencia" (apostolate of intelligence) (Orbaneja 69); that is, proselytizing among the most talented members of society, a practice already recommended by Escrivá in his maxim 16: "Be just commonplace? You, a sheep-like follower? You were born to be a leader! Among us there is no place for the lukewarm" (*The Way* 23). Also, when Elvira justifies the carefully chosen membership because of the rigorous skill set required – efficiency, blind faith, bravery, and sacrificial spirit – her words echo the three axes of the "holiness" that the Father required of aspirant saints: "Holy steadfastness, holy forcefulness and holy shamelessness" (maxim 387, *The Way* 98); blind faith because the opposite is "a sure sign of not possessing the truth" (maxim 394, *The Way* 99). Blind faith is required, according to Elvira, for the noble task of improving the world, of defending a certain idea of civilization, which once again recalls the "apostolate of penetration" that characterizes Opus Dei's apostolic mission (Hutchinson 103). Discordant music punctuates the scene, underlining the malevolent nature of Elvira's words – and the organization's purposes. As if the tone of the speech were not eerie enough, Elvira caresses Anabel's face and breasts, and a disruptive editing cut switches the camera position from the medium long shot employed in most of the scene to a close-up of Elvira's desiring gaze. The film equates – in homophobic fashion – sexual "deviation" with the organization's unorthodox methods, thereby giving a rather carnal interpretation to Escrivá de Balaguer's "holy shamelessness."

La casa sin fronteras presents a secret organization with cultic practices that traps innocent victims who, in the event they do not blindly follow instructions, are castigated with a kind of torture that is reminiscent of the Inquisition trials. The film dwells too much on the sectarian aspects and strips the organization of any spiritual purpose and ecclesiastical connection. This fictional Opus Dei is a holy (and bloody) mafia that operates in a house without scruples, not a religious branch of the Catholic Church. In this sense, it resonates with one of what Opus Dei-friendly historian Ricardo de la Cierva calls "poisoned sources" about Opus Dei (37), which try to deny that it is "un hecho religioso" (a religious question) (86–7). Unlike those "poisoned" accounts that spread "conspiracy theories" (Allen 8) with supporting evidence and details, everything in this film remains on an abstract plane. As Pedro Olea himself admitted, the story was "excesivamente críptica y parabólica, y la gente se aburría por una parte, y no la entendía por otra" (excessively cryptic and parabolic, and people were bored and confused) (Castro 18). This is why the film generated no commercial interest and why, despite its cinematographic merits, it has remained in the murky basement of the history of Spanish cinema.

Thirty-Seven Frames of Freedom

The more relaxed censorship code in the last months of the regime allowed Jordi Grau to make *La trastienda*, which comprises a frontal cinematic representation of Opus Dei. The film focuses on the inner conflicts of Jaime Navarro (Frederick Stafford), a reputable doctor and a devoted supernumerary member of Opus Dei whose religious morals are shaken by his sexual attraction to one of his nurses, Juana Ríos (María José Cantudo). Meanwhile, Jaime's wife, Lourdes (Rosanna Schiafinno), is having an affair with Fernando (Ignacio de Paúl), one of the couple's closest friends. As if propelled by the atmosphere of debauchery at the festival of Sanfermines in Pamplona, Jaime consummates the adultery and causes a scandal. The hypocritical wife rejects Jaime in his attempt to make amends, and the film closes with Jaime departing to start a life on his own.

Seasoned producer José Frade orchestrated an aggressive promotion that promised spectators that *La trastienda* "no es la película de la apertura, sino de la libertad" (is not the film of the *apertura* but the film of freedom) ("La trastienda"). This catchy slogan paid off, and the film became an instant hit, with 2,642,790 tickets sold. Juana's brief nude scene ten minutes into the film seemed to encapsulate that promise of freedom. In the famous scene, Juana comes home and takes her clothes off. As she walks to her bedroom, she plucks an apple from a fruit bowl.

Once in her room, she can be seen in a medium close-up contemplating her own face in a mirror while she bites into the apple. Immediately thereafter, the reverse long shot shows her entire naked body as reflected in the mirror. Interestingly enough, this is not a point-of-view reverse shot, which one would logically expect to follow the close-up, but a detached view of Juana while she is staring at her naked reflection in the mirror. It is significant that this shot is taken from outside the room and in low angle, as if the camera were taking the position of an uninvited voyeur and forcing viewers to become accomplices in a voyeuristic spectacle. The symbolic apple adds an obvious biblical connotation, since it renders Juana as an Eve-like seductress embodying sin who will be the catalyst of the dramatic conflict of the film.

It is hard to think of another second and a half – a total of thirty-seven frames – in the history of Spanish cinema that had a more crucial impact on the commercial run of a film. *La trastienda* benefited from a frequent filmic proposition during the *destape* years that equated the craving for sex with the craving for political freedom. Producers exploited what Brian McNair (11–12) calls the power of "striptease culture" to democratize desire: popular access to the erotic images in this film was presented as a metaphor of the increasing democratization of the public sphere in Spain. This is why Alejandro Melero Salvador mentions *La trastienda* as an example of "the dance of the seven veils" that Spanish cinema played during the transition to progressively uncover layers of sexuality hitherto concealed (14). This was the first time that the censorship board had approved a scene with full frontal nudity in a Spanish feature film, and audiences rushed to movie theatres to witness the occurrence firsthand. In the last years of the regime and in the transition to democracy, screening politics and sex sold tickets, especially if religion was thrown into the equation.

The defining factor of *La trastienda*'s commercial success – female nudity embedded in a "religious crisis" plot – simultaneously became its main impediment in terms of critical reception. Some critics discarded the film as an attempt to cash in on the surplus value of female nudity during these years (Martí 34) and for its "inexistente politización" (nonexistent politicization) ("La trastienda"). Critics did not forgive Grau, a director who began as a bridge figure between the NCE and the School of Barcelona, for his move towards a middlebrow type of filmmaking that, while trying to offer a quality product, also sought a mass market and commercial viability. Like its female lead, *La trastienda* lost all its layers and garments over time, and historians of Spanish cinema barely remember the film as the first to legally show a nude female on the screen. Other than that, as Peter Besas boldly put it, *La trastienda* "had nothing special" (136).

While Jordi Grau was comfortable with the fact that his film had become "a symbol of the *destape*" and embraced his new privileged position in the industry (176, 184) – thanks to the profit and the controversy that the film generated – María José Cantudo always resented becoming an erotic symbol. In fact, she continues to deny that she was ever a *destape* film star. Cantudo has indefatigably refuted that she built her acting career around her physique and justifies her nudity in *La trastienda* as an artistic scene that provided the symbolic context – Juana as the Eve-like embodiment of sexual temptation – necessary to understand the religious conflict of the male lead (José Aguilar 36). Considering how much her star image depended on her erotic appeal, it is hard to give much credibility to her claim. All the media texts that served to construct Cantudo's star image – the films, the promotional material, her interviews in film magazines and tabloids – emphasized the sexual aspect of her performances. One only has to bear in mind how much flesh she showed in both her previous and later film roles – for example, in *El secreto inconfesable de un chico bien* (1976), also directed by Jordi Grau – as well as in her multiple interviews for magazines. In the film magazine *Fotogramas* alone, María José Cantudo appeared semi-nude on the covers of five issues between May 1975 and December 1978. The covers simply teased potential readers with the promise of more nudity to be found in the interviews inside. For example, issue 1386 (May 1975) features a story that is essentially a photographic report of Cantudo posing in a ski resort and wearing only a bikini. The interview in issue 1442 (June 1976) includes abundant pictures of Cantudo wearing only a thong and posing erotically on top of the roulette table in a casino. The first interview was published prior to the shooting of *La trastienda*; the second one appeared a few months after the release of the film. This confirms that, however much Cantudo demands critical attention for her acting merits, her star image before and after *La trastienda* was carved out through her physique and erotic appeal.

To a certain extent, though, Cantudo has a point. There is more to *La trastienda* than her famous nudity. With this film Grau offers the most comprehensive cinematographic picture of Opus Dei's controversial idiosyncrasies and, what is more unusual, of the ethos that it instils in its members. On the surface, it seems as if Grau's goal was to attack Opus Dei as a reactionary organization with a coercive impact on personal freedoms. Both the filmmaker and the female star have recently expressed it in those terms (Grau 176; José Aguilar 36). Yet, I believe that Grau appropriates the dual logic of revelation and concealment that guides erotic cinema to reveal a benevolent side of Opus Dei – "undressed" for the public eye – while the rest of the provincial society of Pamplona, and Spain at the twilight of Francoism, hypocritically "conceal" their depravities. Disguised in erotic scandal and democratic promise, Grau's film encompassed a defence of the Opus Dei ethic and its role in the modernization of Spain during late Francoism.

La trastienda and the Opus Dei Ethic

By comparison with its brief presence in *El buen amor*, and its excessively mythologized portrayal in *La casa sin fronteras*, the representation of Opus Dei in *La trastienda* seems almost like a naturalistic case study. Jaime Navarro is introduced as a model Opus Dei supernumerary. Supernumeraries are third-tier members in the Opus Dei hierarchy – after priests and numeraries. Unlike the numeraries, who hand over all their earnings to the organization, live in Opus Dei residences, and renounce a family life, supernumeraries can get married. They donate only a part of their annual income, usually around 10 per cent (Hutchinson 113), and commit themselves to live virtuously and according to the core message of Opus Dei: they strive to purify the secular world through the performance of their everyday tasks, both in their professional work and in their family life. The first scenes of the film show how Jaime Navarro painstakingly carries out all these activities. He is a highly regarded surgeon in the hospital and complies with his marital and family obligations at home with the same precision. Also, Jaime seeks to sanctify his ordinary life by performing a number of spiritual tasks that the Opus Dei training assigns to its members in what is known as the "plan of life" or "the norms," an individual plan to find "pathways to holiness" (Allen 30). We see Jaime attending Mass every morning before going to work, praying a daily rosary at work, visiting with his spiritual confessor, don Pablo (José Suárez), doing spiritual readings – Escrivá de Balaguer's *Camino* – at night, and practising corporal mortification. What we actually see is the physical result of these mortifications in the wounds on the palms of his hands. Corporal mortification is a common practice among committed Opus Dei laymen – it is required of celibate numeraries and optional in supernumeraries (Allen 166).[6] Opus Dei regards this self-inflicted pain

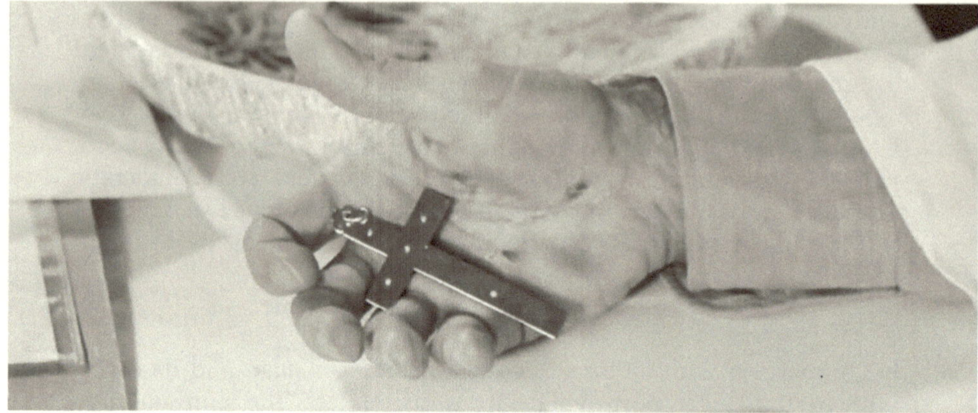

4.1 Corporeal mortification of the Opus Dei supernumerary in *La trastienda* (1975). Permission to reproduce the still from EGEDA.

not as an end in itself, but as a channel to achieve spiritual goals. On a spiritual level, mortification is a symbolic way to link believers with the passion and suffering of Christ (Allen 170). Also, following a time-honoured tradition within Catholicism to attempt to tame the temptations of the body, corporal mortification is, as stated in maxim 227 of *Camino*, "a means of training the body to endure hardship" (Allen 169). For Jaime, mortification is a way of repenting for having carnal desires for Juana.

Jaime's discipline in carrying out all these ordinary tasks of his individual spiritual program goes hand-in-hand with the professional ethic he shows as a surgeon. Jaime's pedigree comes from his methodical planning of his daily activities, which we see him writing down in his diary at night. In addition, several scenes of the film offer details to convey the sense that he is not just another doctor, but one with genuine concern for the well-being of his patients. Nurses praise his careful work in contrast to more mechanical and less humane surgeons, and we see him conscientiously analysing X-rays before giving a prompt diagnosis. Jaime acts following the staple tenet of the Opus Dei organization: members must strive to meet the highest standards in the secular world. *La trastienda* thus goes beyond providing a few brushes with Opus Dei's controversial idiosyncrasies to offer a rather comprehensive picture of the "Opus Dei ethic" that I explained in the introduction.

Jaime embodies Opus Dei members' apostolic mission to sanctify work in the world, to sanctify oneself in work, and to sanctify others with one's work.

Given that *La trastienda* delivers an apology for the Opus Dei ethic, it cannot be taken as "the film of freedom." If anything, we could name it "the film of the developmental technocracy." *La trastienda* was made when Opus Dei's political influence was fading almost to the point of becoming, as Gregorio Peces-Barba provocatively argued in *Cuadernos para el diálogo*, "un cadáver político de muy difícil, por no decir imposible, recuperación" (a political corpse that faced a very difficult, if not impossible, recovery) (38). In my view, the film is an elegy for the participation of the Opus Dei ministers in the modernization process of the technocratic phase of the regime and, concretely, for the impulse towards rationalized planning that these ministers instilled in the Spanish economic and political sphere. After the assassination of Carrero Blanco in December 1973, Carlos Arias Navarro was appointed as president and instantly surprised everyone by sweeping all Opus Dei technocrats out of his government. Arias had a tough time during the two years of his Opus Dei-free administration, which are known as the "gobierno vacío, sin ideas, en permanente deriva" (empty administration, without ideas, permanently adrift) (Mateos and Soto 88), because his administration seemed to function by reacting to events rather than following a credible strategic plan. This lack of political vision combined with several other problems Arias Navarro faced: 1) the political crises as a result of the "Añoveros affair" and the execution of Salvador Puig; 2) the hostility of the Church; 3) the increasing opposition of civil society in favour of democratic plurality; and 4) the economic problems ensuing from the 1973 global oil crisis that put an end to the economic miracle of *desarrollismo*.

La trastienda should be framed within this sociohistorical junction, as a tribute to the key role Opus Dei members played in late Franco society and as a critical pun on their dismissal from the frontline of politics. Jaime stands out in the resolution of the film as the moral victor over his hypocritical wife and the two-faced society of Pamplona that condemns his actions. As Lourdes explains, his biggest error was not cheating on her but doing it openly. The upshot of her rationale is that a hidden affair would have been fine. Also, the film narrative sets up the justification of Jaime's behaviour from the start. The main plot alternates with footage of the different stages of the Sanfermines, shot in documentary fashion with a handheld camera. The climate of debauchery creates a carnivalesque atmosphere conducive to a temporary subversion of norms. Grau has Jaime conveniently give a speech early in the film about the symbolic relevance of Sanfermines as a time to temporarily subvert the social order and let out anxieties. It is almost as if Jaime were forced into his sin by the collective atmosphere.

In this way, the film differentiates between the two adulteries: the almost involuntary and naive act by Jaime versus the clandestine and prolonged affair of Lourdes. Raimundo (Ángel del Pozo), a colleague and friend of Jaime's, justifies the scandal that Jaime's affair generates as a reprisal against Opus Dei. Also, the film dwells on finding a way to forgive Jaime. Don Pablo, Jaime's priest and confessor, deems Jaime's affair an opportunity for redemption and convinces him to stop seeing Juana and to continue performing his duties as promised in his vows to Opus Dei. Interestingly, the camera work corroborates the moral hierarchy the film narrative establishes. The conversations between don Pablo and Jaime, and between Jaime and Raimundo – the three characters who are positively depicted in the film and the three Opus Dei members – are carefully shot in shot / reverse shot sequences that situate the camera at shoulder level and do not privilege anybody's point of view. By contrast, in Jaime's final conversations with both Juana and his wife, the shot / reverse shot structure shows an asymmetrical ordering of the camera angles. Jaime's gaze appears from a high angle perspective, while the reverse, from the female perspective, is consistently shot from low angles. In tune with Opus Dei's notorious gender asymmetries (Armas 68; Carandell 196; Hermet, *Los católicos I* 271), it is as if the camera wants to endorse the moral hierarchy by placing Jaime in a superior position and the female characters on an inferior plane.

Just as Jaime in *La trastienda* is forgiven for his mistake but gets no mercy from the hypocritical social milieu of Pamplona, the Opus Dei technocrats overcame a shameful fault to stay in business for a few more years: the Matesa scandal of political corruption. Run by prominent Opus Dei members, Matesa was a business enterprise that exported loom machinery. The political enemies of Opus Dei revealed in 1969 that the machinery was a cover for the diversion of capital, including some government loans, to fiscal paradises abroad (Hermet, *Los católicos II* 466–7; Hutchinson 131–3; Michael Walsh 147–9). Despite this scandal, Franco surprised everyone by reinforcing the Opus Dei-friendly composition of his cabinet in October 1969 and, in this way, openly favoured the Opus Dei technocrats over the Falangists and other factions. However, once the latter took control of the government, the Opus Dei technocrats could not endure their retaliation. These enemies from within the regime finally succeeded in eliminating Opus Dei from the political vanguard in 1974, but they failed to assume control, especially in stopping the economic recession. The Opus Dei members of the regime administration were rewarded for their religiously infused economic ethos, while their political enemies were penalized. Similarly, in this film Grau undressed his male lead, but to expose his virtues and, thereby, to render him as the moral champion of the narrative. The undressing was not only metaphorical but also quite literal. After Jaime consummates the adultery and the scandal is made public, don Pablo pays him a visit at Juana's apartment to try to convince him to amend his sin. Juana's roommate goes to the bedroom to announce the priest's visit, and a panning camera move displays a long shot of Jaime lying in bed almost naked. Only a pair of stylish black briefs covers Stafford's slim, toned body.

The casting of Frederick Stafford was criticized, as Jordi Grau admitted, for lacking ethnic verisimilitude (Gregori 504). The Czech-born actor was an international star known for a number of high-profile European spy movies, including Alfred Hitchcock's *Topaz* (1969). Evidently, his height (six feet three inches), his toned body, and his chic underwear made him radically different from the male leads Spanish audiences were used to seeing in erotic comedies in those years. Most notably, Alfredo Landa, the star of the cycle of erotic comedies known as "landismo," was short, chubby, and usually wore ill-fitting white boxers. Instead of being a flaw, I believe that Stafford's "non-Spanish" sex-appeal works well to reinforce the reading I am proposing here. He incarnates the Opus Dei-affiliated professionals who penetrated the top spheres of influence from the late 1950s onward. Although Grau does not afford Jaime's character an explicit political dimension, a Spanish spectator could read him as a fictional embodiment of the economic and political elites who modernized the economy and crafted a new image of the regime by downplaying Spain's cultural exceptionality and by co-opting narratives of development that were typically associated with modern European democracies. To the average Spanish viewer, Opus Dei epitomized transnational elites of highly educated members like Jaime who began to colonize the pinnacles of power in Spain and elsewhere. Seen in this light, Stafford's European looks appear as an asset rather than a shortcoming.

Given this favourable depiction of Opus Dei, some reviewers accused Grau of being a covert member of the organization. The magazine

Fotogramas framed an interview with the director by emphasizing Grau's connections with Opus Dei ("El último Opus"). Domènec Font mentioned the director derogatively as "el opusdeísta Jorge Grau" (*Del azul* 260). My goal here has not been to engage in this guessing game and confirm or deny Grau's belonging to or kinship with Opus Dei. I am not interested in an exercise of "religious outing," so to speak, of the filmmaker.[7] Instead, my concern in this section has been to analyse the representational apparatus of the film. In this sense, although many reviewers lambasted the film for sidestepping the public projection of the Opus Dei organization and its association with the political and economic elites ("La trastienda"; Martí 34), and scholars of Spanish cinema pigeonholed it as a *destape* hit, I have shown a different *trastienda* (backroom) of this film. Grau uses eroticism not to distract the spectator from political issues, as in the formulaic patterns of the ordinary *destape* film, but to offer a political criticism of the two-faced society of Pamplona, and allegorically of Spain as a whole, at the twilight of the Franco regime. Instead of the publicized endorsement of pro-democratic values via the liberation of erotic impulses, the film stands out as a requiem for the technocratic phase of the regime and, most specifically, for the Opus Dei participation in the modernization process during the development years.

The Allure of Middlebrow Cinema: Politics, Sex, and Religion

Like other films by young directors of the *Nuevo Cine Español*, *La trastienda* addresses social anxieties about the regulatory powers of religion in Spanish society. However, I have shown how the film was ultimately less a cinematographic testimony against the coercive function of religion than a requiem for the politically disgraced members of Opus Dei at the twilight of the regime. With *La trastienda*, Grau veered from his first films, which were in line with the aesthetic codes and the anti-Francoist stands of the NCE and the School of Barcelona, towards making a middlebrow type of cinema with less foreseeable ideological alliances. In fact, he was one of the pioneers of the new middlebrow trend in Spanish cinema that took an interest in religion in the last few years of the regime. This middlebrow cinema emerged in the early 1970s to cater to a new type of audience: a middle-class, educated, and mostly urban viewer eager to see films that reflected issues of social interest. Historians of Spanish cinema have typically called this middlebrow cinema the "Tercera Vía" (Third Way), because it was conceived as an attempt to move away from both commercial and auteurist cinema (Torreiro, "Del tardofranquismo" 360). As Sally Faulkner has noted, the Third Way "was producer- rather than director-led," steered by entrepreneurial initiatives of producers such as José Frade, Emiliano Piedra, and José Luis Dibildos who commissioned a team of professionals that made films with four distinctive components: "serious subjects; high-culture references; high production values and accessibility" (*A History* 128, 122). Among those serious subject matters, religion featured prominently in two mini-cycles of middlebrow films that need to be understood against the backdrop of the conflictive relations between state and Church at the twilight of the dictatorial regime.

The first was a series of adaptations of nineteenth-century novels which featured priests involved in sexual relationships with women: *Tormento* (Pedro Olea, 1974), *La Regenta* (Gonzalo Suárez, 1974), and *Pepita Jiménez* (Rafael Moreno Alba, 1975). The three films were set in the nineteenth century but were presented as indirect commentaries on the conflict between the state and progressive branches of the Church. These films played the game that Peter Besas described as the "political tease" of films during the late Franco period. In these highly politicized years, Spanish audiences were "thirsty for any break with the status quo" and "anxious to see what the latest limits of expression might be" (94). Overt political dissidence was not yet an option, so the conflicts between state and Church were vicariously suggested through these looks back to another period of Spanish history that was seen as comparable because it also underwent a secularization process, even if that process differed in nature and scope. The secularization of the nineteenth century was caused by an anticlerical movement associated with the attempt of liberal forces to take down the sociopolitical structures of the Ancien Régime ingrained in Spanish society and culture. It fostered a trend towards atheism and, in its most radical forms, a violent reaction against anything religious. By contrast, the secularization that started in the late Franco period, which Alfonso Pérez-Agote calls "the second wave of secularization" in Spain (133), was not a belligerent response but a progressive loss of interest in religion and a weakening of ties to religious institutions by a large number of Spaniards.

The second cycle of religious films was what could be called the "vocational crisis" film, which centred on resignations from the priesthood and on the drastically reduced numbers of young novices entering seminaries in the 1960s. The new social doctrine of Vatican II caused many youngsters to fulfil their yearning to help the community through social activism and lay ministry instead of becoming priests or nuns. Also, broader social issues such as the rise of consumerist values were cited as catalysts of the decline in religious vocations in the development years.[8] As Stanley Payne documents, "[r]enunciations of religious vocation and resignations from the priesthood multiplied by ten during the mid-1960s, then tripled once more by the end of the decade" (199).[9] This sweeping transformation within the clergy offered ample possibilities for filmmaking. Pedro Masó, Vicente Escrivá, and Rafael Romero took advantage of that potential in three films in which the crisis of faith of the clerical characters is prompted by sexual attraction towards a woman: *Un hombre como los demás* (Masó, 1974), *Polvo eres* (Escrivá, 1974), and *Tu Dios y mi infierno* (Romero, 1975). As with the Opus Dei-affiliated protagonist of *La trastienda*, the religious crisis, be that between factions within the Church or between Church and state, is represented in both mini-cycles through a carnal lens and is triggered in each case by sexual temptation. Unable to be more politically explicit because censorship was still operative, these films invited viewers to read between the lines and to project a broader dimension to the sexual conflict.[10]

The sexual content of these films conditioned their reception, as critics have typically dismissed them, sometimes unfairly, as mere exploitative products,[11] but it simultaneously helped them commercially, because they were publicized highlighting their sexual appeal. Besides the allure of sexuality, audiences were drawn to these middlebrow films because they exposed the escalating tensions between the regime's evolving political discourse and the changing Catholic Church. Middlebrow confessional cinema made apparent that religion had become an intricate and even confusing element of public life in the last few years of the regime in Spain that was hard to pigeonhole in one place along the ideological spectrum. This was an innovative treatment of religion for audiences by comparison with each of the films by Carlos Saura and Basilio Martín Patino that I have analysed. Saura and Patino drew on the master Luis Buñuel to denounce the Church's ties to political power and, more importantly, the toxic effects that those bonds had in subjugating civil freedoms as well as basic personal desires such as sexuality. But they sidestepped the shift that Buñuel made following *Nazarín* to explore a potentially modern facet of the sacred in the changing landscape of modernity. Patino and Saura reduced the social impact of religion throughout the whole regime to the schemes of the hierarchy of the crusade Church and, thereby, engaged religion as a mere obstacle to modernity. While it is undeniable that some factions of the Church hierarchy still tried to hold on, even after Vatican II, to the privileges they enjoyed under the regime, reducing the public role of religion in the development years to that dimension eschews part of a richer story. Patino and Saura, like other young directors of the *Nuevo Cine Español* such as Mario Camus in *Los farsantes* (1963) and Miguel Picazo in *La tía Tula* (1964) before them, made films as if the modernization of the Catholic Church with the Vatican II Council had not taken place (Faulkner, *A Cinema* 6). In so doing, they missed an opportunity to extricate the sacred from the monopoly of the war's victors and to show the increasing role religious issues had in weakening the political legitimacy of the regime and in supporting oppositional groups.

Conclusion

Spanish Cinema at the Intersection of Religion and Politics

Throughout this book I have argued that the engagement of Spanish cinema with religion in the 1960s and 1970s showed that the sacred still possessed an influential hold upon Spanish society and political imagination. Beyond the mere defence of traditional values in the wake of the multifaceted processes of modernization and secularization in which the society was inmersed, Spanish cinema addressed the transformation within Spanish Catholicism during and after the Vatican II Council as well as the renewed role of religion in those modernizing processes. In so doing, the film industry was pioneering, relative to other cultural products such as literature. This inquiry has helped me confirm that, contrary to prevailing views about the history of Spanish cinema, religion was a topic of interest for both mainstream and elite film audiences in the 1960s and early 1970s. It has also led me to the somewhat surprising conclusion that commercial films, despite being less aesthetically accomplished and often having a formulaic appearance, delved more than oppositional, art-house films into the fluctuating zeitgeist of the development years regarding the transformations within Spanish Catholicism. Granted, they generally did so with a pro-regime ideological bias and with the intention of accommodating traditional values and the moral authority of Catholicism in a broader national narrative of modernization. As I showed in my analyses, the films were more complex than serving as mere vehicles of regime propaganda. In fact, as I will recapitulate later in these concluding remarks, in the post–Vatican II period, mainstream confessional films began to encapsulate elements that could have led to dissenting reception. For the auteurs of the *Nuevo Cine Español*, however, there was no grey area or possibility of appropriating religion for progressive purposes. As I examined in the previous chapter, acclaimed directors such as Basilio Martín Patino and Carlos Saura dexterously handled the camera work, editing choices, sound devices, and mise-en-scène in their films to depict religion as inherently linked to repression, as a mechanism of social control, as an outright deterrent to modernization, and as a constraint on the society in which they aspired to live.

In the introduction I proposed that the engagement of confessional cinema with religion proved that the signature of the sacred was moved to the space of secular politics in the development years in a different manner than in the first two decades of the regime. Drawing on a brief analysis of Giorgio Agamben's ideas in *The Kingdom and the Glory*, I suggested that confessional cinema increasingly addressed the shift from political theology, which pivoted on the figure of the sovereign invested with divine power (Franco), to economic theology, a managerial paradigm of governance in which the administration of the law matches the divine *oikonomia* (142–3). It is time to assess how this theoretical paradigm helps us to understand the role of religion in the public sphere of the late Franco period by recapping the insights drawn from my analytical chapters.

Confessional films showcased that this shift in the regime's political discourse did not happen overnight, and indeed both paradigms coexisted, arguably until the death of Franco, even though economic theology was more prominent from the 1960s onwards. For example, the state-sponsored film *Franco, ese hombre* that I examined in chapter 1 was made as part of a propaganda campaign and with the intention of highlighting the new modern image of a regime that sought political legitimacy on rational grounds. However, the outcome was a hagiographic documentary that delivered a holy profile of Franco and underlined his divinely invested right to sovereignty. The film urged viewers to keep basing Spanish national identity and Franco's right to sovereign power on a political theology with exclusionary undertones against the enemies of that sacred absolute. Prior to *Franco, ese hombre*, the hagiographic films of the early 1960s such as *Fray Escoba*, *Rosa de Lima*, and *Teresa de Jesús* offered justifications of the traditional legitimacy of the regime and, above all, of the allegedly sacred origin of Spain's national essence. They shaped, through the tactical use of lighting and other aspects of their mise-en-scène such as costume and make-up, an ethno-religious concept of Spanishness embodied by the edifying models of sainthood depicted as national heroes. These hagiographic films contributed to the political sphere by normalizing for a mass audience the essentialist political truths underpinning the political theology adopted by the regime. In my analyses, I have exposed how these idealized celluloid models of sanctity served to reinvigorate a spiritual notion of the Spanish race – *Hispanidad* – that upheld the Spanish imperialist enterprise and a unitary national identity that rested on the exclusion of racial and gender-based otherness.

As time went on, confessional films began to prove that validating almighty sovereignty was not the only role that religious notions could play in the political sphere. By the mid-1960s, the hagiographic film *El señor de La Salle* channelled a critique of political theology through a bold representation of the Bourbon dynasty's excesses of absolutism in France. The radically divergent use of lighting and composition devices in relation to previous hagiographic films was the visual cue to suggest that spectators were watching a hagiopic with unorthodox messages. Made when the first recommendations of Vatican II were coming into public view, this film presented a modern religious leader who advocated for the rights of the poor and the marginalized. Although set in France in the seventeenth century, this film could easily be taken as a jab at the "crusade Church" that underpinned National-Catholicism. Obliquely, one could also interpret the film as a critique of the divine mandate of the sovereign in power.

In the second half of the 1960s, comedies of development praised the economic-managerial paradigm put in place by the newly appointed technocrats in charge of the regime administration. But the comedies of development that I analysed in chapters 2 and 3, such as *Fray Torero, El padre Manolo,* and *Sor Citröen,* also made clear that the successful modernization of the Spanish economy, the thriving consumer society, and the new prosperity enjoyed by Spaniards depended on preserving Spain's Catholic backbone, even if in a renovated post–Vatican II version. In Weberian terms, comedies of development restated that instrumental rationality by itself was not enough to secure the success of the modernization process. Substantive rationality was still part of the equation and informed the administration's development plans. The unique thing is that the technocrats did not incorporate those religious values into their program of modernization by insisting on divine sovereignty. Instead, theological notions appeared in their political discourse through secularized notions of social justice, economic fair play, and morally driven economic development. Crucially, this Catholic-infused modernization was amply celebrated and publicized through media discourses. One of my contentions with *Confessional Cinema* has been that comedies of development were a decisive media form to shape the contours of this new paradigm of power and, even more fascinatingly, to expose the tensions it prompted in relation to changing historical circumstances such as the renewal of the Church with Vatican II. Filtered through the conceptual paradigm I have proposed in this book, the traditionally denigrated stylistic and narrative formulas of the comedies of development acquire a compelling function to symbolize social togetherness and, thereby, to promote social consensus.

Post–Vatican II comedies of development thus challenged perspectives that regard religion only as an anti-modern factor during Francoism, since they contributed to shape the technocrats' discourse regarding the regime's *oikonomia,* which resembled modern forms of government in other Western European countries (minus a democratic form of political representation). If economic theology is a governmental model resting on social consensus, then comedies of development cinematically performed that collective consensus. The endings of *Fray Torero* and *Este cura,* in which the previously divided communities are brought together through religious rituals with symbolic social functions, are paradigmatic examples of this point. By making explicit the link between religion and a modern form of government in the last phase of the Francoist regime, these films urged viewers to test secularist understandings of modernity, including Gonzalo Fernández de la Mora's influential views at that time. The managerial model of economic theology, in which the administration of the law parallels the divine economy (Agamben, *The Kingdom* 142–3), has been called a form of "post-politics" by other scholars following Agamben's lead. With that label they designate "an apolitical paradigm of governmentality" with significant "political consequences" (Diken 139–40). But the crucial point missed by Fernández de la Mora, and by cultural analysts who have taken his managerial model as a normative ideal (in the Weberian sense) to explain the technocrats' political discourse in the 1960s in Spain, is that religion was a central component of this "apolitical" or "post-political" paradigm of governance and was not therefore relocated to the private sphere.

A stimulating line of research that surpasses the scope of this book would be to test Agamben's ideas in the context of post-Franco Spain. In this regard, one could examine how economic theology manifests itself in the democratic period and, moreover, how it has been engaged by Spanish cinema and other forms of visual media. Such a study would start off from a conspicuous fact regarding the public dimension of religion in the non-confessional period after 1979: the power of ecclesiastical institutions and the authority of religious beliefs over secular values have declined considerably. The most apocalyptic views insist on a de-Christianization of democratic Spain fostered from above, especially by the administrations of the socialist party (PSOE), which have supposedly striven to silence the Catholic Church and weaken its ability to intervene in public life (Cárcel Ortí, *¿España neopagana?* 119–22; *Historia* 288–96). Sociological studies have confirmed that church attendance, religious vocations, and the overall clout of ecclesiastical views among Spaniards have been diminishing in the last three decades (Díaz-Salazar and Giner 133; Pérez-Agote 113–18). Irrespective of how one evaluates these facts, it would be reductive to conclude that religion no longer plays a notable role in Spain's politics, society, and culture.

Although the Catholic Church has not entered the political game supporting a specific political party during the democratic period, it has remained a strong pressure group that has tried to influence society and government policies. It has been a major player – often as a resistant factor – in debates and decisions regarding key social issues in Spain such as divorce, abortion, and same-sex marriage. Educational reform and the anti-terrorist pact of the main political parties are two other important issues in which the Church has clashed with the various democratic administrations. A common theme of the public intervention of the Church in post-Franco Spain seems to be its refusal to accept any social reform that entails embracing secular liberal values. To a certain extent, one could argue that the Catholic Church has betrayed its own post–Vatican II motto of coming to grips with modernity, which is leading to an escalating disengagement from organized religion by the younger generations (Pérez-Agote 114; Urrutia Abaigar 123). This would indeed confirm the tenets of the mainline "secularization thesis" of Western modernity that predicted the fading of religion from the public domain. However, as I proposed at the onset of *Confessional Cinema,* we should reframe our approach to the secularization of Spanish society to understand it not through the logic of a "subtraction story" – to borrow again from Charles Taylor – that would pose that once Spaniards discarded their concern with God and the sacred, and once they sloughed off the Church's authority in public affairs, they became truly modern subjects. Instead, we should view secularization as a process of relocation of the scope and the role of religion in modern Spain in such a way that traditional Catholic beliefs now have to compete, often in vain, with secular institutions (the nation-state) and with secular explanations of reality as well as with beliefs from other religious faiths in a context of religious freedom. Religion is still an important element of modern Spanish society, but it is a multilayered and dynamic phenomenon that evolves, and so does its relation to society. Hence, rather than insisting on its disappearance from secular society, we should scrutinize how it renews itself to survive in the new social and political setting of contemporary Spain.

This understanding of secularization allows us to grasp the sway that spirituality and the sacred still hold today in Spanish society, which goes beyond the official, and often reactionary, views of the Catholic Church hierarchy in relation to matters of social interest. While the public dimension of religion in Spain seems to be attached to the notorious controversies in which the ecclesiastical hierarchy typically plays the part of a retrograde force in a national plot of modern emancipation, there are other, more positive – yet less high-profile – aspects of the impact of religion in contemporary Spanish society and culture that merit attention. For example, religious organizations such as Cáritas have played a key humanitarian role in providing support for the victims of the economic crisis affecting Spain and in assisting immigrants who struggle to integrate in the host society.[1] As Bryan Turner asserts, "religious assumptions about suffering and healing have played an important role in shaping human-rights institutions" and in the overall "human-rights agenda" of contemporary societies (xix). Religious roots, even if in the form of secularized ethical values of social justice and human rights, stimulate the cooperative action of non-religious non-profit organizations and social movements that have been essential in helping to maintain the stability of the sociopolitical democratic system in Spain.

Another important dimension of religion in contemporary Spain pertains to the arrival of immigrants and the subsequent pluralization of religious beliefs. Given that sociological studies indicate that immigrant populations are more actively religious than Spaniards (Pérez-Agote 39; Pérez-Agote and Santiago 143–4), how is the interaction with other cultures and religions (e.g., with Islamic worship) shaping Spaniards' cosmovision and their spiritual beliefs? Although Spain cannot be compared with other Western countries in terms of religious pluralism, since all non-Catholic faiths together account for less than 10 per cent of the religiously active population (Martín de Santa Olalla Saludes 16), a fascinating topic for future research would be to examine how Spanish cultural production, and cinema in particular, is representing this new religious pluralism, however limited it may be.

Historians have begun to draw positive conclusions that indicate that religious pluralism has fortified, rather than debilitated, democratic values in Spain (Guia 166). In light of this, how is contemporary Spanish cinema echoing, reinforcing, and/or refuting the broader European anxieties over national identity with respect to the growth of multiculturalism and the assumption by radical secularists and closed-minded Catholics that non-Christian faiths, especially Islam, are incompatible with Western democracy and civil society?

This timely approach to Spanish cinema would complement Elizabeth Scarlett's examination of the diverse responses to the persistence of religion in Spanish society employed by contemporary high-profile filmmakers such as Pedro Almodóvar, Alejandro Amenábar, and Julio Medem. Prominent films of the democratic period have reworked traditional subgenres of religious films, in some cases with iconoclastic undertones, such as hagiographic films – *La noche oscura* (Carlos Saura, 1989), *Teresa, el cuerpo de Cristo* (Ray Loriga, 2007), *There Be Dragons* (Roland Joffé, 2011) – and nun films – *Entre tinieblas* (Pedro Almodóvar, 1983), *Extramuros* (Miguel Picazo, 1985), *Canción de cuna* (José Luis Garci, 1994). However, it is hard to identify religious film cycles or (sub) genres in contemporary Spanish cinema comparable to the ones produced under Franco. As Scarlett rightly points out, what we have are individual responses to the role of the sacred and to the place of the Catholic Church and its historical legacy in contemporary society. Groundbreaking as Scarlett's book is, one could argue that her take on the endurance of religious themes and perspectives in Spanish cinema relies on the secularist assumption that religion is an impediment to Spain's path to modernity, and that Spain "is encumbered with a spectrum of negative collective memories" by contemporary filmmakers (166). Scarlett insists on her astonishment about the fact that the "motifs of Catholicism are never abandoned" in Spanish cinema (168), which she deems "surprising given [Catholicism's] association with the authoritarian side of the Civil War and of Francoism from a democratic vantage point" (171). Apparently, religion can only be represented by filmmakers tied to the wrong side of history, since the persistence of religion is equated with a premodern remnant, almost a regressive state of Spanish society. In fact, when she predicts in her concluding remarks that Spanish filmmakers of the twenty-first century will not likely be concerned about "advocacy of or challenges to Catholicism as a belief system," but only about revealing "covert sexual abuse and human trafficking" in which the Catholic Church or its supporters are involved

(166–7), Scarlett is presuming the self-laudatory narrative of secularist modernity that this book has challenged.

I eagerly anticipate that future studies on Spanish cinema will tackle how the industry addresses the phenomenon of religion not just as a haunting presence that lingers in Spanish society but as a central element of its public sphere. This centrality manifests itself in the significant, yet not necessarily one-directional, role it plays in how Spain responds to new sociopolitical and economic challenges, and to its renewed multicultural composition. Given the aforementioned positive functions of religion, including platforms associated with the Catholic Church, in human rights advocacy and grassroots social movements in Spain (and elsewhere), an important tenet of my project, which I hope further studies will explore in the context of contemporary Spanish cinema and culture, is how religion may be employed, appropriated, or invoked for dissenting and/or progressive purposes. By arguing that confessional cinema during the late Franco period, and especially post–Vatican II comedies, performed the political function of glory, I mean to suggest that they were ritualized media events that exposed that the Spanish political, economic, and social spheres were infused with the sacred. In so doing, they also laid bare a limitation of Émile Durkheim's theory of religion: as ritualized media events, confessional films revealed how hegemonic groups sought media channels as tools to exercise power. When he argued that "religious representations are collective representations that express collective realities" (11), Durkheim missed the symbolic power relations embedded in those representations that shape societal values. This is certainly not the case, as we have seen, with Agamben, who sees how religious beliefs and practices are instrumental to the theological-economic paradigm of power in modern societies. But a caveat to his otherwise compelling theoretical framework for understanding modern political systems is that he does not contemplate the possibility that the same sacred notions that are transferred to the secular political sphere through media channels performing the function of glory could be co-opted for other purposes. Agamben concludes his book by rightly pointing out that modernity has "failed to leave theology behind"; however, one cannot help but wonder if his assumption that the only possible outcome of the relationship between religion and modern politics is "to lead the project of the providential *oikonomia* to completion" (*The Kingdom* 287) does not lead to a conceptual dead end that deactivates, somewhat simplistically, the sway of the sacred to stimulate social and political change in other directions.

This is precisely what I have shown happened in the last few years of the Franco regime. Once the Church began to incorporate post–Vatican II values, it also became implicitly critical of the contours of the economic-theological paradigm in Franco's Spain. Towards the end of the regime, Church and state were no longer inseparable, and the negotiations to revise the concordat had become paralysed. The drastic mutations of Spanish Catholicism both ensued from and fuelled changes in the broader sociopolitical fabric of a country enmeshed in a modernizing process. The Second Vatican Council prompted the Church to dialogue with the modern world, to separate from secular authorities, to seek religious freedom, and to strive for civil rights and democratic plurality. Once it began to apply the Vatican's directives, the Spanish Church became a double agent: while it was trying to become disentangled from Francoism – even helping oppositional groups – it was simultaneously benefiting from the financial and legal privileges of the regime. Although officially the Church still endorsed the regime, the cases of political dissension multiplied. Unlike the 1940s, there were now multiple ideological options within Spanish Catholicism. The post–Vatican II renovation of the Church and the increasing support for democracy within Spanish society were two different yet convergent processes. The Church became, "to the astonishment of many observers, a force of political change," since it anticipated democratic restructuring by advocating for more diversity within civil society (Lannon, "Catholicism" 276). Francisco Franco and President Carrero Blanco were perhaps the most astonished among those observers. Although they gave the technocrats in charge of governing leeway to modernize the official image of the regime, religious notions were still central to the project of socioeconomic development that the technocrats put in place. Both Franco and Carrero Blanco still counted on the Church's backing during the development years. This is why both Franco and Carrero Blanco felt betrayed by a Church whose new direction they did not understand.[2]

Correspondingly, once they began to make room for those conciliar values, confessional films and, above all, post–Vatican II comedies of development encompassed elements that lent themselves to dissident reception. While I cannot claim to know accurately if and how audiences perceived these potentially dissenting values at that time, there is tangible proof that certain confessional films became a thorny presence for the censorship boards. The comedy *Un curita cañón* serves a paradigmatic example of this point. The film exploited a popular and profitable formula that the Spanish film industry adapted from theatre and that had produced box-office hits such as the Cifesa product *El padre Pitillo* (Juan de Orduña, 1955) and the previously discussed post–Vatican II comedy of development *Este cura*: a well-intentioned yet boorish rural priest with a primitive understanding of his apostolic mission confronts the financial and political elite of his rural parish to defend the rights of some vulnerable members of the community. While the formula was amply celebrated in the mid-1950s as a film promoting the official Catholic precepts, the 1974 version, starring Alfredo Landa at the peak of his popularity, was perceived as an ominous product and had trouble with the censorship board.[3] Agustín Rubio Alcover has documented how the script, despite being written by Vicente Escrivá, who had penned the scripts of all of the high-profile religious films produced by Aspa Films in the 1950s, was turned down three times (372–3). Producers were forced to curtail segments of the dialogue that situated the film at the core of the tensions generated by Vatican II and that explicitly suggested that the Church was averse to the political authorities.

Just like its predecessors, *Un curita cañón* worked well at the box-office with almost one million tickets sold in Spain and a subsequent international release in Argentina and Mexico. Although the released version was much more sedate than the initial idea and delivered a consensual resolution in which political and ecclesiastical representatives reached an agreement (religion again as the glue uniting a community), one cannot help but wonder if viewers could see a blatant contrast with their own historical juncture. Unlike the conciliatory solution of this comedy of development, the political authorities of the regime did not yield to the demands of the post–Vatican II Church. This apparently innocuous comedy of development, like other confessional films of the late Franco period examined in this book, suggested that the religious factor, which had been the main scaffolding of the regime in its origins, ended up contributing to the collapse of its political legitimization. Franco died claiming that his authority came directly from God, but confessional cinema ultimately took the side of the majority of the Church in promoting civil rights and democratic values. Unfortunately, this also meant, as I pointed out in chapter 3, accommodating the conservative views on gender and sexuality that the Church still holds today. Confessional cinema towards the end of the development years enabled Spanish audiences to imagine a modern, pro-democratic society on the condition that acutely patriarchal values would still prevail in that society.

Notes

Introduction

1 Letamendi and Seguin explained this foundational fallacy as a Francoist myth that fabricated the origins of Spanish filmmaking linked to the Virgen del Pilar, "a la que se le denominaba como 'la capitana de los ejércitos franquistas' y su basílica era conocida como 'el santuario de la raza'" (they had named her the captain of Franco's army and her temple was the shrine of the Spanish race). For the purposes of promoting National-Catholicism, Gelabert, the first filmmaker in Spain, was not an ideal candidate, since he was "catalán y no identificado con el franquismo, formaba parte de 'esa otra España', la perdedora, que quedó subyugada a los caprichos de los vencedores (falangistas, carlistas y demás combatientes del bando ganador)" (Catalan and not identified with Francoism, he was part of "the other Spain," the one of the losers, who remained subjected to the whims of the winners (Falangists, Carlists, and other soldiers of the winning side) (www.cervantesvirtual.com).

2 Julio Pérez Perucha documents the fusion of civil and clerical forces in the early twentieth century in Spain "para proclamar que el cinema era espectáculo disolvente de la moral y provocador de la insania, la idiotez y la ceguera" (to proclaim that cinema was eroding morality and that it triggered insanity, idiocy, and blindness) (50). See Brad Epps for an account of a similar reactionary position among the intellectual elite in Catalonia related to the *noucentisme* cultural movement (57–8). The Vatican backed those efforts with several documents released during the Pius X's pontificate: *Una delle principali* (1909) prohibited clergy from attending film screenings, and *Postremis hisce annis* (1912) banned the screening of motion pictures in the temple.

3 See Gregory Black and Frank Walsh for well-informed accounts of the crusade of the Catholic Church through the infamous Legion of Decency against the film industry in Hollywood.

4 See Jo Labanyi, "Race," for an insightful analysis of this cycle of missionary films. Although they were produced to promote complicity with the political project of the regime, Labanyi convincingly argues that missionary films also offered the possibility of alternative readings, because spectators could identify with the representations of the "other" in terms of race, gender, and class.

5 The Aspa Films cycle of religious films made by the coalition Gil-Escrivá included *La señora de Fátima* (1951), *Sor Intrépida* (1952), *La guerra de Dios* (1953), *El beso de Judas* (1954), *Murió hace quince años* (1954), *El canto del gallo* (1955), and *Un traje blanco* (1956). The list of national and international awards that this team received for this cycle was impressive. All of them obtained the National Interest classification. Most of them received the award of the Sindicato Nacional del Espectáculo. *La señora de Fátima,* co-produced with Portugal, was an international blockbuster. The success of this film was backed by the next one, *La guerra de Dios,* which earned international recognition, such as the main awards from the International Catholic Organization for Cinema and Audiovisual, the Bronze Lion at the Venice Film Festival, and the Golden Shell at the San Sebastián Film Festival.

6 See chapter 2 of Elizabeth Scarlett's *Religion and Spanish Film* for a thorough analysis of the religious cycle of Aspa Films.

7 For studies on the history and significance of the Semana del Cine Religioso de Valladolid, see the works by Emilio Fuertes Zúñiga and Fernando Herrero, and José María García Escudero's *Palabras a la Semana de Cine Religioso y de Valores Humanos* and *Una política para el cine español* (171–94). García Escudero assesses the impact of this festival in several areas, including the fact that the "Primeras Conversaciones de Cine," held at the Valladolid Festival in 1960, were key to shaping the new censorship regulations implemented in 1964. See also Pedro Rodrigo for the text version of these "Conversaciones de Cine."

8 The following books by García Escudero dealt explicitly with the topic of religious cinema: *Cine social* (1958); *Cine Español* (1962); *Palabras a la Semana de Cine Religioso y de Valores Humanos* (1964); *Excluir, construir, redimir* (1966); and *Una política para el cine español* (1967).

9 There are some notable Spanish practitioners of this theological approach to film (Montserrat Claveras, *La pasión de Cristo en el cine;* Orellana, *Como un espejo;* Orellana and Martínez, *Celuloide posmoderno;* Orellana and Serra,

Pasión de los fuertes; María del Mar Rodríguez Rosell, *Cine y cristianismo*; and Pedro Sánchez Rodríguez, *Dios, la muerte y el más allá en el cine contemporáneo*).

10 A special session of the 2014 Convention of the Modern Language Association entitled "From the Sacred to the Postsecular: Religion and Literary Writing in Twentieth- and Twenty-First-Century Spain" and a panel of the 2015 Cine-Lit Conference entitled "Religion in Spanish Cinema" also suggest that more interest in this topic within Peninsular studies is to come.

11 Also, critiques of post-secularism have noted that it is not clear if its main advocates (Jürgen Habermas and John Rawls in particular) refer to "a change in the attitudes of a large population" or to a change in relation to their own earlier dogmatic secularist notions (Calhoun, Juergensmeyer, and VanAntwerpen 18).

12 This "myth of the Enlightenment" is also tied to the misguided assumption that the Enlightenment was only a secular question. As Craig Calhoun reminds us, although "there was a largely secular branch of eighteenth-century philosophy" (clearly the most influential one), "the Enlightenment was also a movement among religious thinkers" ("Afterword" 125). For two notable approaches to this religiously informed Enlightenment, see Israel Joachim and David Sorkin.

13 To offset this fallacy, Casanova suggests that we turn to counter-examples such as Japan and the United States, two societies in which social modernization and the differentiation of spheres have not resulted in a decline in the actively religious population (*Public* 27).

14 Although it would be impossible to summarize here the vast bibliography on the political ties between Franco's regime and the Catholic Church, some key studies that have examined the topic in depth are the books by Feliciano Blázquez; Julián Casanova Ruiz, *La Iglesia*; Romina De Carli; Guy Hermet, *Los católicos* I and II; Feliciano Montero; Stanley Payne; Hilari Raguer Suñer; Juan José Ruiz Rico; Luis Suárez; and the contributions by Julián Casanova Ruiz and Mike Richards to the volume *Unearthing Franco's Legacy* (ed. Carlos Jerez-Farrán and Samuel Amago).

15 Noël Valis has criticized the same secularist prejudices in relation to interpretations of the nineteenth- and early twentieth-century Spanish novel "under the somewhat belated and dismal impact of Michel Foucault," which have regarded religion as a coercive force inherently aligned with repressive power structures (5). While I share Valis's view about the need to approach the study of the interface between religion and cultural production from a less prejudiced and more nuanced

position, I would not reduce it all to an unfortunate application of a "reductive Foucauldianism" (241), however influential Foucault might have been in Peninsular studies. Interestingly enough, the late Foucault has enjoyed a renewed interest in the context of religious studies debates. For example, Ivan Strenski delineates a helpful distinction between the "First" and "Final" Foucault (from the second and third volumes of *History of Sexuality* onwards) that lays out the influence of the "Final" Foucault within Religious Studies debates. Also, Foucault's "repressive hypothesis" has been helpful for scholars who have taken the "secularization thesis" to task. For example, Wendy Brown claims that Foucault's "repressive hypothesis" has in some respects informed Charles Taylor's "subtraction argument" and his critique of the secularization thesis as a grand narrative of modernization ("The Sacred" 89).

16 See Laura Zenobi, *La construcción del mito de Franco* for a recent detailed study on the crafting of Franco's charisma as a leader.

17 The undesirable subjects, the *homo sacer* in Agamben's theory, were maintained in a "zone of indistinction" deprived of their *bios*, their right to participate in the political sphere, and reduced to be simply *zoē*, that is, to mere natural life, what Agamben refers to as "bare life" (*Homo Sacer* 6, 1).

18 Foucault further argues that this does not mean that sovereignty and discipline cease to exist. Quite the reverse, they become all the more important because they serve the best interest of the people. Expanding on his previous positions, and reacting to misguided interpretations of his ideas, Foucault warns against conceptualizing one template of power relations to replace a previous one. Instead of thinking of rational government as a replacement for disciplinary society and the latter as a replacement for sovereign society, we should see things as a triangle, "sovereignty-discipline-government," in which the three components work together for the common good of the target population. Disciplinary institutions such as the army and the police remain important but refashioned – through the "art" of governing – for pragmatic ends, as apparatuses that benefit the whole social fabric, in this case ensuring security (101).

19 In his 1960 lecture "Política comercial española," Ullastres asserted: "Lo que tenemos que hacer nosotros es llevar nuestro desarrollo moral, individual y social paralelamente a nuestro desarrollo económico; no va lo económico si no marcha paralelamente lo moral" (What we need to do is to make our moral, individual, and social development parallel to our economic development; the economy won't improve without parallel moral progress) (quoted in Amando de Miguel 335).

20 There are academic studies of this impact of Vatican II in relation to the modernization process in late Franco society from the diverse angles of history (Blázquez; Brassloff; Callahan; Cárcel Ortí, *Historia*; Cooper; Cuenca Toribio; De Carli; Lannon, *Privilege*; Martín de Santa Olalla Saludes; Montero Moreno; Payne; Piñol; Raguer Suñer; Suárez), political theory (Linz; Lombardía; Ruiz Rico), sociology (José Casanova, *Public*; Vázquez, Medín, and Méndez) and theology (Álvarez Bolado, *El experimento, Teología*).

21 Italian cultural historian Emilio Gentile has led this line of inquiry by claiming in his influential *Politics as Religion* (2006) that the sacralization of politics is a crucial feature not only in totalitarian regimes but also in modern mass societies. Gentile reformulates the distinction between "political religion," which Juan José Linz, among others, theorized as a usual component of authoritarian regimes such as early Francoism entailing a sacralization of politics in a fundamentalist way (109), and "civil religion," typical in modern democratic societies and involving a "shared civic creed" that does not impose any individual political movement or religious faith over others (Gentile 140). Gentile contends that, while this analytical distinction is still operative and necessary, both concepts are ideal types, and in reality all political systems, including democracies, exist with some form of hybrid between both of them (140).

22 Agamben is not using here the term "economy" as we would today to mean "production, distribution, exchange and consumption of goods and services," but in a broader sense to refer to the "organization" and "administration" of a community. This is why he always employs the Greek term *oikonomia* to establish that distinction. As Carlo Salzani points out in a review of Agamben's book, the "Greek term *oikonomia* means 'administration of the house' (oikos) and is opposed, in the Greek politico-philosophical tradition, to the 'political' activity in the proper sense, the art of ruling the city (polis)" (229). The repercussion of this is that Agamben is conceptualizing the functioning of modern politics through a paradigm that is more administrative than political, even if it has tangible political implications.

23 Teresa's arm had been co-opted by Francoist factions since the days of the Civil War. During the military operations to occupy the city of Málaga in February 1937, a Nationalist soldier supposedly found the relic in the suitcase of a Republican colonel. The retrieval of the relic was instantly used for the interpretation of the Civil War in spiritual terms to justify each Nationalist victory as a result of divine protection for the crusade (Di Febo 63). As a politically instilled synecdoche, one body part – the arm – stood

for the whole saint, who guided the spiritual crusaders to victory. Furthermore, the Nationalist propagandists orchestrated a campaign to claim that, since all providential events happen for a reason, this retrieval occurred during the war because Franco was the "natural recipient" of the relic. The arm relic was used for a symbolic exchange of charisma that epitomized the communion between throne and altar under Franco, who indeed got to keep the relic with him in the Palacio del Pardo until his death.

24 For studies that focus specifically on the way Buñuel approached religion in his films, see Ian Christie; Gwynne Edwards, *A Companion*; Víctor Fuentes (especially chapter 10 of *Los mundos*); Vicente Sánchez Biosca ("Scenes" and *Luis Buñuel*); Libby Saxton; Elizabeth Scarlett; and Santos Zunzunegui, to name but a few key authors. For a recent reading of *Viridiana* that briefly engages this film as a contrastive refutation of the secularization thesis of modernity in Spain, see Nathan Richardson's *Constructing Spain* (158–68). Apart from the extensive work by Spanish film scholars, Buñuel's films, especially *Nazarín* and *Viridiana*, have been a factor in conversations in the broader field of religion and film (see, for example, Aitken 194–209; Ivan Butler 190–7; Ferlita 151–6).

1 Lighting Sainthood in theTime of Technocracy

1 Valeria Camporesi documents that *Molokai* had a run of 105 days in commercial theatres (123), but there is no reliable ticket sales data available. Box-office figures were not systematically collected in Spain until 1965. This was the result of the *Ley de Control en las Taquillas* (1964) that García Escudero implemented as part of his new *política cinematográfica*, with the goal of documenting the impact of the new policies on the Spanish industry. Until then, the only data to estimate the commercial success of films was the number of weeks they were shown in commercial theatres. Any film that was shown for longer than six weeks in Madrid theatres was considered a "película de éxito" (box-office hit) (Camporesi 81). Because of this absence of box-office results, I will provide the number of weeks shown in theatres as the only measure of commercial success for some of the hagiographic films discussed in this chapter. For films released in 1965 and beyond, I will provide the data made available by the database of the Ministerio de Cultura (http://www.mecd.gob.es).

2 For example, in their brief analysis of *Fray Escoba* and *Cristo Negro* (Ramón Torrado, 1963), a hagiographic and a missionary film, respectively, José Luis Castro de Paz and Jaime Pena Pérez argue that Ramón Torrado

"chega tarde ó xénero, pero a película responde ó pé da letra ás características nacional-evanxelizadoras que se encontraban na raíz de boa parte das produccións citadas da década anterior" (arrives late to the genre, but the film follows to the letter the national-evangelizing features underpinning a good number of productions of the previous decade) (76).

3 *Aquella joven de blanco* was based on the best-selling novel *The Song of Bernadette*, written in 1942 by Franz Werfel, a Jewish author who escaped Nazi Czechoslovakia. The novel was previously adapted by Henry King in a 1943 Hollywood blockbuster with the same title starring Jennifer Jones as Bernadette in an Oscar-winning performance. The Spanish adaptation was not as successful, but the 352,215 tickets sold were still fine for a low-budget film.

4 Although some scholars have attributed to Francoism the infamous honour of hijacking Teresa de Ávila's historical figure as the saint of the Spanish race (Joseph Pérez 12), in reality the regime only reactivated an old stereotype. As Giuliana Di Febo has shown, the racial construction of the myth of Teresa goes back to the initial process of canonization of the saint in 1609–10, in relation to the discussions over the lineage of Teresa that were crucial in that very process. The favourable testimonies freed Teresa from suspicions of being a *cristiana nueva* and proved her "pure race" as a *cristiana vieja*, not descending from converted Jews or Moors (73–4). The consummation of this symbolic labelling of Teresa as the saint of the Spanish race took place in 1922, coinciding with the third centenary of Teresa's canonization by Pope Gregory XV. At a time when Spain was trying to re-energize the myths of its national identity in racial terms, Teresa was a suitable symbol to hold the ideological function of unifying all Hispanic cultures (85). She could carry the flag for Catholic Hispanic cultures because she was the quintessential Counter-Reformation saint. Teresa endorsed two of the main directives of the Council of Trent: moderation in corporal penances and observance of enclosure for her female order.

5 The reception of the film contributed to diminishing the intellectual stature of Teresa de Avila. In an otherwise favourable review of the film in *Radiocinema*, Alejandro de España pointed out: "Tal vez de las mujeres sea Santa Teresa la más representativa de la literatura universal, pese a que no releía sus escritos y que en algunos de ellos se observaba una falta de hilación, que era tanto como subrayar el temperamento místico de la escritora, más entregada a la verdad de Dios que a Dios por el camino de las vanidades literarias" (Among all women writers, Saint Teresa was perhaps the most representative one, even though she did not edit her

writing and some of it lacked coherence, which underscored the mystic character of the writer, more devoted to the truth of God than to finding God through literary vanities) (9).

6 In a *Tel Quel* article, Roland Barthes famously asserted that "toute biographie est un roman qui n'ose pas dire son nom" (every biography is a novel that dares not speak its name) (89).

7 The figure of Rosa's mother, though, is one of the wrinkles of Rosa's holy *vida* that the film irons out to make it fit the rigid gender roles in vogue in Francoist Spain. Frank Graziano documents how the very first hagiography of Rosa de Lima by Pedro de Loayza, who was also one of Rosa's confessors, reports the torments that Rosa suffered from her own mother, María de Oliva, who tried to marry off her daughter and reacted unkindly to her inclination to a religious life (45). Within the context of fervent idealization of the maternal figure under Franco, such a negative portrayal of a mother was not advisable. This is why Elorrieta's film offers a more sedate version of the mother. While she tries to convince Rosa to marry Carlos and is concerned about the toll that fasting and penances could take on her daughter, the filmic mother is warmhearted and affectionate toward Rosa. She limits her role of reprimanding Rosa for her disobedience to asking her to obey the patriarchal authority of her father.

8 The film also contains flagrant historical inaccuracies: the narrative starts in 1580 depicting Martín as a grown boy when, in reality, he would have been barely one year old; Martín de Porres and his sister were sent to Guayaquil by their father to be educated for about two years instead of the ten years that the film records. The most ominous inaccuracy has to do with the Caribbean accents of René Muñoz and Esther Zulema in a film set in colonial Peru.

9 This is factually correct. As Leo Marie Preher documented in a dissertation that approached the figure of Martín de Porres from a sociological point of view: "Feeling that he was not worthy to become a regular lay brother of the First Order, Martin asked to be admitted as a Tertiary dedicated to the manual household duties of the convent" (15).

10 When it seemed that it was time to put the missionary film to rest, the Spanish film industry once again found a way to refashion it in 1972, when Pedro María Herrero made *Cao-Xa*, set in Vietnam. Asia had already been explored in previous Spanish missionary films such as *La mies es mucha* (José Luis Sáenz de Heredia, 1949), *Sor Intrépida* (Rafael Gil, 1952), and *Una cruz en el infierno* (José María Elorrieta, 1956). Like the latter, *Cao-Xa* did not link the sacrifices of the Spanish missionaries to a Spanish colonial project, but rather to a philanthropic pursuit of (capitalist and Western) human

rights. In the aftermath of the decolonization of Equatorial Guinea, a colonial-missionary film would have been a tough sell. Devoid of colonial garments, the film was still ideologically crammed. Along the lines of its predecessor *Una cruz en el infierno*, *Cao-Xa* used the missionary alibi to produce an anti-communist pamphlet. Mixing documentary and drama, the film was shot on location in Cao Xa, a Vietnamese village that was besieged by the communist National Liberation Front. Binary oppositions deliver the heavy-handed ideological message of the film: bloody communists take over the poor, devastated North, while the South, at the time still under the protection of capitalist nations, is portrayed by shots of the thriving city of Saigon. A shot of a boy selling Coca-Cola bottles in the streets encapsulates the pro-Western future that the film hoped for after the Vietnamese conflict (wishful thinking soon to be undone by the outcome of the war).

11 Franco went even further in his speech to the Consejo Nacional on 9 April 1964, when he deemed the social peace attained under his leadership not only the direct result of his successful preservation of peace but also a pioneering initiative for the type of reform that the Church was just beginning to promote with the Vatican II Council (Preston 715). With this rather bold rhetorical move, Franco was switching his symbolic position in relation to the Catholic Church from ally to luminary.

12 Regarding the inclusion of Franco's closing interview, Sáenz Heredia stated the following in an interview with Antonio Castro: "Creo que es la única entrevista filmada que existe con Franco, la primera vez que se hace la biografía de un Jefe de Estado en vida, y que termina con la intervención del propio protagonista" (I think this is the only filmed interview with Franco, the first time that the biography of a head of state is made while he is alive and the only one that ends with the intervention of the protagonist) (Castro 377).

13 Franco signed executions almost to his dying day. The last ones were those of three members of FRAP and two of ETA on 27 September 1975. These executions backfired for Franco, since they caused a strong international reaction against the regime.

14 José Luis Sáenz de Heredia tried to complete Franco's hagiographic profile in 1975 with *El último caído*, another documentary hagiography thought of as a final homage to Franco – and to the regime – after Franco's death. As Nancy Berthier has documented, Sáenz de Heredia planned to present Franco as a victim, buried in the Valle de los Caídos along with fellow Spaniards from both sides of the war. With this gesture, the Valle de los Caídos monument would be framed as the ultimate proof of Franco's ability

to reconcile and unite all factions of the ideological spectrum under the peace and prosperity of his regime. Also, with this final homage the filmmaker claimed to be marking the path Spain should take in the post-Franco period: incorporating the traditional values embodied by the holy leader (Berthier, "*El último*" 537). But Sáenz de Heredia could not deliver his project because of some health issues and some desertions, including lack of support from the new King, Juan Carlos, who did not respond to a letter asking for an interview to be included in the documentary (546).

15 One could trace countless examples of metaphors linking light to knowledge in the religious and secular cultural traditions, beginning with the Bible (Dyer, *White* 108–9). The epitome of that long-standing tradition comes, of course, in the eighteenth century, which came to be known as the Enlightenment (*Siglo de las luces* in Spanish).

16 The significance of this speech in the film is reinforced in the English version (*Saint John Baptist de La Salle: Patron Saint of Teachers*), since the voiceover narrator, Andre (Marc Michel), repeats it so that spectators leave with that message in their minds. This English-language version, released in DVD format in 2010 by Ignatius Press, is a shorter version that is framed, unlike the one released in Spain, by an initial and final commentary by the narrator.

17 Amadori's film is actually not the last instalment of the cycle. Another high-profile hagiopic, *Cotolay*, was produced the next year. José Antonio Nieves Conde was commissioned to produce this hagiography of Francis of Assisi for the commemoration of the *Año Xacobeo* in 1966. Thus, the film had to highlight the saint's work in founding a Franciscan convent in Santiago de Compostela. *Cotolay* was produced and released with ample publicity, had a decent commercial run (552,039 spectators), and was awarded the *Primer Premio del Sindicato*, but it failed to achieve its primary goal – to be the Spanish film industry's contribution to the *Año Xacobeo* – since it could not be released until 1967. Nieves Conde resented making this film, which he deemed "un embolado, un film de necesidad" (a jam, a film made by necessity) (Llinás 122). See Ramón Herrera Torres (23–8) and José María Folgar de la Calle for detailed accounts of the production, shooting, and commercial release of *Cotolay*.

2 Praying for Development in Post–Vatican II Comedies

1 The law significantly deviated from Vatican II recommendations. Article 2 of the law stated that other faiths were tolerated as long as they did not interfere – by trying to proselytize – with Catholicism, still considered

the only faith of the Spanish nation. As Ángel Francisco Carrillo noted in the pages of *Cuadernos para el diálogo*, this was an offensive declaration against non-Catholic Spaniards, because it presupposed that they were not really "Spanish" (42). Moreover, article 9 of the law basically prohibited any public manifestation or teaching of non-Catholic faiths. Far from the Vatican II recommendations, the Spanish law typified two different statuses of freedom and, consequently, two categories of citizenship in terms of religious beliefs. Non-Catholic Spaniards were still discriminated against as second-class citizens and denied the chance to declare their faith in the public arena.

2 This seed would only grow faster in the following years. Influential Catholic cultural platforms, such as the journals *Razón y Fe*, *Signo*, *Vida Nueva*, and *El Ciervo*, positioned themselves along conciliar lines. Despite the relative freedom Catholic publications enjoyed, some of them were forced to shut down. See the well-informed study by Carlos Barrera ("Revistas católicas") for data on the financial sanctions these Catholic publications had to face between 1966 and 1975, and on the shutting down of *Signo*, *Juventud Obrera*, *Voz del Trabajo*, and *Aún* due to pressures from both the ecclesiastical hierarchy and government officials. New publications such as *Cuadernos para el Diálogo* were created (1963) with the explicit goal of providing a public forum in which a plurality of views could debate matters related to religious and political issues. The influence of *Cuadernos* on the cultural field of late Francoism symbolically marked a sort of rehearsal for a democratic scenario in which the Church contributed to an increasingly secularized public sphere (Lannon, *Privilege* 244).

3 In her study *Para grandes y chicos: Un cine para todos los españoles (1940–1990)*, Valeria Camporesi offered data to prove that in the late 1960s Spanish cinema was widely supported by audiences. The year 1968 was the peak of spectators of national films with 30 per cent of the total share of moviegoers and 123 million tickets sold (76).

4 The recent book *El "cine de barrio" tardofranquista* (2012), written by a collaborative research team led by Miguel Ángel Huerta Floriano and Ernesto Pérez Morán, is the most comprehensive study of this subgenre and provides commentary on a hundred comedies of development. For other recent approaches that have reassessed this subgenre, see Crumbaugh; Annabel Martín, "Miniskirts" and "El viaje"; Nieto Ferrando, "Entre el turismo"; Jorge Pérez; and Renard.

5 That formal petition did not materialize until 1977, once Spain could show evidence that it was transitioning toward a democratic system. Spain did not become a member until 1 January 1986.

6 The Citroën 2CV, popularly known in Spain as "un dos caballos," is one of the most utilitarian and profitable cars in the history of the automobile. It was meant to be an economical car that peasants would be able to afford, and was created with the goal of being "an umbrella on four wheels" (www.geocities.com/Motor-City/Shop/6846/). Sales began in 1948 and, due to its commercial success with almost four million vehicles sold, the 2CV continued to be made until 1990. Today it is a cult automobile, one of the few that has a fan club, called 2CVGB, founded in 1978 and with around three thousand members (http://www.2cvgb.co.uk).

7 Of those, approximately 2 million migrated to Madrid, 1.8 million to Barcelona, and the rest to other urban centres such as Seville, Bilbao, and Zaragoza (Riquer i Permanyer 263). The migration figures for those years were supplemented with the migrants to other countries, which were over one million between 1961 and 1973. According to John Hooper, those numbers were as high as 620,000 in France, 270,000 in West Germany, 136,000 in Switzerland, 78,000 in Belgium, 40,000 in Britain, and 33,000 in Holland (20).

8 By 1967 Spain was experiencing a boom in its automobile industry. Adrian Shubert reminds us that the automobile industry in Spain "barely existed" until the creation of SEAT in 1950, and by 1973 it produced more than 700,000 automobiles per year, of which 20 per cent were exported (208). Borja de Riquer i Permanyer also notes that "Spanish levels of car ownership rose from 500,000 (one car [for] every fifty-five inhabitants) in 1960, to over 3.3 million (one [for] every nine) in 1974" (265).

3 Gender and Modernization in Nun Films

1 There is no data about the commercial run of the first three films I list, but we do know that the post-1965 nun films were all box-office hits: *Encrucijada para una monja* (2,673,726 tickets sold), *Sor Citroën* (1,992,032), *Sor Ye-Yé* (2,065,747), *Las cuatro bodas de Marisol* (2,506,832), *La novicia rebelde* (1,346,691), and *Una monja y un Don Juan* (933,859).

2 The revision of the Civil Code, announced on 24 April 1958, removed some legal barriers of the Civil Code of 1889 that limited women's rights. Granted, the new code still maintained biological inequalities that kept women subordinated to the patriarchal authority of their fathers and husbands. For instance, women had to remain in the parental household until the age of twenty-five unless they got married or entered a convent. But other gender-based restrictions were eliminated. For example, the new code allowed married women to be guardians and testamentary witnesses

provided that they had their husbands' permission (Morcillo, *True Catholic* 67). The most significant reforms that affected women had to do with their renewed role as emergent labour force. The 1961 Women's Political, Professional, and Employment Rights Law supported equal opportunities for women in the work environment. Actually, such egalitarianism was not complete. Anny Brooksbank Jones reminds us that "the Law acknowledged women's equal political, professional, and labour rights (including the right to equal pay for equal work) while excluding them from certain professions – among them the Forces and the Judiciary – on the grounds that these involved activities which might offend or brutalise women's sensibilities" (77). Besides, the liberalization of labour laws was not accompanied by other necessary modifications, such as changes "in the regulation of sexuality and reproduction" (Valiente 111), and, tellingly, until 1975 women still needed marital permission to work or to hold a valid passport to travel abroad.

3 Although the Spanish context is not comparable to that of other Western countries, feminist activists were already quite visible in the late 1960s in Spain. In 1965 the *Movimiento Democrático de Mujeres*, later known as *Movimiento de Liberación de la Mujer*, was created to express their solidarity with political prisoners. Among their activities, there were public lectures and workshops to educate women on a variety of topics of interest, including sexual education.

4 For a severe assessment of nun films according to this gender dichotomy (masculine = rational, aesthetically worthy; feminine = sentimental, B movie type), see Les and Barbara Keyser. For these critics, nun films "rarely attempt to make audiences think; their sagas are normally melodramas designed to make audiences feel and feel and feel" (141).

5 The case of *Sor Intrépida* falls within a trend in Spanish cinema of the late 1940s and early 1950s that Jo Labanyi has described as "feminizing the nation." In fostering identification with female images onscreen as well as in a certain feminization of masculine roles, Spanish popular films endorsed a switch in the official image for the nation "from the military values of wartime and of early 1940s fascist propaganda to a 'privatized' domestic model of masculinity appropriate to peacetime under dictatorial rule" ("Feminizing" 181).

6 *Sor Angélica* (1934, 1954), *Sor Intrépida* (1952), and *La hermana San Sulpicio* (1952) are other salient examples of *enfermeras-monjas* in Spanish cinema.

7 Commenting on the defenceless situation of married women in cases of domestic violence during Francoism, John Hooper explains that "[l]eaving the family home for even a few days constituted the offence of desertion,

which meant – among other things – that battered wives could not take refuge in the homes of their friends or relatives without putting themselves on the wrong side of the law" (167).

8 Gubern dates the beginning of this cycle as early as 1948 with *En un rincón de España* (Jerónimo Mihura). Like *La orilla* two decades later, the second film of this cycle, *El santuario no se rinde* (Arturo Ruiz Castillo, 1949), also dressed the conciliatory rhetoric in religious apparel. During the 1964 commemorative campaign of Twenty-Five Years of Peace, José María García Escudero fostered the revival of the cycle with a call for film scripts that would reconsider the war in assuaging terms (Gubern, *La guerra* 148). For another study on this cycle of Spanish cinema, see Jorge Marí.

9 "[H]emos descubierto un modo de comer más apasionadamente, que une a las mismas ventajas alimenticias de antes el extraordinario gozo de los sabores mezclados, con lo que se consigue un indudable atractivo, por lo menos durante algún tiempo" (We have discovered a way of eating with more passion, one that combines previous nutritional benefits with the extraordinary pleasure of mixed flavours. The result carries an unquestionable appeal, at least for a while) ("Editorial" 5).

10 As with other folkloric divas of Spanish cinema, such as Carmen Sevilla in *La hermana San Sulpicio*, Lola Flores in *La hermana Alegría* (1954), Marisol in *Las cuatro bodas de Marisol*, and even Sara Montiel in *Pecado de amor* (Luis César Amadori, 1962) and *Esa mujer* (Mario Camus, 1969), dressing the star Rocío Dúrcal in nun attire somewhat sanitized her star persona, even if by that time the effort seemed rather pointless. Most of the *folclóricas* ended up betraying the decent image that the industry tried to safeguard for them: Carmen Sevilla became one of the queens of the first *destape* films; Marisol posed nude for *Interviú* in 1976, and Lola Flores in 1983; Rocío Dúrcal ended her acting career with explicit lesbian scenes in *Me siento extraña* (1977); as for Sara Montiel, it would have taken many more nun roles to sanitize the erotic myth attached to her star persona.

11 None other than Pedro Almodóvar crafts a very similar scene in *La mala educación* (2004), but this time with two schoolboys as the subjects of mutual desire, thus redefining the love-in-the-church scene with a queer twist. The schoolmates Ignacio (Nacho Pérez) and Enrique (Raúl García) fall in love with each other, and one of the steps in that process takes place in the church. They exchange looks during Mass, as Enrique turns his head a number of times and looks up at the choirboys to make eye contact with the object of his affection. The similarities between the scenes are conspicuous, with only one modification: the third wheel in the party. In *La novicia rebelde*, the Virgin Mary presides, and implicitly approves, the visual

encounter between the loving subjects. In Almodóvar's film, the third wheel is a priest who rejoices in ecstasy while Ignacio is singing, and who will soon compete for Ignacio's affection. I am not aware of whether or not Almodóvar had Lucia's film in mind when making *La mala educación*, but it is hard for a present-day viewer not to visually associate the two scenes. Also, my interpretation is not as off the cuff as it may initially seem, if we consider Almodóvar's own words in relation to his inspiration for the nuns of *Entre tinieblas* (*Dark Habits*, 1983): "In those days, my references came mainly from cinema. I had in mind Sara Montiel in her roles as a nun, and also a certain type of Spanish pop cinema where nuns could be seen rescuing or educating young women. Those films were a kind of musical comedy, and were used to further the careers of promising young actresses, such as Marisol or Rocío Dúrcal, who were set to become stars. *Dark Habits* is a nod in the direction of that religious pop cinema" (Strauss 182).

Almodóvar is famous, among other stylistic trademarks, for retrieving elements from his previous films (and from the archive of his cultural and sentimental education). Marsha Kinder aptly terms this trademark "retroseriality," since Almodóvar's films seem to provide "variations of the same genetic material" ("All about the Brothers" 268). Given that in the previous quote Almodóvar confessed that he had films like *La novicia rebelde* in mind when he made *Entre tinieblas*, it is not preposterous to think that this admitted source of "religious pop cinema" re-emerged (in retroserial fashion) in *La mala educación*.

4 Naratives of Suspicion: Religion in the *Nuevo Cine Español*

1 One could see Father Echarri's condemnation of knowledge and intellectual curiosity as reminiscent of the argument that historian Hugh Thomas recounts between José Millán Astray and Miguel de Unamuno, which was held at the *paraninfo* (great hall) of the University of Salamanca on 12 October 1936. In response to Unamuno's words, Millán Astray infamously shouted: "¡Mueran los intelectuales!" (Death to intellectuals!).

2 Religious iconography and critical mentions were already present in Saura's previous films. Two prominent examples included the representation of religious fervour during Francoism as excessive, as seen in the Holy Week processions that he depicts in *Peppermint Frappé* (1967), and the images of religious martyrdom in *Stress es tres, tres* (1968).

3 José María Caparrós Lera argues that Procusa (1958–65) was mistakenly considered an Opus Dei production company when in reality it was run

by a diverse group of intellectuals that included figures associated with the NCE such as Antonio Mercero, José María Forqué, and Elías Querejeta (145). While Caparrós is right in that Procusa was an independent business enterprise, it no less true that a number of prominent Opus Dei members were part of its executive board, such as Alberto Ullastres, Fernando Lázaro, and José María Villota.

4 That international pedigree did not pay off at the box office. Although the Ministerio de Cultura's website offers the number of tickets sold for this film (48,780), these figures are not reliable, given that *El buen amor* was released before box-office figures began to be systematically collected.

5 In a more recent interview, Olea finally admitted that when he was writing the script with Juan Antonio Porto, they were already thinking about the potential interpretation of the international sect in the film as Opus Dei (López Echevarrieta 70).

6 Maxim 227 of *Camino* states this clearly: "If you realize that your body is your enemy, and an enemy of God's glory since it is an enemy of your sanctification, why do you treat it so softly?" (*The Way* 62–3).

7 Jordi Grau has never hidden his connections with Opus Dei during his early career, but he has denied that he was ever a member of the religious organization. See his recently published memoirs for an explanation of the extent of his ties with Opus Dei (62).

8 The editorial of issue 1695 (June 1974) of *Ecclesia* argued that the decline in religious vocations was caused by two interrelated sets of reasons: 1) internal (to the Church) reasons, such as the identity crisis in the clergy, vertiginous changes in methods of formation of the clergy, and internal divisions within religious organizations; and 2) external factors, such as the rise of materialism, consumerism, and secularization ("Ante la Asamblea" 4).

9 "In 1963 only 167 priests abandoned their vocation in Spain. By 1965 the figure reached 1,189 and then hit the all-time high of about 3,700 in 1969–70" (Payne 199).

10 A number of films employed sexually charged plots during the first years of the transition to address the public conflict between ecclesiastical and civil powers. While the more permissive context allowed blatant political messages, Spanish cinema continued to conceptualize religious crisis and its broader sociopolitical impact in sexual terms, but showing increasingly more flesh. The most renowned cases were those of *El sacerdote* (Eloy de la Iglesia, 1978) and *Cartas de amor de una monja*. Other ventures in a similar direction included *Cara al sol que más calienta* (Jesús Yagüe, 1977), which depicted Opus Dei as a mafia that used illegal businesses to pay for sexual orgies with prostitutes; *La portentosa vida del padre Vicente* (Carles Mira,

1978); and *La boda del señor cura* (Rafael Gil, 1979), a retrograde film used by Rafael Gil, former religious film pundit, to argue that the decadence of the Church as seen in the decline of religious vocations was caused by the cancer of Marxism within young clergy.

11 Of the literary adaptations mini-cycle, Gonzalo Suárez's *La Regenta* has received the most negative responses for reducing the plot, as Cristina Martínez Carazo explains, to the consummation of adultery (193). Sally Faulkner argues that the case of *Tormento*, also publicized as and criticized for exploiting sexual themes, is quite different and unfortunate, since the romance between the protagonist, Amparo (Ana Belén), and the priest (a secondary character in the film played by Javier Escrivá) leads to "the dullest sequences of the film, and the single soft-focus moment of passion between the two (which of course appears in the publicity material) is risibly contrived" (*A History* 128). However, historians of Spanish cinema have tended to focus only on this and to bypass the significant cinematic qualities of Pedro Olea's adaptation.

Conclusion: Spanish Cinema at the Intersection of Religion and Politics

1 The self-report on their 2012 activities (*Memoria*) revealed that Cáritas has a wide network of more than 70,000 volunteers who helped more than 1,300,000 persons in need of social assistance such as housing, food, employment, and so on.

2 Take the following words pronounced by Carrero Blanco in a *Consejo de Ministros* in December 1972 as proof that both he and Franco were increasingly out of touch with the renewed mission of Spanish Catholicism: "Ningún gobernante, en ninguna época de nuestra Historia, ha hecho más por la Iglesia Católica que Vuestra Excelencia, y ello, y esto es muy importante, sin otra mira que el mejor servicio de Dios y de la Patria, al que habéis consagrado vuestra vida con ejemplar entrega. Es lamentable que con el transcurso de los años algunos, entre los que se encuentran quienes por su condición y carácter menos debieran hacerlo, hayan olvidado esto o no quieran recordarlo" (No other head of the state, in any era of our history, has done more for the Catholic Church than Your Excellency, and you have done it, and this is crucial, only for the benefit of God and the Fatherland to which you have dedicated your life. It is unfortunate that with the passage of years, you encounter those who, though their condition makes them less likely to do so, have forgotten this or don't want to remember it) ("El Vicepresidente" 31–2).

3 Perusing the issues of *Primer Plano* between May 1954 and March 1955, I found no less than thirteen articles, all of them with a celebratory tone, devoted to the preparation, shooting, post-production, and commercial release of *El padre Pitillo.* The last one, published in issue 751, praised the film for depicting "un cura muy nuestro, muy español" (a very Spanish priest). Let us remember that *Primer Plano* was a film magazine created to disseminate the views of the Falange on the role of cinema for the reconstruction of the *New Spain* (Triana-Toribio 39). Therefore, the splash made by this quasi-official cultural platform about this film proves that in the mid-1950s the rebellious attitude of the priest against the rural oligarchy was not seen as dissent but rather as proof of the felicitous Catholicization of Spanish society.

Filmography

¡A mí la legión!, dir. Juan de Orduña, prod. Cifesa, 1942.
Agustina de Aragón, dir. Juan de Orduña, prod. Cifesa, 1950.
Akelarre, dir. Pedro Olea, prod. Amboto P.C., S.L., 1984.
Alba de América, dir. Juan de Orduña, prod. Cifesa, 1951.
El ángel exterminador, dir. Luis Buñuel, prod. Producciones Gustavo Alatriste, 1962.
Aquella joven de blanco, dir. León Klimovsky, prod. Estela Films, 1965.
Atraco a las tres, dir. José María Forqué, prod. Hesperia Films, 1962.
Balarrasa, dir. José Antonio Nieves Conde, prod. Aspa Films, 1951.
La becerrada, dir. José María Forqué, prod. Inter Lagar, S.A., 1963.
El beso de Judas, dir. Rafael Gil, prod. Aspa Films, 1954.
¡Bienvenido, Mister Marshall!, dir. Luis García Berlanga, prod. UNINCI, 1952.
La boda del señor cura, dir. Rafael Gil, prod. 5 Films, 1979.
El bosque del lobo, dir. Pedro Olea, prod. Amboto P.C., S.L., 1970.
El buen amor, dir. Francisco Regueiro, prod. Jet Films, S.A., 1963.
La campana del infierno, dir. Claudio Guerín, prod. Hesperia Films / Les Films La Boétie, 1973.
Canción de cuna, dir. José María Elorrieta, prod. Luis Saiz Fernández, 1961.
Canción de cuna, dir. José Luis Garci, prod. Nickel Odeon, 1994.
Canción de juventud, dir. Luis Lucia, prod. Época Films, 1962.
Canciones para después de una guerra, dir. Basilio Martín Patino, prod. Julio Antonio López Pérez, 1971.
El canto del gallo, dir. Rafael Gil, prod. Aspa Films, 1955.
Cao-Xa, dir. Pedro María Herrero, prod. Sella Films, S.L., 1972.
Cara al sol que más calienta, dir. Jesús Yagüe, prod. Lotus Film Internacional / Películas Mexicanas, 1977.
Cartas de amor de una monja, dir. Jordi Grau, prod. Constan Films, S.L., 1978.

La casa sin fronteras, dir. Pedro Olea, prod. Amboto P.C., S.L., 1972.
Caudillo, dir. Basilio Martín Patino, prod. Reta, S.A., 1974.
Cerca del cielo, dir. Domingo Viladomat, prod. Columbus Films, 1951.
La ciudad no es para mí, dir. Pedro Lazaga, prod. Pedro Masó, 1966.
Cotolay (El niño y el lobo), dir. José Antonio Nieves Conde, prod. Midega Films, S.A., 1966.
Cría cuervos, dir. Carlos Saura, prod. Elías Querejeta, 1975.
Cristina Guzmán, dir. Luis César Amadori, prod. Cámara Producciones Cinematográficas, 1968.
El Cristo del océano, dir. Ramón Fernández, prod. José María Reyzabal Larroy / Cinematográfica Pelimex, S.A. / Devon Film, 1971.
Cristo negro, dir. Ramón Torrado, prod. Cooperativa Cine España, 1963.
Una cruz en el infierno, dir. José María Elorrieta, prod. Universitas Films, 1956.
Las cuatro bodas de Marisol, dir. Luis Lucia, prod. Guión Producciones Cinematográficas, 1967.
Un curita cañón, dir. Luis María Delgado, prod. Talia Films, 1974.
Dawn of the Dead, dir. George A. Romero, prod. Laurel Group, 1978.
Del amor y otras soledades, dir. Basilio Martín Patino, prod. Cesáreo González / Eco Films, 1969.
Del rosa ... al amarillo, dir. Manuel Summers, prod. Eco Films / Impala, S.A., 1963.
El desencanto, dir. Jaime Chávarri, prod. Elías Querejeta, 1976.
Encrucijada para una monja, dir. Julio Buchs, prod. Izaro Films / Filmes Cinematrográfica / Sargon Film, 1967.
Entre tinieblas, dir. Pedro Almodóvar, prod. Tesauro, S.A., 1983.
En un rincón de España, dir. Jerónimo Mihura, prod. Emisora Films, 1948.
Esa mujer, dir. Mario Camus, prod. Marciano de la Fuente Rodríguez, 1969.
Este cura, dir. Enrique Carreras, prod. Cesáreo González, 1968.
Extramuros, dir. Miguel Picazo, prod. Blau Films, 1985.
Los farsantes, dir. Mario Camus, prod. IFI España, S.A., 1963.
La fe, dir. Rafael Gil, prod. Suevia Films, 1947.
Franco, ese hombre, dir. José Luis Sáenz de Heredia, prod. Chapalo Films, 1964.
Fray Escoba, dir. Ramón Torrado, prod. Cooperativa Cine España, 1961.
Fray Torero, dir. José Luis Sáenz de Heredia, prod. Cesáreo González, 1966.
La gran familia, dir. Fernando Palacios, prod. Pedro Masó, 1962.
La guerra de Dios, dir. Rafael Gil, prod. Aspa Films, 1953.
La hermana Alegría, dir. Luis Lucia, prod. Cesáreo González / Benito Perojo, 1954.
La hermana San Sulpicio, dir. Florián Rey, prod. Perseo Films, 1927.
La hermana San Sulpicio, dir. Florián Rey, prod. CIFESA, 1934.

La hermana San Sulpicio, dir. Luis Lucia, prod. Producciones Benito Perojo, 1952.

Un hombre como los demás, dir. Pedro Masó, prod. Pedro Masó / Impala, S.A., 1974.

Un hombre llamado Flor de Otoño, dir. Pedro Olea, prod. José Frade Producciones Cinematográficas, 1978.

Inés de Villalonga, 1870, dir. Jaime J. Balcázar, prod. Producciones Balcázar, S.A., 1979.

Isidro, el Labrador, dir. Rafael Salvia, prod. Cooperativa Cinematográfica Walkiria, 1964.

Los jueces de la Biblia, dir. Francisco Pérez Dolz, prod. Pia Sociedad de San Pablo / Paolo Films, 1966.

King of the Zombies, dir. Jean Yarbrough, prod. Monogram Pictures, 1941.

Ladri di biciclette, dir. Vittorio de Sica, prod. Producciones de Sica, 1948.

Las Leandras, dir. Eugenio Martín, prod. Cámara Producciones Cinematográficas, 1969.

Locura de amor, dir. Juan de Orduña, prod. Cifesa, 1948.

Los que fuimos a la guerra, dir. Julio Diamante, prod. Saroya Films, 1963.

El maestro de esgrima, dir. Pedro Olea, prod. Altube Filmeak, S.L. / Origen Producciones Cinematográficas, S.A., 1992.

La mala educación, dir. Pedro Almodóvar, prod. El Deseo, S.A., 2004.

La manigua sin Dios, dir. Arturo Ruiz Castillo, prod. Taurus Films, 1949.

Melocotón en almíbar, dir. Antonio del Amo, prod. Antonio del Amo, 1960.

Me siento extraña, dir. Enrique Martí Maqueda, prod. Oscar Guarido Tizón, 1977.

La mies es mucha, dir. José Luis Sáenz de Heredia, prod. Chapalo Films, 1949.

Milagro a los cobardes, dir. Manuel Mur Oti, prod. José Luis Renedo Tamayo, 1962.

Misión blanca, dir. Juan de Orduña, prod. Colonial Aje, 1946.

Molokai, dir. Luis Lucia, prod. Europea de Cine, S.A., 1959.

Una monja y un don Juan, dir. Mariano Ozores, prod. Producciones Internacionales Cinematográficas, 1973.

Murió hace quince años, dir. Rafael Gil, prod. Aspa Films, 1954.

Nazarín, dir. Luis Buñuel, prod. Producciones Barbachano Ponce, 1958.

Night of the Living Dead, dir. George A. Romero, prod. Image Ten / Laurel Group, 1968.

El niño de las monjas, dir. José Calvache Walken, prod. Regia Films, 1925.

El niño de las monjas, dir. José Buchs, prod. Exclusivas Diana, 1935.

El niño de las monjas, dir. Ignacio Iquino, prod. IFI Producción S.A., 1959.

Noche de verano, dir. Jordi Grau, prod. Productores Cinematográficos Unidos / Domiziana Internazionale Cinematográfica / David Film, 1963.

La noche oscura, dir. Carlos Saura, prod. Iberoamericana Films, 1989.

La novicia rebelde, dir. Luis Lucia, prod. Cámara Producciones Cinematográficas, S.A., 1971.

Nueve cartas a Berta, dir. Basilio Martín Patino, prod. Eco Films, 1966.

Nuevo en esta plaza, dir. Pedro Lazaga, prod. Pedro Masó, 1966.

La orilla, dir. Luis Lucia, prod. Producciones Internacionales Cinematográficas Asociadas / Producciones Benito Perojo, 1970.

Oscuros sueños de agosto, dir. Miguel Picazo, prod. Cesáreo González, 1967.

El padre Coplillas, dir. Ramón Comas, prod. Sello Blanco, S.A. / Estudio 8, 1969.

El padre Manolo, dir. Ramón Torrado, prod. Arturo González Rodríguez, 1966.

El padre Pitillo, dir. Juan de Orduña, prod. Cifesa, 1955.

The Passion of Joan of Arc, dir. Carl Theodor Dreyer, prod. Société générale des films, 1928.

Pecado de amor, dir. Luis César Amadori, prod. Cesáreo González / Producciones Benito Perojo / Transmonde Film, 1962.

Pepita Jiménez, dir. Rafael Moreno Alba, Emaus Films, 1975.

Peppermint Frappé, dir. Carlos Saura, prod. Elías Querejeta, 1967.

Piedra de toque, dir. Julio Buchs, prod. Jesús Rubiera González, 1963.

Pim, pam, pum ... ¡Fuego!, dir. Pedro Olea, prod. José Frade Producciones Cinematográficas, 1975.

Polvo eres, dir. Vicente Escrivá, prod. Aspa Films, 1974.

La portentosa vida del padre Vicente, dir. Carles Mira, prod. Carlos Mira, 1978.

La prima Angélica, dir. Carlos Saura, prod. Elías Querejeta, 1974.

Proceso a Jesús, dir. José Luis Sáenz de Heredia, prod. Aldebarán Films, S.A., 1973.

Queridísimos verdugos, dir. Basilio Martín Patino, prod. Turner Films, S.A., 1973.

Raza, dir. José Luis Sáenz de Heredia, prod. Consejo de la Hispanidad, 1942.

Raza, el espíritu de Franco, dir. Gonzalo Herralde, prod. Producciones Septiembre, S.A., 1977.

La Regenta, dir. Gonzalo Suárez, prod. Emiliano Piedra, 1974.

Reina Santa, dir. Rafael Gil, prod. Cesáreo González, 1947.

Riña en un café, dir. Fructuós Gelabert, prod. Fructuós Gelabert, 1897.

Rosa de Lima, dir. José María Elorrieta, prod. Cooperativa Cinematográfica Unión, 1961.

El sacerdote, dir. Eloy de la Iglesia, prod. Óscar Guarido Tizón / Carlos Goyanes, 1978.

Saint John Baptist de La Salle: Patron Saint of Teachers, dir. César Amadori, prod. Europea de Cinematografía, S.A., 1965.

Salida de la misa de doce del Pilar, dir. Eduardo Gimeno, 1899.

El santuario no se rinde, dir. Arturo Ruiz Castillo, prod. Valencia Films, 1949.

¡Se armó el belén!, dir. José Luis Sáenz de Heredia, prod. Hidalgo, P.C., 1969.

Sebastianne, dir. Derek Jarman, prod. Cinegate / Disctac / Megalovision, 1976.

El secreto inconfesable de un chico bien, dir. Jordi Grau, prod. José Frade Producciones Cinematográficas, S.A., 1976.

El señor de La Salle, dir. Luis César Amadori, prod. Europea de Cinematografía, S.A., 1965.

La señora de Fátima, dir. Rafael Gil, prod. Aspa Producciones Cinematográficas, S.A., 1951.

Simón del desierto, dir. Luis Buñuel, prod. Producciones Gustavo Alatriste, 1965.

The Song of Bernadette, dir. Henry King, prod. Twentieth-Century Fox, 1943.

Sor Angélica, dir. Francisco Gargallo, prod. Selecciones Capitolio, 1934.

Sor Angélica, dir. Joaquín Romero Marchent, prod. IFI Producción, 1954.

Sor Citröen, dir. Pedro Lazaga, prod. Pedro Masó, 1967.

Sor Intrépida, dir. Rafael Gil, prod. Aspa Films, 1952.

Sor Ye-Yé, dir. Ramón Fernández, prod. Cooperativa Cinematográfica Astro / Filmex, 1967.

The Sound of Music, dir. Robert Wise, prod. Robert Wise Productions / Argyle Enterprises, 1965.

Stress es tres, tres, dir. Carlos Saura, prod. Elías Querejeta, 1968.

Teresa de Jesús, dir. Juan de Orduña, prod. Cooperativa Cinematográfica Agrupa Films, 1961.

Teresa, el cuerpo de Cristo, dir. Ray Loriga, prod. Artédis / Future Film Production / Lola Films, 2007.

There Be Dragons, dir. Roland Joffé, prod. Antena 3 Films / Mount Santa Fe, 2011.

La tía Tula, dir. Miguel Picazo, prod. Eco-Surco, 1964.

Topaz, dir. Alfred Hitchcock, prod. Universal Pictures, 1969.

Tormento, dir. Pedro Olea, prod. José Frade Producciones Cinematográficas, 1974.

Un traje blanco, dir. Rafael Gil, prod. Aspa Films, 1956.

La trastienda, dir. Jordi Grau, prod. José Frade Producciones Cinematográficas, S.A., 1975.

Tristana, dir. Luis Buñuel, prod. Talia Films / Época Films / Selenia Cinematográfica / Les Films Corona, 1970.

Tu Dios y mi infierno, dir. Rafael Romero-Marchent, prod. Lotus Films Internacional, S.L. / Distribuidora Centroamericana de Películas y Films, 1975.

El turismo es un gran invento, dir. Pedro Lazaga, prod. Pedro Masó, 1968.

Venus de fuego, dir. Germán Llorente, prod. Arte 7 Producción, 1979.

La vieja memoria, dir. Jaime Camino, prod. Profilmes, 1977.

Viento de siglos, dir. Enrique Gómez, prod. Nueva Films, 1945.

Viridiana, dir. Luis Buñuel, prod. UNINCI / Films 59 / Producciones Gustavo Alatriste, 1961.

La Voie Lactée, dir. Luis Buñuel, prod. Greenwich Films Productions / Fraia Films, 1968.

Works Cited

2CVBG Club. http://www.2cvgb.co.uk.

Abajo de Pablo, Juan Julio de. *Mis charlas con José Luis Sáenz de Heredia.* Valladolid: Quirón Ediciones, 1996.

Agamben, Giorgio. *Homo Sacer: Sovereign Power and Bare Life.* Trans. Daniel Heller-Roazen. Stanford: Stanford University Press, 1998.

– *The Kingdom and the Glory: For a Theological Genealogy of Economy and Government.* Stanford: Stanford University Press, 2011.

Agel, Henri. *El cine y lo sagrado.* Madrid: Rialp, 1960.

Aguilar, José. *Las estrellas del destape y la transición: El cine español se desnuda.* Madrid: T&B Editores, 2012.

Aguilar, Paloma. *Memory and Amnesia: The Role of the Spanish Civil War in the Transition to Democracy.* London: Berghahn Books, 2002.

Agustín, José. "La casa sin fronteras (Lluvia)." In *Cuentos completos (1968–2002)*, 91–111. Mexico, D.F.: Editorial Joaquín Mortiz, 2002.

Aitken, Tom. "Sacrilege, Satire or Statement of Faith? Ways of Reading Luis Buñuel's *Viridiana*." In *Cinéma Divinité: Religion, Theology and the Bible in Film*, ed. Eric Christianson, Peter Francis, and William Telford, 194–209. London: SCM Press, 2005.

Allen, John. *Opus Dei: An Objective Look behind the Myths and Reality of the Most Controversial Force in the Catholic Church.* New York: Doubleday, 2005.

Alonso, Carlos. *The Burden of Modernity: The Rhetoric of Cultural Discourse in Spanish America.* New York: Oxford University Press, 1998.

Alonso, Julián. "'El Señor de La Salle', un film de categoría internacional." *Cinestudio* 21 (1964): 36–7.

Altman, Rick. *The American Film Musical.* Bloomington: Indiana University Press, 1987.

Altman, Rick, ed. *Film/Genre.* London: British Film Institute, 1999.

– *Genre: The Musical*. London: Routledge, 1981.

Álvarez Bolado, Alfonso. *El experimento del Nacional-Catolicismo (1939–1975)*. Madrid: Editorial Cuadernos para el Diálogo, 1976.

– *Teología Política desde España. Del nacionalcatolicismo y otros ensayos*. Bilbao: Editorial Desclée de Brouwer, 1999.

Andrin, Muriel. "Back to the 'Slap': Slapstick's Hyperbolic Gesture and the Rhetoric of Violence." In *Slapstick Comedy*, ed. Tom Paulus and Rob King, 226–35. New York: Routledge, 2010.

"Ante la Asamblea Plenaria." *Ecclesia* 1695 (1974): 3–4.

Armas, Isabel de. *Ser mujer en el Opus Dei*. Madrid: Ediciones Foca, 2002.

Arroita, Marcelo. "*Aquella Joven de Blanco*, de León Klimovsky." *Film Ideal* 167 (1965): 322.

Asad, Talal. *Formations of the Secular: Christianity, Islam, Modernity*. Stanford: Stanford University Press, 2003.

Ashbrook Harvey, Susan. "Martyr Passions and Hagiography." In *The Oxford Handbook of Early Christian Studies*, ed. Susan Ashbrook Harvey and David Hunter, 603–27. Oxford: Oxford University Press, 2008.

Ashton, Gail. *The Generation of Identity in Late Medieval Hagiography: Speaking the Subject*. London: Routledge, 2000.

Ayfre, Amédée. *Dios en el cine*. Madrid: Rialp, 1958.

Backscheider, Paula. *Reflections on Biography*. Oxford: Oxford University Press, 1999.

Bakhtin, Mikhail. *The Dialogic Imagination*. Austin: University of Texas Press, 2001.

Barbáchano, Carlos. *Francisco Regueiro*. Madrid: Filmoteca Española, 1989.

Barbeito Carneiro, María Isabel. "Feminist Attitudes and Expression in Golden Age Spain: From Teresa de Jesús to María de Guevara." In *Recovering Spain's Feminist Tradition*, ed. Lisa Vollendorf, 48–69. New York: Modern Language Association, 2001.

Barrera, Carlos. *Historia política de la España reciente (1962–2000)*. Multilva Baja: Newbook Ediciones, 2000.

– "Revistas católicas y conflictos con el poder político en el tardofranquismo." *Anuario de Historia de la Iglesia* 10 (2001): 101–42.

Barthes, Roland. "Réponses." *Tel Quel* 47 (1971): 89–107.

Battersby, W.J. *De La Salle: A Pioneer of Modern Education*. London: Longmans, Green and Co., 1949.

Bazin, André. "Cinema and Theology." In *Bazin at Work: Major Essays and Reviews from the Forties and Fifties*, ed. Bert Cardullo, 61–72. New York: Routledge, 1997.

Beck, Jay, and Vicente Rodríguez Ortega. "Introduction." In *Contemporary*

Spanish Cinema and Genre, 1–23. Manchester: Manchester University Press, 2009.

Beckford, James. *Social Theory and Religion*. Cambridge: Cambridge University Press, 2003.

Bellido López, Adolfo. *Basilio Martín Patino: Un soplo de libertad*. Valencia: Filmoteca De la Generalitat Valenciana, 1996.

Benjamin, Walter. "The Work of Art in the Age of Mechanical Reproduction." In *Illuminations: Essays and Reflections*, 217–51. New York: Schocken Books, 1988.

Bergan, Ronald. "Whatever Happened to the Biopic?" *Films and Filming* 346 (1983): 21–2.

Berger, Michael. "Women Drivers: The Emergence of Folklore and Stereotypic Opinions Concerning Feminine Automotive Behavior." *Women's Studies International Forum* 9.3 (1986): 257–63.

Berthier, Nancy. "José Luis Sáenz de Heredia, admirador de Franco. *Franco, ese hombre* y *El último caído*." In *El destino se disculpa: El cine de José Luis Sáenz de Heredia*, ed. José Luis Castro de Paz and Jorge Nieto Ferrando, 207–17. Valencia: Ediciones de la Filmoteca, 2011.

– "*El último caído* de Sáenz de Heredia, un poema documental sobre Franco." In *El espíritu del caos. Representación y recepción de las imágenes durante el Franquismo*, ed. Laura Gómez Vaquero and Daniel Sánchez Salas, 529–57. Madrid: Ocho y Medio, 2009.

Besas, Peter. *Behind the Spanish Lens: Spanish Cinema under Fascism and Democracy*. Denver: Arden Press, 1985.

Bird, Michael. "Film as Hierophany." In *Religion in Film*, ed. John R. May and Michael Bird, 3–22. Knoxville: University of Tennessee Press, 1982.

Bishop, Ryan. *Comedy and Cultural Critique in American Film*. Edinburgh: Edinburgh University Press, 2013.

Black, Gregory. *The Catholic Crusade against the Movies, 1940–1975*. Cambridge: Cambridge University Press, 1997.

Blázquez, Feliciano. *La traición de los clérigos en la España de Franco*. Madrid: Trotta, 1991.

Boisvert, Donald. *Sanctity and Male Desire: A Gay Reading of Saints*. Cleveland: Pilgrim Press, 2004.

Bordwell, David, and Kristin Thompson. *Film Art: An Introduction*. Fifth ed. New York: McGraw-Hill, 1997.

Botti, Alfonso. *Cielo y dinero: El nacionalcatolicismo en España (1881–1975)*. Madrid: Alianza, 1992.

Bourdieu, Pierre. *Distinction: A Social Critique of the Judgement of Taste*. Cambridge, MA: Harvard University Press, 1984.

Brassloff, Audrey. *Religion and Politics in Spain: The Spanish Church in Transition, 1962–1996*. New York: St Martin's Press, 1998.

Brooksbank Jones, Anny. *Women in Contemporary Spain*. Manchester: Manchester University Press, 1997.

Brown, Wendy. "Introduction." In *Is Critique Secular? Blasphemy, Injury, and Free Speech*, ed. Talal Asad et al., 7–19. Berkeley: Townsend Center for the Humanities, 2009.

– "The Sacred, the Secular, and the Profane: Charles Taylor and Karl Marx." In *Varieties of Secularism in a Secular Age*, ed. Michael Warner, Jonathan VanAntwerpen, and Craig Calhoun, 83–104. Cambridge, MA: Harvard University Press, 2010.

Buchanan, Tom. "How 'Different' Was Spain? The Later Franco Regime in International Context." In *Spain Transformed: The Late Franco Dictatorship, 1959–1975*, ed. Nigel Townson, 85–96. Basingstoke: Palgrave Macmillan, 2010.

Butler, Ivan. *Religion in the Cinema*. New York: A.S. Barnes, 1969.

Butler, Judith. "The Sensibility of Critique: Response to Asad and Mahmood." In *Is Critique Secular? Blasphemy, Injury, and Free Speech*, ed. Talal Asad et al., 101–36. Berkeley: Townsend Center for the Humanities, 2009.

Calhoun, Craig. "Afterword: Religion's Many Powers." In *The Public of Religion in the Public Sphere*, ed. Eduardo Mendieta and Jonathan VanAntwerpen, 118–34. New York: Columbia University Press, 2011.

– "Secularism, Citizenship, and the Public Sphere." In *Rethinking Secularism*, ed. Craig Calhoun, Mark Juergensmeyer, and Jonathan VanAntwerpen, 75–91. Oxford: Oxford University Press, 2011.

Calhoun, Craig, Mark Juergensmeyer, and Jonathan VanAntwerpen. "Introduction." In *Rethinking Secularism*, ed. Craig Calhoun, Mark Juergensmeyer, and Jonathan VanAntwerpen, 3–30. Oxford: Oxford University Press, 2011.

Callahan, William. *The Catholic Church in Spain, 1875–1998*. Washington: Catholic University of America Press, 2000.

Camporesi, Valeria. *Para grandes y chicos: Un cine para todos los españoles (1940–1990)*. Madrid: Ediciones Turfan, 1993.

Caparrós Lera, José María. "Sobre Procusa (1958–1965), una iniciativa de coproducciones europeas y de cortometrajes." In *El productor y la producción en la industria cinematográfica*, ed. Javier Marzal Felici and Francisco Javier Gómez Tarín, 143–64. Madrid: Editorial Complutense, 2009.

Carandell, Luis. *Vida y milagros de monseñor Escrivá de Balaguer, fundador del Opus Dei*. Barcelona: Laia, 1975.

Cárcel Ortí, Vicente. *¿España neopagana? Análisis de la situación y discursos del Papa en las visitas "ad limina"*. Valencia: EDICEP, 1992.

– *Historia de la Iglesia en la España contemporánea (siglos XIX y XX)*. Madrid: Ediciones Palabra, 2002.

– *La Iglesia y la transición española*. Valencia: EDICEP, 2003.

Cáritas. *Memoria 2012*. http://www.caritas.es/memoria2012/.

Carr, Raymond, and Juan Pablo Fusi. *Spain: Dictatorship to Democracy*. London: George Allen and Unwin, 1981.

Carreño, José María. "Dos películas de Pedro Olea." *Fotogramas* 1284 (1973): 74.

Carrillo, Ángel Francisco. "Interpretación española de la declaración conciliar sobre libertad religiosa." *Cuadernos para el diálogo* 6 (1967): 40–6.

Casanova, José. "The Opus Dei Ethic and the Modernization of Spain." Diss. New School for Social Research, 1982.

– *Public Religions in the Modern World*. Chicago: University of Chicago Press, 1994.

Casanova Ruiz, Julián. "The Faces of Terror: Violence during the Franco Dictatorship." In *Unearthing Franco's Legacy: Mass Graves and the Recovery of Historical Memory in Spain*, ed. Carlos Jerez-Farrán and Samuel Amago, 90–120. Notre Dame: University of Notre Dame Press, 2010.

– *La Iglesia de Franco*. Madrid: Temas de Hoy, 2001.

Casas, Quim, and Casimiro Torreiro. "Entrevista." In *Un cineasta llamado Pedro Olea*, ed. Jesús Angulo, Carlos Heredero, and José Luis Rebordinos, 85–111. San Sebastián: Filmoteca Vasca, 1993.

Castro, Antonio. *El cine español en el banquillo*. Valencia: Fernando Torres, 1974.

Castro de Paz, José Luis, and Jaime Pena Pérez. *Ramón Torrado: Cine de consumo no franquismo*. A Coruña: Xunta de Galicia, 1993.

Charney, Leo, and Vanessa Schwartz, eds. *Cinema and the Invention of Modern Life*. Berkeley: University of California Press, 1995.

Chuliá, Elisa. "Cultural Diversity and the Development of a Pre-Democratic Civil Society in Spain." In *Spain Transformed: The Late Franco Dictatorship, 1959–1975*, ed. Nigel Townson, 163–81. New York: Palgrave Macmillan, 2010.

Christie, Ian. "Buñuel against 'Buñuel': Reading the Landscape of Fanaticism." In *Luis Buñuel: New Readings*, ed. Peter William Evans and Isabel Santaolalla, 128–42. London: British Film Institute, 2004.

Cierva, Ricardo de la. *El Opus Dei: Controversia y camino*. Madrid: ARC Editores, 1996.

"Cinema y espíritu." *SIPE* 50 (1942): n.p.

Clarke, Deborah. *Driving Women: Fiction and Automobile Culture in Twentieth-Century America*. Baltimore: Johns Hopkins University Press, 2007.

Claveras, Montserrat. *La pasión de Cristo en el cine*. Madrid: Ediciones Encuentro, 2010.

Collins, Jim. "Toward Defining a Matrix of the Musical Comedy: The Place of the Spectator within the Textual Mechanisms." In *Genre: The Musical*, ed. Rick Altman, 134–46. London: Routledge, 1981.

Colmeiro, José. *Memoria histórica e identidad cultural: De la postguerra a la postmodernidad*. Barcelona: Anthropos, 2005.

Colón Perales, Carlos. *Un cine para tres Españas: El cine y los toros (1929–1960)*. Seville: Fundación Real Maestranza de Caballerías de Sevilla, 2005.

Comaroff, Jean, and John Comaroff. "Alien Nation: Zombies, Immigrants, and Millennial Capitalism." *South Atlantic Quarterly* 101.4 (2002): 779–805.

"Concurso de Guiones Cinematográficos sobre las Misiones Españolas." *SIPE* 212 (1946): 48.

Cooper, Norman. "The Church: From Crusade to Christianity." In *Spain in Crisis*, ed. Paul Preston, 48–81. Hassocks, Sussex: Harvester Press, 1976.

Corbière, Emilio. *Opus Dei: El Totalitarismo Católico*. Buenos Aires: Editorial Sudamericana, 2002.

Cresswell, Tim. *In Place/Out of Place: Geography, Ideology, and Transgression*. Minneapolis: University of Minnesota Press, 1996.

Crumbaugh, Justin. *Destination Dictatorship: The Spectacle of Spain's Tourist Boom and the Reinvention of Difference*. Albany: State University of New York Press, 2009.

Cuenca Toribio, José Manuel. *Iglesia y cultura en la España del siglo XX*. Madrid: Editorial ACTAS, 2012.

Deacy, Christopher. *Faith in Film: Religious Themes in Contemporary Cinema*. Aldershot: Ashgate, 2005.

– *Screen Christologies: Redemption and the Medium of Film*. Cardiff: University of Wales Press, 2001.

Debord, Guy. *The Society of Spectacle*. Detroit: Black & Red, 1983.

De Carli, Romina. *El derecho a la libertad religiosa en la transición democrática de España (1963–1978)*. Madrid: Centro de Estudios Políticos y Constitucionales, 2009.

de Certeau, Michel. *The Writing of History*. New York: Columbia University Press, 1988.

De León, Fray Luis. *La perfecta casada. Obras completas de Fray Luis de León*. Ed. Félix García. Madrid: Biblioteca de Autores Españoles, 1944.

Deleyto, Celestino. *The Secret Life of Romantic Comedy*. Manchester: Manchester University Press, 2009.

Delgado García, Alfredo. "El ferrocarril de La Robla." 6 Sept. 2006. http://www.laercina.com/historia.htm.

Delgado Ruiz, Manuel. *De la muerte de un Dios: La fiesta de los toros en el universo simbólico de la cultura popular*. Barcelona: Península, 1986.

Dellinger, Kirsten, and Christine Williams. "Makeup at Work: Negotiating Appearance Rules in the Workforce." *Gender and Society* 11.2 (1997): 151–78.
Derrida, Jacques. "La loi du genre / The Law of Genre." *Glyph/Textual Studies* 7 (1980): 176–232.
Deveny, Thomas. *Cain on Screen: Contemporary Spanish Cinema*. Metuchen, NJ: Scarecrow Press, 1993.
Di Febo, Giuliana. *La Santa de la Raza. Teresa de Ávila: Un culto barroco en la España franquista (1937–1962)*. Barcelona: Icaria, 1988.
Díaz, Elías. *Pensamiento español en la era de Franco*. Madrid: Tecnos, 1983.
Díaz-Salazar, Rafael, and Salvador Giner, eds. *Religión y sociedad en España*. Madrid: Centro de Investigaciones Sociológicas, 1993.
Diken, Bülent. "Religious Antinomies of Post-Politics." In *The Post-Political and Its Discontents: Spaces of Depoliticisation, Spectres of Radical Politics*, ed. Japhy Wilson and Erik Swyngedouw, 126–45. Edinburgh: Edinburgh University Press, 2014.
D'Lugo, Marvin. *The Films of Carlos Saura: The Practice of Seeing*. Princeton: Princeton University Press, 1991.
D'Lugo, Marvin, and Paul Julian Smith. "Auteurism and the Construction of the Canon." In *A Companion to Spanish Cinema*, ed. Jo Labanyi and Tatjana Pavlović, 113–51. London and Malden, MA: Wiley-Blackwell, 2013.
DuPont, Denise. *Writing Teresa: The Saint from Ávila at the fin-de-siglo*. Lewisburg: Bucknell University Press, 2012.
Durkheim, Émile. *The Elementary Forms of Religious Life*. Oxford: Oxford University Press, 2001.
Dyer, Richard. "Entertainment and Utopia." In *Genre: The Musical*, ed. Rick Altman, 175–89. London: Routledge, 1981.
– *White*. London: Routledge, 1997.
"Editorial." *Cinema Universitario* 7 (1958): 5.
Edwards, Gwynne. *A Companion to Luis Buñuel*. Woodbridge: Tamesis, 2005.
– *Indecent Exposures: Buñuel, Saura, Erice and Almodóvar*. London: Marion Boyars, 1995.
Epps, Brad. "Echoes and Traces: Catalan Cinema, or Cinema in Catalonia." In *A Companion to Spanish Cinema*, ed. Jo Labanyi and Tatjana Pavlović, 50–80. Malden, MA: Wiley-Blackwell, 2013.
Un equipo de religiosas. "La monja, ese extraño personaje." *Cuadernos para el diálogo* (1965): 69–70.
Escrivá de Balaguer, José María. *Conversaciones con Mons. Escrivá de Balaguer*. México: Ediciones Rialp, 1968.
– *The Way*. New York: Scepter, 1979.
España, Alejandro de. "Teresa de Jesús." *Radiocinema* 531–2 (1962): 9, 11.

Evans, Peter William. "*Cría cuervos* and the Daughters of Fascism." *Vida Hispánica* 33 (1984): 17–22.

Faulkner, Sally. *A Cinema of Contradiction: Spanish Film in the 1960s*. Edinburgh: Edinburgh University Press, 2006.

– *A History of Spanish Cinema: Cinema and Society 1910–2010*. London: Bloomsbury, 2013.

Felix, Sara. "EAP Programmes Feeding the Living Dead of Academia: Critical Thinking as a Global Antibody." In *Zombies in the Academy*, ed. Andrew Whelan, Ruth Walker, and Christopher Moore, 189–202. Bristol: Intellect, 2014.

Ferlita, Ernest. "Luis Buñuel." In *Religion in Film*, ed. John R. May and Michael Bird, 151–6. Knoxville: University of Tennessee Press, 1982.

Fernández de la Mora, Gonzalo. *El crepúsculo de las ideologías*. Madrid: Rialp, 1965.

Feuer, Jane. *El musical de Hollywood*. Madrid: Verdoux, 1992.

Folgar de la Calle, José María. "*Cotolay*: historia cinematográfica do paso de Francisco de Asís por Compostela." In *Homenaje a José García Oro*, ed. Miguel Romaní Martínez and María Ángeles Novoa Gómez, 425–36. Santiago de Compostela: Servicio de Publicaciones de la Universidad de Santiago de Compostela, 2002.

Font, Domènec. *Del azul al verde: El cine español durante el franquismo*. Barcelona: Avance, 1976.

– "Canciones para después de una guerra, de Basilio Martín Patino." *Dirigido por* 36 (1976): n.p.

Foucault, Michel. "Governmentality." In *The Foucault Effect: Studies in Governmentality*, ed. Graham Burchell, Colin Gordon, and Peter Miller, 87–104. Chicago: University of Chicago Press, 1991.

Fraga Iribarne, Manuel. *El desarrollo político*. Barcelona: Grijalbo, 1971.

– *Horizonte español*. Madrid: Editora Nacional, 1965.

Friedberg, Anne. *Window Shopping: Cinema and the Postmodern*. Berkeley: University of California Press, 1993.

Fuentes, Víctor. *Buñuel, del surrealismo al terrorismo*. Seville: Editorial Renacimiento, 2013.

– *Los mundos de Buñuel*. Madrid: Akal, 2000.

Fuertes Zúñiga, Emilio. "La evolución del cine religioso. La Semana de Valladolid (1956–1974)." *Anuario de Historia de la Iglesia* 14 (2005): 435–9.

Galán, Diego. "El cine 'político' español." In *Siete trabajos de base sobre el cine español*, ed. Enrique Braso et al., 87–107. Valencia: Fernando Torres, 1975.

– *Venturas y desventuras de La prima Angélica*. Valencia: Fernando Torres, 1974.

García Escudero, José María. *Cine español*. Madrid: Rialp, 1962.

– *Cine social*. Madrid: Taurus, 1958.
– *Excluir, construir, redimir*. Valladolid: Semana Internacional de Cine Religioso y de Valores Humanos, 1966.
– "La imagen cinematográfica de Franco." *Archivos de la Filmoteca* 42–3 (2002–3): 162–73.
– *Palabras a la Semana de Cine Religioso y de Valores Humanos*. Valladolid: Semana de Cine Religioso, 1964.
– *Una política para el cine español*. Madrid: Editora Nacional, 1967.
García Ochoa, Santiago. "El automóvil en el cine español: valor iconográfico y conceptual en la obra de Carlos Saura." Diss. Universidad de Santiago de Compostela, 2004.
García Rivera, Alex. *St. Martín de Porres: The "Little Stories" and the Semiotics of Culture*. Maryknoll, NY: Orbis Books, 1995.
Gentile, Emilio. *Politics as Religion*. Princeton: Princeton University Press, 2006.
Geocities Motor. https://smallbusiness.yahoo.com/geocities.
Giménez Caballero, Ernesto. *Genio hispánico y mestizaje*. Madrid: Editora Nacional, 1965.
Gómez Pérez, Rafael. *Política y religión en el régimen de Franco*. Barcelona: DOPESA, 1976.
González Ballesteros, Teodoro. *Aspectos jurídicos de la censura cinematográfica en España*. Madrid: Universidad Complutense, 1981.
Gortari, Carlos. "Pudor y sensibilidad." *Cinestudio* 125 (1973): 32–6.
Grace, Pamela. *The Religious Film: Christianity and the Hagiopic*. Malden, MA: Wiley-Blackwell, 2009.
Graham, Helen. "Gender and the State: Women in the 1940s." In *Spanish Cultural Studies: An Introduction. The Struggle for Modernity*, ed. Helen Graham and Jo Labanyi, 182–95. Oxford: Oxford University Press, 1995.
Grau, Jordi. *Confidencias de un director de cine descatalogado*. Madrid: Calamar Ediciones, 2014.
Graziano, Frank. *Wounds of Love: The Mystical Marriage of Saint Rose of Lima*. Oxford: Oxford University Press, 2004.
Gregori, Antonio. *El cine español según sus directores*. Madrid: Cátedra, 2009.
Gubern, Román. *La censura: Función política y ordenamiento jurídico bajo el Franquismo (1936–1975)*. Barcelona: Ediciones Península, 1981.
– *La guerra de España en la pantalla: De la propaganda a la Historia*. Madrid: Filmoteca Española, 1986.
Guerrero, Fernando. "Magisterio auténtico y conciencia moral." *Ecclesia* 1412 (1968): 29–33.
Guia, Aitana. *The Muslim Struggle for Civil Rights in Spain: Promoting Democracy through Migrant Engagement, 1985–2010*. Chicago: Sussex Academic Press, 2014.

Guillén, Abraham. *La "élite" del poder en España: La sociedad secreta del "Opus Dei"*. Montevideo: Editorial Aconcagua, 1973.

Habermas, Jürgen. "Religion in the Public Sphere." *European Journal of Philosophy* 14.1 (2006): 1–25.

Halbwachs, Maurice. *The Collective Memory*. New York: Harper, 1980.

Hampe Martínez, Teodoro. "Santa Rosa de Lima y la identidad criolla en el Perú colonial." *Revista de Historia de América* 121 (1996): 7–26.

Handley, Charles. "History of Motion-Picture Lighting." In *A Technological History of Motion Pictures and Television*, ed. Raymond Fielding, 120–4. Berkeley: University of California Press, 1967.

Hardcastle, Anne. "The Guilt of the Innocent: Memory, History and Trauma in Saura's *Cría cuervos* and Matute's *Primera memoria*." *Letras Peninsulares* 17.2.3 (2004): 387–403.

Harper, Rowena. "Being Post-Death at Zombie University." In *Zombies in the Academy*, ed. Andrew Whelan, Ruth Walker, and Christopher Moore, 27–38. Bristol: Intellect, 2014.

Hayward, Susan. *Cinema Studies: The Key Concepts*. London: Routledge, 2000.

Hebdige, Dick. *Hiding in the Light: On Images and Things*. London: Routledge, 1988.

Heredero, Carlos. *Las huellas del tiempo: Cine español 1951–1961*. Madrid / Valencia: Filmoteca Nacional / Filmoteca de la Generalitat Valenciana, 1993.

Hermet, Guy. *Los católicos en la España franquista I: Los actores del juego político*. Madrid: Siglo XXI, 1985.

– *Los católicos en la España franquista II: Crónica de una dictadura*. Madrid: Siglo XXI, 1985.

Hernández Les, Juan. *El cine de Elías Querejeta: Un productor singular*. Bilbao: Ediciones Mensajero, 1986.

Hernández Ruiz, Javier, and Pablo Pérez Rubio. "Un universo proteico y multiforme: la comedia costumbrista del desarrollismo." In *El paso del mundo al sonoro: Actas del IV Congreso de la A.E.H.C.*, 311–20. Madrid: Editorial Complutense, 1993.

Herrera Torres, Ramón. *Cine Jacobeo: El Camino de Santiago en la pantalla*. Bilbao: Ediciones Mensajero, 2008.

Herrero, Fernando. *20 años de historia del cine a través de la Semana Internacional de Cine de Valladolid*. Valladolid: XXII Semana Internacional de Cine, 1977.

Higginbotham, Virginia. *Spanish Film under Franco*. Austin: University of Texas Press, 1988.

Hobsbawm, Eric. "Introduction: Inventing Traditions." In *The Invention of Tradition*, ed. Eric Hobsbawm and Terence Ranger, 1–14. Cambridge: Cambridge University Press, 1983.

Hooper, John. *The New Spaniards*. London: Penguin, 1995.

Hopewell, John. *Out of the Past: Spanish Cinema after Franco*. London: British Film Institute, 1986.

Hubner, Laura, Marcus Leaning, and Paul Manning. *The Zombie Renaissance in Popular Culture*. New York: Palgrave Macmillan, 2014.

Huerta Floriano, Miguel Ángel, and Ernesto Pérez Morán, eds. *El "cine de barrio" tardofranquista: Reflejo de una sociedad*. Madrid: Biblioteca Nueva, 2012.

Hutchinson, Robert. *Their Kingdom to Come: Inside the Secret World of Opus Dei*. New York: Thomas Dunne Books, 2006.

Jakobsen, Janet R., and Ann Pellegrini. "Introduction: Times Like These." In *Secularisms*, 1–35. Durham, NC: Duke University Press, 2008.

Jameson, Fredric. *The Political Unconscious: Narrative as a Socially Symbolic Act*. Ithaca: Cornell University Press, 1982.

Janosik, Mary Ann. "Madonnas in Our Midst: Representations of Women Religious in Hollywood Film." *U.S. Catholic Historian* 15.3 (1997): 75–98.

Jeffreys, Sheila. *Beauty and Misogyny: Harmful Cultural Practices in the West*. New York: Routledge, 2005.

Joachim, Israel. *The Radical Enlightenment*. Oxford: Oxford University Press, 2001.

Jurado Morales, José. "*La prima Angélica* de Carlos Saura en el contexto del tardofranquismo." *Hispanic Research Journal* 12.4 (2011): 357–68.

Kalberg, Stephen. "Introduction." In *Max Weber: Readings and Commentary on Modernity*, 1–47. Malden, MA: Blackwell, 2005.

Karnick, Kristine Brunovska. "Commitment and Reaffirmation in Hollywood Romantic Comedy." In *Classical Hollywood Comedy*, ed. Kristine Brunovska Karnick and Henry Jenkins, 123–46. New York: Routledge, 1995.

Karnick, Kristine Brunovska, and Henry Jenkins, eds. *Classical Hollywood Comedy*. New York: Routledge, 1995.

Katznelson, Ira, and Gareth Stedman Jones. "Introduction: Multiple Secularities." In *Religion and the Political Imagination*, 1–22. Cambridge: Cambridge University Press, 2010.

Kaufmann, Michael. "Post-Secular Puritans: Recent Retrials of Anne Hutchinson." *Early American Literature* 45.1 (2010): 31–59.

Kaye, Richard. "Losing His Religion: Saint Sebastian as a Contemporary Gay Martyr." In *Outlooks: Lesbian and Gay Sexualities and Visual Cultures*, ed. Peter Horne and Reina Lewis, 86–105. London: Routledge, 1996.

Keller, Patricia. "Letters from the City: Writing Boundaries in *Nueve cartas a Berta* (1965)." *Bulletin of Hispanic Studies* 90.8 (2013): 945–64.

Keyser, Les, and Barbara Keyser. *Hollywood and the Catholic Church: The Image of Roman Catholicism in American Movies*. Chicago: Loyola University Press, 1984.

Kinder, Marsha. "All about the Brothers: Retroseriality in Almodóvar's Cinema." In *All about Almodóvar: A Passion for Cinema*, ed. Brad Epps and Despina Kakoudaki, 267–94. Minneapolis: University of Minnesota Press, 2009.

– "The Children of Franco in the New Spanish Cinema." *Quarterly Review of Film Studies* 8.2 (1983): 57–76.

Kleinberg, Aviad. *Flesh Made Word: Saints' Stories and the Western Imagination.* Cambridge, MA: Harvard University Press, 2008.

Koehlinger, Amy. *The New Nuns: Racial Justice and Religious Reform in the 1960s.* Cambridge, MA: Harvard University Press, 2007.

Kuhns, Elizabeth. *The Habit: A History of the Clothing of Catholic Nuns.* New York: Doubleday, 2003.

Labanyi, Jo. "Feminizing the Nation: Women, Subordination and Subversion in Post-Civil War Spanish Cinema." In *Heroines without Heroes: Reconstructing Female and National Identities in European Cinema, 1945–51*, ed. Ulrike Sieglohr, 163–83. London: Cassell, 2000.

– "Memory and Modernity in Democratic Spain: The Difficulty of Coming to Terms with the Spanish Civil War." *Poetics Today* 28.1 (2007): 89–116.

– "Race, Gender, and Disavowal in Spanish Cinema of the Early Franco Period: The Missionary Film and the Folkloric Musical." *Screen* 38.3 (1997): 215–27.

Lannon, Frances. "Catholicism and Social Change." In *Spanish Cultural Studies: An Introduction. The Struggle for Modernity*, ed. Helen Graham and Jo Labanyi, 276–82. Oxford: Oxford University Press, 1995.

– *Privilege, Persecution, and Prophecy: The Catholic Church in Spain 1875–1975.* Oxford: Clarendon Press, 1987.

LaRubia-Prado, Francisco. "Franco as Cyborg: The Body Re-Formed by Politics: Part Flesh, Part Machine." *Journal of Spanish Cultural Studies* 1.2 (2000): 135–52.

Letamendi, Jon, and Jean-Claude Seguin. "*Salida de misa de doce del Pilar de Zaragoza*: la fraudulenta creación de un mito franquista." *Actas del VII Congreso de la A.E.H.C.* Madrid: Academia de las Artes y Ciencias Cinematográficas de España, 1999. Accessed online on Biblioteca Virtual Cervantes: www.cervantesvirtual.com.

Lindvall, Terry. *Sanctuary Cinema: Origins of the Christian Film Industry.* New York: New York University Press, 2007.

Linz, Juan José. "The Religious Use of Politics and / or the Political Use of Religion: Ersatz Ideology versus Ersatz Religion." In *Totalitarianism and Political Religions*, ed. Hans Maier, 107–25. London: Routledge, 2004.

Llinás, Francisco. *José Antonio Nieves Conde: El oficio del cineasta.* Valladolid: Semana Internacional del Cine, 1995.

Lombardía, Pedro. "Actitud de la Iglesia ante el Franquismo." In *Iglesia Católica y Regímenes Autoritarios y Democráticos*, ed. Iván Ibán, 81–102. Madrid: EDERSA, 1987.

Longhurst, Alex. "Culture and Development: The Impact of 1960s 'Desarrollismo'." In *Contemporary Spanish Cultural Studies*, ed. Barry Jordan and Rikki Morgan-Tamosunas, 17–28. London: Arnold, 2000.

López Echevarrieta, Alberto. *El cine de Pedro Olea*. Valladolid: Semana Internacional de Cine de Valladolid, 2006.

López Hernández-Herrera, Francisco. "El Concilio habló de la mujer." *Ecclesia* 1699 (1974): 25–6.

López Rodó, Laureano. *Nuevo horizonte del desarrollo*. Madrid: Aguilar, 1972.

– *Política y desarrollo*. Madrid: Aguilar, 1970.

Losilla, Carlos. "Su ciclo literario: Marginación y conformismo." In *Un cineasta llamado Pedro Olea*, ed. Jesús Angulo, Carlos Heredero, and José Luis Rebordinos, 61–70. San Sebastián: Filmoteca Vasca, 1993.

Lyden, John. *Film As Religion: Myths, Morals, and Rituals*. New York: New York University Press, 2003.

Maeztu, Ramiro de. *Defensa de la Hispanidad*. Madrid: Gráfica Universal, 1934.

Marí, Jorge. "La hora perdida: Memoria, olvido, reconciliación y representatibilidad en *España otra vez*." In *Un Hispanismo para el siglo XXI: Ensayos de crítica cultural*, ed. Rosalía Cornejo Parriego and Alberto Villamandos, 241–60. Madrid: Biblioteca Nueva, 2011.

Marsh, Clive, and Gaye Ortiz, eds. *Explorations in Theology and Film*. Oxford: Blackwell, 1997.

Marsh, Steven. *Popular Spanish Film under Franco: Comedy and the Weakening of the State*. New York: Palgrave Macmillan, 2006.

Marshall, Jonathan Paul. "The Intranet of the Living Dead: Software and Universities." In *Zombies in the Academy*, ed. Andrew Whelan, Ruth Walker, and Christopher Moore, 119–36. Bristol: Intellect, 2014.

Martí, Octavi. "La trastienda." *Dirigido por…* 32 (1976): 34–5.

Martín, Annabel. "Miniskirts, Polka Dots, and Real-State: What Lies under the Sun?" In *Spain Is (Still) Different: Tourism and Discourse in Spanish Identity*, ed. Eugenia Afinoguénova and Jaume Martí-Olivella, 219–43. Lanham, MD: Lexington Books, 2008.

– "El viaje sin retorno: turismo y disidencia identitaria en el cine español de los 60." In *Turistas de película: Sus representaciones en el cine hispánico*, ed. Antonia del Rey-Reguillo, 65–89. Madrid: Biblioteca Nueva, 2013.

Martín Arias, Luis. "Lo táurico, lo fílmico: una aproximación analítica." In *Pantalla y ruedo*, ed. Louis Delluc et al., 39–61. Córdoba: Filmoteca de Andalucía, 1992.

Martín Descalzo, José Luis. *Dios es alegre. (Antología del humor posconciliar).* Madrid: Editorial PPC, 1971.

Martin-Márquez, Susan. "De *Cristo negro* a Cristo hueco: formulaciones de raza y religión en la Guinea española." In *Memoria colonial e inmigración: La negritud en la España posfranquista,* ed. Rosalía Cornejo-Parriego, 53–78. Barcelona: Bellaterra, 2007.

– *Disorientations: Spanish Colonialism in Africa and the Performance of Identity.* New Haven: Yale University Press, 2008.

Martín de Santa Olalla Saludes, Pablo. *El Rey, la Iglesia y la Transición.* Madrid: Sílex, 2012.

Martínez Bretón, Juan Antonio. *Influencia de la Iglesia Católica en la cinematografía española (1951–1962).* Madrid: Harofarma, 1987.

Martínez Carazo, Cristina. *De la visualidad literaria a la visualidad fílmica: La Regenta de Leopoldo Alas "Clarín".* Gijón: Libros del Pexe, 2006.

Mateos, Abdón, and Alvaro Soto. *El final del franquismo, 1959–1975: La transformación de la sociedad española.* Madrid: Temas de Hoy, 1997.

May, John. "Visual Story and the Religious Interpretation of Film." In *Religion in Film,* ed. John R. May and Michael Bird, 23–43. Knoxville: University of Tennessee Press, 1982.

McLeod, Hugh. *The Religious Crisis of the 1960s.* Oxford: Oxford University Press, 2007.

McNair, Brian. *Striptease Culture: Sex, Media and the Democratisation of Desire.* London: Routledge, 2002.

Medina, Alberto. *Exorcismos de la memoria: Políticas y poéticas de la melancolía en la España de la transición.* Madrid: Ediciones Libertarias, 2001.

Melero Salvador, Alejandro. *Placeres ocultos: Gays y lebianas en el cine español de la transición.* Madrid: Notorius Ediciones, 2010.

Mendieta, Eduardo, and Jonathan VanAntwerpen, eds. *The Power of Religion in the Public Sphere.* New York: Columbia University Press, 2011.

Miguel, Amando de. *Sociología del Franquismo.* Barcelona: Editorial Euros, 1975.

Miguel, Santiago. "La casa sin fronteras." *Cinestudio* 125 (1973): 37.

Millerson, Gerald. *Lighting for Television and Film.* Third edition. Oxford: Focal Press, 1991.

Ministerio de Cultura. http://www.mcu.es.

"La mística Rosa de Rima." *Cinestudio* 2 (1962): 28.

Monaco, James. *How to Read a Film: Movies, Media, and Beyond.* New York: Oxford University Press, 1981.

Montero, Feliciano. *La Iglesia: De la colaboración a la disidencia (1956–1975).* Madrid: Ediciones Encuentro, 2009.

Montero Moreno, Antonio. "Cómo vivió la Iglesia los últimos cincuenta años de vida de España." In *Iglesia y poder público: Actas del VII Simposio de Historia de la Iglesia en España y América*, ed. Paulino Castañeda and Manuel Cociña y Abella, 193–9. Córdoba: Publicaciones Cajasur, 1997.

Morcillo, Aurora. *The Seduction of Modern Spain: The Female Body and the Francoist Body Politic*. Lewisburg: Bucknell University Press, 2010.

– *True Catholic Womanhood: Gender Ideology in Franco's Spain*. Dekalb: Northern Illinois University Press, 2000.

Morgan, Ronald. *Spanish American Saints and the Rhetoric of Identity, 1600–1810*. Tucson: University of Arizona Press, 2002.

Morin, Edgar. *The Stars*. Trans. Richard Howard. Minneapolis: University of Minnesota Press, 2005.

Mujica, Bárbara. *Teresa de Ávila: Lettered Woman*. Nashville: Vanderbilt University Press, 2009.

Myers, Kathleen Ann. *Neither Saints nor Sinners: Writing the Lives of Women in Spanish America*. Oxford: Oxford University Press, 2003.

Nahum García Martínez, Alberto. *El cine de no-ficción en Martín Patino*. Madrid: Ediciones Internacionales Universitarias, 2008.

Neale, Steve. *Genre and Hollywood*. New York: Routledge, 2000.

Neale, Steve, and Frank Krutnik. *Popular Film and Television Comedy*. New York: Routledge, 1990.

Nichols, Bill. *Representing Reality: Issues and Concepts in Documentary*. Bloomington: Indiana University Press, 1991.

Nieto Ferrando, Jorge. "Entre el turismo y el aperturismo. A partir de *La España otra vez* de Jaime Camino (1968)." In *Turistas de película: Sus representaciones en el cine hispánico*, ed. Antonia del Rey-Reguillo, 91–106. Madrid: Biblioteca Nueva, 2013.

– *Posibilismos, memoria y fraudes: El cine de Basilio Martín Patino*. Valencia: Ediciones de la Filmoteca, 2006.

Nieto Jiménez, Rafael. *Juan de Orduña: Ciencuenta años de cine español (1924–1974)*. Santander: Hispanoscope Shangrila Textos Aparte, 2014.

Nolan, Steve. *Film, Lacan and the Subject of Religion: A Psychoanalytic Approach to Religious Film Analysis*. London: Continuum, 2009.

Nora, Pierre. *Realms of Memory: Rethinking the French Past*. New York: Columbia University Press, 1996.

Nowell-Smith, Geoffrey. *Making Waves: New Cinemas of the 1960s*. New York: Continuum, 2008.

Orbaneja Aragón, Fernando de. *Opus Dei: La Santa coacción*. Barcelona: Ediciones B, 2007.

Orellana, Juan. *Como en un espejo: Drama humano y sentido religioso en el cine contemporáneo*. Madrid: Ediciones Encuentro, 2007.

Orellana, Juan, and Juan Pablo Serra. *Pasión de los fuertes: La mirada antropológica de diez maestros del cine*. Madrid: Editoriales Dossat, 2005.

Orellana, Juan, and Jorge Martínez Lucena. *Celuloide posmoderno: Narcisismo y autenticidad en el cine actual*. Madrid: Ediciones Encuentro, 2010.

Pack, Sasha. *Tourism and Dictatorship: Europe's Peaceful Invasion of Franco's Spain*. New York: Palgrave, 2006.

Pagano, David. "The Space of Apocalypse in Zombie Cinema." In *Zombie Culture: Autopsies of the Living Dead*, ed. Shawn McIntosh and Marc Leverette, 71–86. Lanham, MD: Scarecrow Press, 2008.

Palacio, Manuel, and Carmen Ciller. "The Cinema of José Luis Sáenz de Heredia and the Transition (1969–1975): Images of Women and the Dialectics between Tradition and Modernity." *Studies in Hispanic Cinemas* 8.1 (2011): 51–67.

Pastor, E. "*Fray Torero*, de José Luis Sáenz de Heredia." *Cartelera Turia* 148 (1966): n/p.

Pastor Martín, Ernesto. "El nudo gordiano de *Canciones para después de una guerra*." In *El cine español durante la Transición democrática (1974–1983)*, ed. Arturo Lozano Aguilar and Julio Pérez Perucha, 287–304. Madrid: Academia de las Artes y las Ciencias Cinematográficas de España, 2005.

Pavlović, Tatjana. "España cambia de piel (1954–1964): The Mobile Nation." *Journal of Spanish Cultural Studies* 5.2 (2004): 213–26.

– *The Mobile Nation: España cambia de piel (1954–1964)*. Bristol: Intellect, 2011.

Payne, Stanley. *Spanish Catholicism: An Historical Overview*. Madison: University of Wisconsin Press, 1984.

Peces-Barba, Gregorio. "Sobre el aperturismo." *Cuadernos para el diálogo* 125 (1974): 38–9.

Pérez, Jorge. "Vestida para medrar: Rocío Dúrcal y la modernidad por debajo de las rodillas." In *Un hispanismo para el siglo XXI: Ensayos de crítica cultural*, ed. Rosalía Cornejo Parriego and Alberto Villamandos, 81–101. Madrid: Biblioteca Nueva, 2011.

Pérez, Joseph. *Teresa de Ávila y la España de su tiempo*. Madrid: Algaba, 2007.

Pérez-Agote, Alfonso. *Cambio religioso en España: Los avatares de la secularización*. Madrid: Centro de Investigaciones Sociológicas, 2012.

Pérez-Agote, Alfonso, and José Santiago. *La nueva pluralidad religiosa*. Madrid: Ministerio de Justicia, 2009.

Pérez Lozano, José María. *Un católico va al cine*. Barcelona: Juan Flors, 1966.

Pérez Millán, Juan Antonio. *La memoria de los sentimientos: Basilio Martín Patino y su obra documental*. Valladolid: Semana Internacional del Cine, 2002.

Pérez Perucha, Julio. "Narración de un aciago destino (1896–1930)." In *Historia del cine español*, ed. Román Gubern et al., 19–121. Madrid: Cátedra, 1995.

Piñol, Josep. *La transición democrática de la Iglesia católica española*. Madrid: Editorial Trotta, 1999.

Prada, Joaquín de. "Molokai." *Cinema Universitario* 12 (1960): 64–5.

Preston, Paul. *Franco: A Biography*. New York: Basic Books, 1994.

Preher, Sr. Leo Marie. "The Social Implications in the Work of Blessed Martin de Porres." Diss. The Catholic University of America, 1941.

Primer Plano. "*El padre Pitillo*." *Primer Plano* 751 (1955).

Prout, Ryan. "Between *automoción patria* and Maternal Combustion: Driving through Change in *Sor Citröen* (1967)." *International Journal of Iberian Studies* 24.2 (2011): 109–27.

Quintana, Ángel. "A Poetics of Splitting: Memory and Identity in *La prima Angélica* (Carlos Saura, 1974)." In *Burning Darkness: A Half Century of Spanish Cinema*, ed. Joan Ramón Resina, 83–96. Albany: State University of New York Press, 2008.

– "Y el Caudillo quiso hacerse hombre. La retórica épica e inconográfica en *Franco, ese hombre*." *Archivos de la Filmoteca* 42–3 (2002–3): 175–89.

Raguer Suñer, Hilari. *Réquiem por la cristiandad: El Concilio Vaticano II y su impacto en España*. Barcelona: Península, 2006.

Rancière, Jacques. *Dissensus: On Politics and Aesthetics*. London: Continuun, 2010.

Renard, Santiago. "Las reinas Cristinas conquistan España. Cine, turismo, sexo e identidad." In *Turistas de película: Sus representaciones en el cine hispánico*, ed. Antonia del Rey-Reguillo, 107–27. Madrid: Biblioteca Nueva, 2013.

Richards, Mike. "Grand Narratives, Collective Memory, and Social History: Public Uses of the Past in Postwar Spain." In *Unearthing Franco's Legacy: Mass Graves and the Recovery of Historical Memory in Spain*, ed. Carlos Jerez-Farrán and Samuel Amago, 121–45. Notre Dame: University of Notre Dame Press, 2010.

Richardson, Nathan. *Constructing Spain: The Re-imagination of Space and Place in Fiction and Film, 1953–2003*. Lewisburg: Bucknell University Press, 2012.

– *Postmodern Paletos: Immigration, Democracy, and Globalization in Spanish Narrative and Film, 1950–2000*. Lewisburg: Bucknell University Press, 2002.

Riley, Maria. "Religious Life and Women's Issues." In *Journey in Faith and Fidelity: Women Shaping Religious Life for a Renewed Church*, ed. Nadine Foley, 242–59. New York: Continuum, 1999.

Ríos Carratalá, Juan. *Lo sainetesco en el cine español*. Alicante: Publicaciones de la Universidad de Alicante, 1997.

Ripoll, Juan. "¿Forma o contenido?" *Film Ideal* 37 (1959): 7.

Riquer i Permanyer, Borja de. "Social and Economic Change in a Climate of Political Immobilism." In *Spanish Cultural Studies: An Introduction. The Struggle for Modernity*, ed. Helen Graham and Jo Labanyi, 259–71. Oxford: Oxford University Press, 1995.

Rivett, Sarah. "Early American Religion in a Postsecular Age." *PMLA* 128.4 (2013): 989–96.

Rodrigo, Pedro. *Conversaciones de cine de Valladolid*. Madrid: Editorial Razón y Fe, 1965.

Rodríguez Rosell, María del Mar. *Cine y cristianismo*. Murcia: Universidad Católica San Antonio, 2002.

Rolph, Wendy. "*¡Bienvenido, Mister Marshall!* (Berlanga, 1952)." In *Spanish Cinema: The Auteurist Tradition*, ed. Peter William Evans, 8–18. Oxford: Oxford University Press, 1999.

Rowe, Erin Kathleen. *Saint and Nation: Santiago, Teresa of Avila, and Plural Identities in Early Modern Spain*. University Park: Pennsylvania State University Press, 2011.

Rubio Alcover, Agustín. *Vicente Escrivá: Película de una España*. Valencia: Ediciones de la Filmoteca, 2013.

Ruiz Muñoz, María Jesús. "Cómo ha cambiado el convento. Desde *La Hermana San Sulpicio* hasta *Teresa, el cuerpo de Cristo*, pasando por otros conventos del cine español." *Quaderns* 5 (2010): 93–100.

Ruiz Rico, Juan José. *El papel político de la Iglesia Católica en la España de Franco*. Madrid: Tecnos, 1977.

"Sacerdocio y Curascope." *Cinema Universitario* 3 (1956): 3.

Sáenz de Heredia, José Luis. *Fray Torero*. 1965.

Salzani, Carlo. "The Kingdom and the Glory: For a Theological Genealogy of Economy and Government." *Journal of Contemporary European Studies* 20.2 (2012): 229–30.

Sánchez Biosca, Vicente. *Luis Buñuel: Viridiana*. Barcelona: Paidós, 1999.

– "Scenes of Liturgy and Perversión in Buñuel." In *Luis Buñuel: New Readings*, ed. Peter William Evans and Isabel Santaolalla, 173–86. London: British Film Institute, 2004.

Sánchez Rodríguez, Pedro. *Dios, la muerte y el más allá en el cine contemporáneo: Una mirada a las películas con ojos de fe*. Madrid: PPC Editorial y Distribuidora, 2007.

Sánchez Vidal, Agustín. *El cine de Carlos Saura*. Zaragoza: Caja de Ahorros de la Inmaculada, 1988.

Santa Teresa, Silverio de. *Santa Teresa de Jesús: Síntesis suprema de la Raza*. Madrid: Biblioteca Nueva, 1939.

Sanz Ferreruela, Fernando. *Catolicismo y cine en España (1936–1945)*. Zaragoza: Institución Fernando el Católico, 2013.

– "Reconstruyendo la memoria histórica en la pantalla. La presencia de lo religioso en el franquismo a través de la obra documental de Basilio Martín Patino en los años setenta: *Canciones para después de una guerra* (1971), *Queridísimos verdugos* (1973) y *Caudillo* (1975)." *Artigrama* 20 (2005): 487–510.

Saxton, Libby. "Between God and the Machine: Buñuel's Cine-Miracles." In *A Companion to Luis Buñuel*, ed. Rob Stone and Julián Gutiérrez Albilla, 414–30. Malden, MA: Wiley-Blackwell, 2013.

Scarlett, Elizabeth. *Religion and Spanish Film: Luis Buñuel, the Franco Era, and Contemporary Directors*. Ann Arbor: University of Michigan Press, 2015.

Schatz, Thomas. *Hollywood Genres: Formulas, Filmmaking, and the Studio System*. Philadelphia: Temple University Press, 1981.

Schleich, Kathryn. *Hollywood and Catholic Women: Virgins, Whores, Mothers, and Other Images*. New York: iUniverse, 2003.

Schmitt, Carl. *Political Theology*. Chicago: University of Chicago Press, 2005.

Schrader, Paul. *Transcendental Style in Film: Ozu, Bresson, Dreyer*. New York: Da Capo Press, 1976.

Schüssler Fiorenza, Elisabeth. "Breaking the Silence – Becoming Visible." In *Women – Invisible in Church and Theology*, ed. Elisabeth Schüssler Fiorenza and Mary Collins, 3–16. Edinburgh: T. & T. Clark, 1985.

Shubert, Adrian. *A Social History of Modern Spain*. London: Unwin Hyman, 1990.

Sieburth, Stephanie. *Inventing High and Low: Literature, Mass Culture, and Uneven Modernity in Spain*. Durham, NC: Duke University Press, 1994.

Simerka, Barbara. "Feminist Epistemology and Pedagogy in Teresa of Ávila." In *Approaches to Teaching Teresa of Ávila and the Mystics*, ed. Alison Weber, 107–13. New York: Modern Language Association of America, 2009.

"Sor Ye-Yé." Cine Asesor 58–9 (1968).

Sorkin, David. *The Religious Enlightenment*. Princeton: Princeton University Press, 2008.

Stone, Rob. *Spanish Cinema*. Harlow: Longman, 2002.

Stott, Andrew. *Comedy: The New Critical Idiom*. New York: Routledge, 2005.

Strauss, Frédéric. *Almodóvar on Almodóvar*. London: Faber & Faber, 1996.

Strenski, Ivan. "Religion, Power, and Final Foucault." *Journal of the American Academy of Religion* 66.2 (1998): 345–67.

Suárez, Luis. *Franco y la Iglesia: Las relaciones con el Vaticano*. Madrid: Homo Legens, 2011.

Suenens, Leon Joseph. *The Nun in the World: Religious and the Apostolate*. London: Burns & Oates, 1963.

Sullivan, Rebecca. *Visual Habits: Nuns, Feminism, and American Popular Culture*. Toronto: University of Toronto Press, 2005.

Sutton, Martin. "Patterns of Meaning in the Musical." *Genre: The Musical*. Ed. Rick Altman, 190–6. London: Routledge. 1981.

Tapia, María del Carmen. *Beyond the Threshold: A Life in Opus Dei*. New York: Continuum, 1997.

Taylor, Charles. *A Secular Age*. Cambridge, MA: Harvard University Press, 2007.
– "Why We Need a Radical Redefinition of Secularism." In *The Power of Religion in the Public Sphere*, ed. Eduardo Mendieta and Jonathan VanAntwerpen, 34–59. New York: Columbia University Press, 2011.
Thomas, Hugh. *The Spanish Civil War*. New York: Modern Library, 2001.
Torreiro, Casimiro. "Del tardofranquismo a la democracia (1969–1982)." In *Historia del cine español*, ed. Román Gubern et al., 341–98. Madrid: Cátedra, 2004.
– "¿Una dictadura liberal? (1962–1969)." In *Historia del cine español*, ed. Román Gubern et al., 295–340. Madrid: Cátedra, 2004.
– "Murió Antonio Garisa, un comediante competente." *El País*, 9 August, 1989. http://elpais.com/diario/1989/08/09/cultura/618616808_850215.html.
Torrella, José. "¿Films de exaltación religiosa o cristianización del cine?" *Otro Cine* 1.2 (1952): 4–5.
Torres, Augusto M. *Diccionario del cine español*. Madrid: Espasa, 1996.
Tortella, Gabriel. *The Development of Modern Spain: An Economic History of the Nineteenth and Twentieth Centuries*. Cambridge, MA: Harvard University Press, 2000.
Townson, Nigel. "Introduction." In *Spain Transformed: The Late Franco Dictatorship, 1959–1975*, 1–29. Basingstoke: Palgrave Macmillan, 2010.
Tranche, Rafael R., and Vicente Sánchez-Biosca. *NO-DO: El tiempo y la memoria*. Madrid: Filmoteca Española/Cátedra, 2001.
"La trastienda." *Cartelera Turia* 642 (1976): n.p.
Triana-Toribio, Núria. *Spanish National Cinema*. London: Routledge, 2003.
Tuñón de Lara, Manuel. *El hecho religioso en España*. Paris: Éditions de la Librairie du Globe, 1968.
Turner, Bryan. *Religion and Modern Society: Citizenship, Secularisation and the State*. Cambridge: Cambridge University Press, 2011.
Tusell, Javier. *La dictadura franquista*. Madrid: El País, 2007.
"El último Opus de Jorge Grau." *Fotogramas* 1440 (1976).
Urrutia Abaigar, Víctor. "Church and State after Transition to Democracy: The Case of Spain." In *The Secular and the Sacred: Nation, Religion and Politics*, ed. William Safran, 122–36. London: Frank Cass, 2003.
Valentine, Mary Hester. *The Post-Conciliar Nun*. New York: Hawthorn Books, 1968.
Valiente, Celia. "Implementing Women's Rights in Spain." In *Globalization, Gender, and Religion: The Politics of Women's Rights in Catholic and Muslim Contexts*, ed. Jane H. Bayes and Nayereh Tohidi, 107–25. New York: Palgrave, 2001.
Valis, Noël. *Sacred Realism: Religion and the Imagination in Modern Spanish Narrative*. New Haven: Yale University Press, 2010.

Vaquerizo García, Luis. *La censura y el Nuevo Cine Español*. Alicante: Publicaciones de la Universidad de Alicante, 2014.

Vatican. *Apostolicam Auctositatem: Decree on the Apostolate of the Laity*. http://w2.vatican.va/content/vatican/en.html.

– *Dignitatis Humanae: Declaration on Religious Freedom*. 1965.

– *Gaudium et Spes: Pastoral Constitution on the Church in the Modern World*. 1965.

– *Humanae Vitae: Encyclical on the Regulation of Birth*. 1968.

– *Lumen Gentium: Dogmatic Constitution on the Church*. 1964.

– *Mater et Magistra: Encyclical on Christianity and Social Progress*. 1961.

– *Pacem in Terris: Encyclical on Establishing Universal Peace in Truth, Justice, Charity, and Liberty*. 1963.

– *Perfectae Caritatis: Decree on the Adaptation and Renewal of Religious Life*. 1965.

Vázquez, Jesús, Félix Medín, and Luis Méndez. *La Iglesia española contemporánea*. Madrid: Editora Nacional, 1973.

"El Vicepresidente del gobierno destaca los servicios prestados por el régimen a la Iglesia Católica." *ABC* 8 December 1972, 31–2.

Viestenz, William. *By the Grace of God: Francoist Spain and the Sacred Roots of Political Imagination*. Toronto: University of Toronto Press, 2014.

Villarejo, Amy. *Film Studies: The Basics*. London: Routledge, 2007.

Virilio, Paul. *Speed and Politics: An Essay in Dromology*. New York: Semiotext(e), 1986.

Vives, Juan Luis. *Instrucción de la mujer cristiana*. Buenos Aires: Espasa Calpe, 1940.

Walsh, Frank. *Sin and Censorship: The Catholic Church and the Motion Picture Industry*. New Haven: Yale University Press, 1996.

Walsh, Michael. *Opus Dei: An Investigation into the Secret Society Struggling for Power within the Roman Catholic Church*. New York: HarperCollins, 1992.

Warner, Marina. *From the Beast to the Blonde*. London: Chatto & Windus, 1994.

Weber, Alison. "The Creation of Feminist Consciousness: Teaching Teresa of Ávila in a Women Writers Course." In *Approaches to Teaching Teresa of Ávila and the Spanish Mystics*, 157–65. New York: Modern Language Association of America, 2009.

Weber, Max. *Economy and Society*. Ed. Guenther Roth and Claus Wittich. New York: Bedminster Press, 1968.

– *From Max Weber: Essays in Sociology*. Ed. H.H. Gerth and C. Wright Mills. New York: Oxford University Press, 1946.

– *The Methodology of Social Sciences*. Glencoe, IL: Free Press, 1949.

– *The Protestant Ethic and the Spirit of Capitalism*. New York: Charles Scribner's Sons, 1958.

Whelan, Andrew, Ruth Walker, and Christopher Moore. *Zombies in the Academy*. Bristol: Intellect, 2014.

Whittaker, Tom. *The Films of Elías Querejeta: A Producer of Landscapes*. Cardiff: University of Wales Press, 2011.

Williams, Raymond. *Marxism and Literature*. Oxford: Oxford University Press, 1977.

Woods Peiró, Eva. "Rehearsing for Modernity in *¡Bienvenido, Mister Marshall!* (Luis García Berlanga, 1952)." In *Burning Darkness: A Half Century of Spanish Cinema*, ed. Joan Ramon Resina, 9–26. Albany: SUNY Press, 2008.

– *White Gypsies: Race and Stardom in Spanish Musicals*. Minneapolis: University of Minnesota Press, 2012.

Wright, Melanie. *Religion and Film: An Introduction*. London: I.B. Tauris, 2007.

Ynfante, Jesús. *La prodigiosa aventura del Opus Dei*. París: Ruedo Ibérico, 1970.

Zenobi, Laura. *La construcción del mito de Franco*. Madrid: Cátedra, 2011.

Žižek, Slavoj. *Did Somebody Say Totalitarianism?* London: Verso, 2001.

Zunzunegui, Santos. *Los felices sesenta*. Barcelona: Paidós, 2005.

Index

TORONTO IBERIC

1 Anthony J. Cascardi, *Cervantes, Literature, and the Discourse of Politics*
2 Jessica A. Boon, *The Mystical Science of the Soul: Medieval Cognition in Bernardino de Laredo's Recollection Method*
3 Susan Byrne, *Law and History in Cervantes' Don Quixote*
4 Mary E. Barnard and Frederick A. de Armas (eds), *Objects of Culture in the Literature of Imperial Spain*
5 Nil Santiáñez, *Topographies of Fascism: Habitus, Space, and Writing in Twentieth-Century Spain*
6 Nelson Orringer, *Lorca in Tune with Falla: Literary and Musical Interludes*
7 Ana M. Gómez-Bravo, *Textual Agency: Writing Culture and Social Networks in Fifteenth-Century Spain*
8 Javier Irigoyen-García, *The Spanish Arcadia: Sheep Herding, Pastoral Discourse, and Ethnicity in Early Modern Spain*
9 Stephanie Sieburth, *Survival Songs: Conchita Piquer's* Coplas *and Franco's Regime of Terror*
10 Christine Arkinstall, *Spanish Female Writers and the Freethinking Press, 1879–1926*

11 Margaret Boyle, *Unruly Women: Performance, Penitence, and Punishment in Early Modern Spain*
12 Evelina Gužauskytė, *Christopher Columbus's Naming in the* diarios *of the Four Voyages (1492–1504): A Discourse of Negotiation*
13 Mary E. Barnard, *Garcilaso de la Vega and the Material Culture of Renaissance Europe*
14 William Viestenz, *By the Grace of God: Francoist Spain and the Sacred Roots of Political Imagination*
15 Michael Scham, Lector Ludens*: The Representation of Games and Play in Cervantes*
16 Stephen Rupp, *Heroic Forms: Cervantes and the Literature of War*
17 Enrique Fernandez, *Anxieties of Interiority and Dissection in Early Modern Spain*
18 Susan Byrne, *Ficino in Spain*
19 Patricia M. Keller, *Ghostly Landscapes: Film, Photography, and the Aesthetics of Haunting in Contemporary Spanish Culture*
20 Carolyn A. Nadeau, *Food Matters: Alonso Quijano's Diet and the Discourse of Early Modern Food in Spain*
21 Cristian Berco, *From Body to Community: Venereal Disease and Society in Baroque Spain*
22 Elizabeth R. Wright, *The Epic of Juan Latino: Dilemmas of Race and Religion in Renaissance Spain*
23 Ryan D. Giles, *Inscribed Power: Literary Amulets in Medieval and Early Modern Iberia*
24 Jorge Pérez, *Confessional Cinema: Religion, Film, and Modernity in Spain's Development Years, 1960–1975*

www.ingramcontent.com/pod-product-compliance
Lightning Source LLC
LaVergne TN
LVHW090154080826
844660LV00013B/811/J